ZOLA AND THE CRAFT OF FICTION
(Essays in Honour of F.W.J. Hemmings)

F.W.J. Hemmings

ZOLA AND THE CRAFT OF FICTION
(Essays in Honour of F.W.J. Hemmings)

Edited by
ROBERT LETHBRIDGE and
TERRY KEEFE

Leicester University Press
(a division of Pinter Publishers)
Leicester, London and New York

First published in Great Britain in1990 by Leicester University Press
(a division of Printer Publishers Ltd)

Editorial offices
Fielding Johnson Building, University of Leicester,
University Road, Leicester, LE1 7RH

Trade and other enquiries
25 Floral Street, London, WC2E 9DS

British Library Cataloguing in Publication Data
A CIP cataloguing record for this book is available from the British Library
ISBN 0-7185-1312-6

Library of Congress Cataloging-in-Publication Data
Applied for

Typeset by Communitype Communications Ltd.
Printed and bound in Great Britain by Biddles of Guildford and Kings Lynn

CONTENTS

ABBREVIATIONS

RM   Emile Zola, *Les Rougon-Macquart*, 5 vols, ed. Henri Mitterand (Paris, Gallimard, 'Bibliothèque de la Pléiade', 1960–7).

OC   Emile Zola, *Œuvres complètes*, 15 vols, ed. Henri Mitterand (Paris, Cercle du livre précieux, 1966–70).

Corr.   Emile Zola, *Correspondance*, ed. Bard Bakker *et al.* (Presses universitaires de Montréal, 1978–).

B.N., N.a.f., Bibliothèque Nationale (Paris), Nouvelles acquisitions françaises.

The place of publication of all books cited is Paris, unless otherwise stated.

PREFACE

The essays in this book were originally presented (in abbreviated form) as papers to the conference on 'Zola and the Craft of Fiction', held at Fitzwilliam College, Cambridge, in March 1988. This was timed to celebrate the 25th anniversary of the colloquium hosted by the French Institute in London in 1963, which was the first of numerous international conferences during a period which has seen an unprecedented interest in Zola and his work. Professor F.W.J. Hemmings, of the University of Leicester, one of the very first English-speaking scholars to produce substantial and rigorous commentary on the works of the novelist, continued to enlarge our understanding of Zola throughout that period, and both the 1988 occasion and this book have been organized as a tribute to his scholarship.

Neither would have been possible without the assistance of the following: the Master and Fellows of Fitzwilliam College, Cambridge; Peter Boulton, formerly Secretary of Leicester University Press; Jean Khalfa, Délégué Culturel of the French Embassy in London; Chantal Morel, of the Institut Français du Royaume Uni; Professor Peter Bayley, of the Department of French, University of Cambridge; Professor David Baguley, of the University of Western Ontario; Sheila Green; Lynda Thurston; and Judith Angell, who improved the text while reproducing it.

R.D.L.
T.K.

JOHN HEMMINGS: A PORTRAIT

Terry Keefe

Frederic William John Hemmings was born in 1920 in Southampton, where his father was Headmaster of Taunton's School. He received his own secondary education there from 1930 to 1938, except for a year's break in 1932–3, which he spent on an exchange at the Ecole des Roches in Normandy. His interest in France and things French, as well as his knowledge of the French language (at first, inevitably, schoolboy slang) date from this time.

He went up to Exeter College, Oxford on an Open Scholarship in French and German in October 1938 and, since postponement of military service was allowed for all students, was able to complete his three-year course in spite of the outbreak of war, taking a First in 1941. His tutor was Herbert Hunt, with whom he was subsequently to keep in permanent touch. Indeed, after Hunt's death, he was to be involved not only in the production of the *Festschrift*, published by Leicester University Press, but also in the revision of a translation of a Balzac novel that Hunt had been working on before he died. Although study of French literature in Oxford at this time did not extend beyond 1870, and Zola had published only one important novel before that date, *Thérèse Raquin*, Hunt advised John to read this and had him write an essay on it.

From his second year in Oxford onwards John was learning Russian, which at this stage there was particular encouragement to take up, and in his final year he undertook a special subject on Chekhov. He hoped for some kind of interpreter's job in the Navy on leaving Oxford, but eventually joined the Army Intelligence Corps, which involved compulsory infantry training (in Yorkshire), and then a field security course in Winchester, including motor cycle rough-riding! In the spring of 1942 he was sent on a cipher course in Bedford, from which he was posted to Bletchley Park, the British communications headquarters. In a group of about twenty, he participated in the process of breaking the ciphers for traffic between German SS Army headquarters and Army Corps - one stage below the work on Enigma, which was being carried on at Bletchley Park on one of the very first computers ever constructed. Only while examining records after the German collapse did he become aware of the Enigma activity, so tight had been the security, though it was based on little more than one's word of honour.

He was demobilized in 1946, receiving a Further Education and Training

Scholarship of £110 per year to go back to Oxford for postgraduate work. Cataloguing and supervising borrowing for one evening a week in the Russian library at the Taylorian provided a modest supplement to his income, and he also carried out some tutorial work in French for Exeter College. However, John's major preoccupation was now his thesis concerning the Russian novel in France from 1870 onwards. This topic had been decided after consultation with Gustave Rudler, but was a natural development of his earlier study of Russian. His D.Phil was completed in 1949 and gave rise to his first academic publication, *The Russian Novel in France, 1884–1914*, published by Oxford University Press the following year. His research on the late nineteenth century led him directly on to detailed work on Zola.

Very few academic appointments in French were being made at this time, although two posts were eventually filled in Bangor by John's fellow Oxford postgraduates, Grimsley and Barber, and John himself was appointed to an assistant lectureship at the University College of Leicester in 1948. At this time Leicester was preparing undergraduates for London University degrees, and John was required to teach all of the post-Renaissance literature set for the General degree, as well as language work. He was to hold a permanent post at Leicester for 37 years until retirement in 1985, by which time Leicester (an independent university since 1957) had grown nearly tenfold.

Around 1950 the French department at Leicester began running Thursday afternoon lectures on twentieth-century authors neglected by the London syllabus. This led to play-readings of modern dramas and preparation during the students' year abroad for departmental productions of French plays. John produced the first, *Antigone*, in 1952 and half a dozen others. Performances of Ionesco's *La Cantatrice chauve* in 1958 turned into a very special occasion, since John had to step into the major part of Mister Smith for two evenings at very short notice, when a student actor fell ill. These were his only appearances ever on the stage: a programme note asked for the audience's indulgence for the shortcomings of the producer, who had had to replace a student!

When Leicester became autonomous, the old London General degree was converted into a Combined Studies degree of Honours standard, and John was appointed as Senior Tutor for the course. He held this post for a number of years, until being elected as the first non-professorial Dean of Arts in August 1963. In October 1963 he was awarded the personal title and status of Professor of French Literature, the first appointment to a personal Chair at the University of Leicester. (He had been made Reader at the exceptionally early age of 34 in 1954.) Over and above his university duties and his research, in August 1964 John took on the reviewing of current English fiction for the *New Statesman*. Regularly every six weeks over a two-year period, he received a parcel of books containing about 30 hardback novels, from which half a dozen at most had to be chosen for review. From August 1968 to May 1970 he was to carry out the same kind of reviewing for *The Listener*.

John accepted the invitation of Victor Brombert to spend the session 1966–7 as a Visiting Professor at the University of Yale, taking the opportunity to visit other parts of the United States and delivering lectures in Virginia, Brown University, Ann Arbor, Michigan, Toronto and California.

As he was giving only three courses per week at Yale, he felt guilty at the amount of time at his disposal and began returning essays to graduate students on an individual basis - only to be told that this was not in accord with American practice and would generate expectations that could not be met! On the other hand, he found the end-of-year oral examinations, in which students could be asked to discuss in French, in front of a panel of five, any aspect of French literature from the Middle Ages to Sartre, extremely fierce. After the year at Yale John received a number of invitations to take up chairs in Canada and the United States, but was concerned that the administration involved would sooner or later take away significant time from his research.

In 1965–6, he was involved in a curious episode concerning a Russian writer who had been influenced by Stendhal, Valery Tarsis. Tarsis had been employed in the Soviet Union as a translator, but was also a genuine creative writer. Some of his works that could not be published in the Soviet Union were being brought out in translation in the West and it came to John's attention that Tarsis, who was at the time in a psychiatric institution, would benefit greatly from a formal invitation to visit a British university. As Dean of the Faculty of Arts, he duly issued such an invitation to Leicester, and some six months later, after an initial refusal, learned that Tarsis was to be allowed to come to England. This was the first case of an intellectual being permitted to leave the Soviet Union, and the visit to Leicester was surrounded by a great flurry of publicity. Tarsis, however, was not a major writer and faded fairly quickly from sight.

In 1970 staff movements at Leicester led to John's being asked to take over the headship of the French Department. Being very actively engaged in preparing works for publication at the time, he was reluctant to do so, but eventually agreed out of a sense of duty, seeing that there was a specific job to be done. During what turned out to be a nine-year period of office as head, he led the Leicester French Department imaginatively, considerably broadening its base by establishing a number of new joint degree courses for undergraduates. He also managed to take on time-consuming tasks in addition to his administrative responsibilities. Over this time he made three visits to Canada as an assessor for what was originally called the Canada Council for the Arts, then later the Social Sciences and Humanities Research Council for Canada. In November 1975 he advised on the setting-up and funding of a special centre for Naturalist Studies, its first task being the establishing and publication of Zola's correspondence. There was a follow-up visit in October 1980, and in January 1981 a further trip in connection with a proposal for a Corpus d'Editions Critiques, a series of French–Canadian texts. John took early retirement from his post at Leicester in summer 1982, but continued teaching part-time for a three-year period as an Associate Professor.

Throughout his teaching career John sustained a remarkable research output and he has actively continued his work since taking full retirement. The pattern of his academic interest in nineteenth-century France is easy to trace and goes back directly to work for his doctoral thesis. Broadly speaking, the promoting of the Russian novel in France at the end of the nineteenth century could be seen to come from those on the political Right with a religious orientation, and this led John to focus, for purposes of balance and contrast, on Zola, a major figure of the Left whose works he was to some extent already familiar with, but about whom very little indeed had been written by the beginning of the 1950s. After the publication of his influential *Emile Zola* in 1953, he continued working on the author, raising new points and queries (including some concerning the manner of Zola's death), and producing, in collaboration with Robert Niess, a much-used and much-appreciated edition of *Les Salons d'Emile Zola* (for which his knowledge of Russian was especially useful, enabling him to translate back from the Russian some of the material that Zola had submitted to a publication in St Petersburg). The second edition of his *Emile Zola*, published in 1966, was very different from the first, taking account of research published in the intervening years and offering a more coherent interpretation of Zola's work as a whole by tracing certain recurring themes back to his childhood. The bibliography of John's writings testifies to the range of his subsequent publications on Zola, which extends from detailed work on the origins of particular novels to fully developed interpretations. His articles on Zola's fiction, moreover, were explicitly complemented by a biography, *The Life and Times of Emile Zola*, published by Elek in 1977.

Being among the very first scholars to work on Zola's newly accessible manuscripts in the 1950s, he was able to cast fresh light on the genesis of the *Rougon-Macquart*. He also opened up major fields of inquiry into Zola's work as a journalist and his relations with contemporary artists. As the nature of literary criticism itself has changed in recent years, John's interests have simultaneously been moving more into the area of social history. Nevertheless, his interest in Zola has endured and he has continued to publish articles on the author, the latest being 'Sur quelques sources "inconscientes" de *La Terre*' in 1987.

Following the first edition of his *Emile Zola*, John developed a particular interest in Stendhal, and it is worth stressing what a substantial contribution he made to Stendhal scholarship between 1961 and 1987, producing a detailed study of Stendhal's novels for the Clarendon Press in 1964, as well as some seventeen articles. He also published a study of Balzac in New York in 1967. His early study of the Russian novel in France and then particular French novelists gradually developed into a broader investigation of culture and society in nineteenth-century France, which yielded two major books. In 1971 Batsford brought out *Culture and Society in France, 1848–1898*, but were unable to publish the volume covering the period 1789–1848, which was completed soon afterwards. John revised and updated this companion volume some years later, for publication by the Leicester University Press (1987). The broadening-out of his interests, however, in no way prevented him from continuing to write on individual French authors. In the sixteen years between the two volumes on French culture and society, he published a book on Alexandre Dumas in 1979 and one on Baudelaire in 1982. He also edited a work on *The Age of Realism*, for Penguin Books in 1974, and produced a further dozen or so articles for academic journals.

During the last few years of his teaching career, John gave an extremely successful final-year course on the theatre world in nineteenth-century

France, the particular aspect of cultural life on which he had come to focus, and this has become his major research interest. He considers the theatre world to constitute a more original and open area of research than any he has engaged in for some years. Covering a period of 150 years (1760–1910), his work in this area is clearly a considerable undertaking. It has already resulted in a number of detailed articles on specific features of the subject, but the central project is that of a long volume. This will not be a literary study as such, but will fall quite squarely in the realm of social history. Above all, it will describe the growth of an industry - theatre being the only major form of collective amusement or entertainment open to the French public in the period concerned - and examine, among other issues, the rise of the commercial theatre, which largely replaced state-controlled theatres; the nature and behaviour of audiences; the acting profession; questions of authorship; and stage machinery. He has been greatly aided in his research by the existence in the Leicester University Library of a special French Memoirs collection, which he himself was partly responsible for establishing.

Acquaintance with Hunt and with Rudler - himself a disciple of Lanson - gives John Hemmings links that reach back to the very oldest traditions of French teaching in British universities. Yet his own teaching career continued until 1985 and spanned a period of enormous change. He sees the rate of expansion in British universities in the 1960s and 1970s as having significantly altered the nature of personal and professional relationships in universities, and is conscious that expectations concerning undergraduates' knowledge dropped considerably during this period. Yet he willingly accepts that such expansion had to take place. Moreover, any of his former colleagues can testify that his ideals regarding availability to students and the need to take a personal interest in each of his tutees never wavered. He has always been horrified at the sight of academics, however famous, turning undergraduates away.

Equally, to the very end of his teaching career John continued to learn from his students, at least to the extent of being spurred on in his own research by the particular questions that they asked. His own central concern has always been to extend his learning and to pass on knowledge through both teaching and published research. His complete devotion and total commitment to his subject have always been such that the less important trappings of academic life have been kept firmly in perspective. Few academics of eminence have been less inclined to consider university professors as creatures to be treated with particular respect and regarded with awe. And yet few academics have managed to blend as harmoniously as John Hemmings administrative achievements of a high order, consistently stimulating undergraduate teaching, and research work of great substance and distinction. His unique contribution to Zola scholarship over some thirty-five years is but one of the more obvious measures of an immensely successful university career, for which many colleagues, numerous researchers and scores of undergraduates will continue to be grateful.

PUBLICATIONS BY JOHN HEMMINGS

(a) Writings on Zola

1952

'The Genesis of Zola's *La Joie de vivre*', *French Studies*, VI, 114–25.

1953

Emile Zola, Oxford: Clarendon Press. 308 pp.

1854

'The Origins of the Terms *naturalisme, naturaliste*', *French Studies*, VIII, 109–21.

1955

'Zola on the Staff of *Le Gaulois*', *Modern Language Review*, L, 25–9.

1956

'The Present Position in Zola Studies', *French Studies*, X, 97–122.

'Zola's Apprenticeship to Journalism, 1865–1870', *PMLA*, LXXI, 340–54.

'Zola, *Le Bien public* and *Le Voltaire*', *Romanic Review*, XLVII, 103–16.

1958

'Zola, Manet and the Impressionists, 1875–1880', *PMLA*, LXXIII, 407–17.

1959

'Un *Salon* inconnu d'Emile Zola' (with R.J. Niess), *Revue des Sciences humaines*, fasc. 92, pp. 521–9.

Les Salons d'Emile Zola, recueillis, annotés et présentés par F.W.J. Hemmings et R.J. Niess et précédés d'une étude sur 'Emile Zola: critique d'art' de F.W.J. Hemmings. Geneva: Droz; Paris: Minard. 277 pp.

'The Secret Sources of *La Faute de l'abbé Mouret*', *French Studies*, XIII, 226–39.

'Zola and *L'Education sentimentale*', *Romanic Review*, L, 35–40.

1960

'Emile Zola et Louise Solari', *Revue d'histoire littéraire de la France*, LX, 60–1.

1961

'Zola: pour ou contre Stendhal?', *Les Cahiers naturalistes*, no. 19, 107–12.

1963

'Zola par delà la Manche et l'Atlantique: essai bibliographique', *Les Cahiers naturalistes*, no. 23, 299–312.

'Les sources d'inspiration de Zola conteur', *Les Cahiers naturalistes*, nos 24–5, 29–44.

1965

'Emile Zola et le théâtre scandinave de son temps', *Les Cahiers naturalistes*, no. 29, 25–33.

1966

Emile Zola, second edition. Oxford: Clarendon Press. 329 pp.

'The Elaboration of Character in the *ébauches* of Zola's *Rougon-Macquart* Novels', *PMLA*, LXXXI, 286–96.

1967

'La critique d'un créateur: Zola et Malot', *Revue d'histoire littéraire de la France*, LXVII, 55–67.

'Emile Zola: romancier innovateur', *Les Cahiers naturalistes*, no. 33, 1–11.

1968

'Emile Zola et la religion, à propos de *La Faute de l'abbé Mouret*', *Europe*, nos 468–9, 129–35.

'*Le Candidat* de Flaubert dans la critique d'Emile Zola', *Revue des Sciences humaines*, fasc. 131, 465–75.

1969

'Fire in Zola's Fiction: variations on an elemental theme', *Yale French Studies*, no. 42, 26–37.

1970

Emile Zola, Oxford paperbacks. 331 pp.

1971

'Intention et réalisation dans les *Rougon-Macquart*', *Les Cahiers naturalistes*, no. 42, 93–108.

'The Present Position in Zola Studies', pp. 596–623 & 951–4 in, Charles B. Osburn, *The Present State of French Studies*. Metuchen, N.J.: Scarecrow Press.

1972

'Emile Zola devant l'Exposition Universelle de 1878', *Cahiers de l'Association internationale des études françaises*, no. 24, 131–53.

1976

'De *Jack* à *Germinal*. Le prolétaire vu par Alphonse Daudet et Emile Zola', *Les Cahiers naturalistes*, no. 50, 107–14.

1977

The Life and Times of Emile Zola. London: Paul Elek. 192 pp.

1979

Emile Zola, Chronist und Ankläger seiner Zeit. Munich: Blanvalet Verlag. 285 pp.

1980

'De *Germinal* à *Messidor*: la valeur idéologique d'un livret d'opéra', *Cahiers de l'UER Froissart*, no. 5, 11–17.

1981

'Le père d'Emile Zola et les chemins de fer d'Autriche', *Les Cahiers naturalistes*, no. 55, 156–69.

1985

'Zola et les Folies-Bergère', *Les Cahiers naturalistes*, no. 59, 175–80.

1986

'Emile Zola', pp. 93–100 in, D. Baguley, ed., *Critical Essays on Emile Zola*. Boston, Mass.: G. K. Hall.

1987

'Sur quelques sources "inconscientes" de *La Terre*', *Les Cahiers naturalistes*, no. 61, 15–25.

(b) Other Writings on Nineteenth-Century French Literature and Culture

1950

The Russian Novel in France, 1884-1914. Oxford University Press. 250 pp.

'Dostoevsky in Disguise: the 1888 French version of *The Brothers Karamazov*', *French Studies*, IV, 227–38.

1961

'Baudelaire, Stendhal, Michel-Ange et Lady Macbeth', *Stendhal Club*, no. 11, 85–98.

'Deux débuts de Julien Sorel', *Stendhal Club*, no. 12, 151–6.

1962

'Stendhal, self-plagiarist', *L'Esprit créateur*, II, 19–25.

'Julien Sorel and Julian the Apostate', *French Studies*, XVI, 229–44.

'Proust et Stendhal', *Stendhal Club*, no. 16, 176–7.

'Stendhal relu par Zola au temps de "l'Affaire" (documents inédits)', *Stendhal Club*, no. 16, 302–10.

1963

'A Note on the Origins of *La Chartreuse de Parme*', *Modern Language Review*, LVIII, 392–5.

'Quelques observations sur les procédés de l'invention chez Stendhal', *Stendhal Club*, no. 21, 47–62.

1964

Stendhal: a study of his novels, Oxford: Clarendon Press. xvii + 232 pp.

1965

The Uses of Literature: an inaugural lecture, Leicester University Press. 21 pp.

1966

'L'Unité artistique de *La Chartreuse de Parme*', pp. 223–1, in *Communications présentées au congrès stendhalien de Civitavecchia.* Florence: Sansoni; Paris: Didier.

1967

Balzac: an interpretation of 'La Comédie humaine'. New York: Random House. xxx + 189 pp.

1968

'Stendhal et le plaisir du roman', *Livres de France*, XIX, 129–35.

1970

'Emma and the Maw of Wifedom', *L'Esprit créateur*, X, 13–23.

1971

Culture and Society in France, 1848–1898. London: Batsford. 280 pp.

1972

'Marie de Verneuil et le marquis de Montauran: un cas classique de "cristallisation" stendhalienne', pp. 17–28 in *Stendhal et Balzac: actes du VIIe congrès international stendhalien*, Aran: Editions du Grand-Chêne.

'Balzac's *Les Chouans* and Stendhal's *De l'Amour*', pp. 99–110 in *Balzac and the Nineteenth Century*, Leicester University Press.

'Stendhal's Fourth Circle', *Forum for Modern Language Studies*, VIII, 230–6.

1973

'Les deux *Lamiel*, nouveaux aperçus sur les procédés de composition de Stendhal romancier', *Stendhal Club*, no. 60, 287–316.

1974

The Age of Realism. Harmondsworth: Penguin Books. 415 pp.

1976

'Est-il bon, est-il méchant?: les catégories morales dans la *Vie de Henry Brulard*', pp. 47–53 in *Stendhal et les problèmes de l'autobiographie*. Presses Universitaires de Grenoble.

1977

City Blues (Le Spleen de Paris). Eighteen Prose Poems by Charles Baudelaire translated with an introduction and notes. Melton Mowbray: Brewhouse Press. 67 pp.

1978

The Age of Realism. Sussex: The Harvester Press; New Jersey: Humanities Press. 415 pp.

1979

The King of Romance: a portrait of Alexandre Dumas. London: Hamish Hamilton; New York: Scribner's. 231 pp.

'Constant's *Adolphe*: internal and external chronology', *Nineteenth-Century French Studies*, VII, pp. 153–64.

1980

'A Focal Figure in the Romantic *fraternité des arts*: Sardanapalus', pp. 1–12 in *Literature and Society: studies in nineteenth- and twentieth-century French literature*, presented to R.J. North. Birmingham: John Goodman.

1982

Baudelaire the Damned, London: Hamish Hamilton. 251 pp.

1983

'Stendhal, 1783–1842: to the Happy Few', *The Unesco Courier*, XXXVI, pp. 11–14.

1984

'El bestiario de Baudelaire', *Revista de Occidente*, no. 42, 151–65.

1985

'Alexandre Dumas père', pp. 710–43 in, Jacques Barzun, ed., *European Writers: the romantic century*, VI. New York: Scribner's.

1986

'La claque: une institution contestée', *Revue d'Histoire du Théâtre*, XXXVIII, 293–309.

1987

Culture and Society in France, 1789–1848. Leicester University Press. 342 pp.

'Stendhal: anglophile ou anglophobe?', in *Stendhal et l'Angleterre*. Liverpool University Press, pp. 1–11.

'Child Actors on the Paris Stage in the Eighteenth and Nineteenth Centuries', *Theatre Research International*, XII, 9–22.

'Co-authorship in French plays of the Nineteenth Century', *French Studies*, XLI, 37–51.

'The training of actors at the Paris Conservatoire during the nineteenth century', *Theatre Research International*, XII, 241–53.

1988

'Stendhal et Sieyès à travers Sainte-Beuve' (with M.G. Forsyth), *Stendhal Club*, no. 114, 102–112.

1989

'Two English Theatre Buffs in Pre-Revolutionary France'. *French Studies Bulletin*, no. 31, 4–7; no. 32, 8–10.

'Playwrights and Play-Actors: the controversy over *Comités de Lecture* in France, 1757–1910', *French Studies*, XLIII, 405–22.

'Applause for the Wrong Reasons: the use of *application* for political purposes in Paris theatres, 1780–1830', *Theatre Research International*, XIV, 256–70.

'Marcel Proust', in *European Writers: The Twentieth Century*, III. New York: Scribner's, 254–68.

INTRODUCTION

Robert Lethbridge

The title of this book merely *invokes* Percy Lubbock's. The latter's *The Craft of Fiction*, published in 1921, makes no mention of Zola, and our intention is neither to repair an 'oversight', nor to measure the author of *Les Rougon-Macquart* against Lubbock's criteria. It is no longer possible to subscribe to the view that 'in all our talk about novels we are hampered and held up by our unfamiliarity with what is called their technical aspect'.[1] Such frustrations are now more likely to be located in the technicality of the 'talk'. In the 'narratological age' in which we live (or the jargon we have just come through), the 'craft' of fiction has a quaintness which is not simply an indication of changing critical terminology. To be sure, we find ourselves far removed from Lubbock's lament that 'the want of a received nomenclature is a real hindrance'.[2] But the term itself conjures up the pre-industrial world of the village workshop, of the artisan bent over material minutely and painstakingly fashioned. It is a world described in *Le Rêve* (*RM*, IV, 846–9), usually seen as the most uncharacteristic of all Zola's novels, and the very delicacy of skilled procedures does not, at first sight, seem compatible with F.W.J. Hemmings's summary of the 'salient features' of Zola's work: 'solidity of foundation, balance and symmetry, ascending and descending lines, vistas, patches of light and shadow, and, above all, hugeness of dimension'.[3]

The imprecise connotations of 'craft', however, need to be contextualized rather than associatively pursued. It is worth remembering Lubbock's admission (in the preface to the 1954 edition of his book) that between art and craft there was barely a 'true working distinction' to be made, and that 'the homely note of the craft' was primarily designed to call attention to fictional shapes and authorial methods, 'to the thing that has been made and the manner of its making'.[4] It is arguable, indeed, that *The Craft of Fiction* acquired its influential status mainly as a result of what Lubbock later called his 'happy' choice of title.[5] For all the charming instability of the book's language,[6] a certain Anglo-American tradition long remained in its debt. Situated between Jamesian theory and practice, on the one hand, and E.M. Forster's attempted systematization, on the other, of the 'genius and insight' with which Lubbock had laid 'a sure foundation for the aesthetics of fiction',[7] that tradition has subsequently been refined, of course, by modern (and largely French) critical enquiry.[8] The essays in this book bear witness to that renewal, but they also remain faithful to the general spirit (though not to the formulations) of *The Craft of Fiction*. Each in its own particular way is addressed to some aspect of Lubbock's central question: how are fictional constructions made?[9]

The Craft of Fiction is informed by the notion of a writer's workmanlike operations, and seldom, if ever, has a novelist left us with such a wealth of material as Zola with which to answer that question.[10] The fact that Zola's voluminous *work*-notes have been preserved, and are accessible for consultation,[11] thus provides analysis of design (in both senses of the word) with supporting evidence more firmly grounded than simply the abstraction from realistic illusion posited by Lubbock. Yet, paradoxically, during Zola's lifetime, and for more than half a century after his death in 1902, bringing together his kind of fiction and the resonance of 'craft' seemed like a contradiction in terms.

Zola himself went to considerable lengths to prevent such a juxtaposition, not least because of his encouragement of that inclination, of which Lubbock speaks, 'to forget, if we can, that the book is an object of art, and to treat it as a piece of the life around us'.[12] It is a strategy which can only be understood in the context of his work's contemporary reception. For, to the repeated charges of exaggeration (underlying those of immorality), Zola's denials increasingly have recourse to an artless 'but scientifique' and 'copie exacte et minutieuse de la vie' (*OC*, I, 520). And this is equally true of the self-definition implied in his alignment of other artists under the banner of a militant Naturalism. Craftsmanship has no place within its rigorously mimetic ambitions.

Or, at least, this is one critical position that Zola adopts. He replied to accusations that Manet's art, for example, was only a vulgar transcription of life by stressing that *Olympia* was indeed informed by a realism which challenged the idealized generalizations of tradition.[13] As his opponents insisted that obscenity resulted from a perverse distortion of reality, Zola found himself denying that any such distortion had taken place, justifying the painting's formal arrangement in the name of an objective realism devoid of interpretative significance. This would be confirmed in *Le Roman expérimental*, in the view 'qu'on donne aujourd'hui une prépondérance exagérée à la forme' (*OC*, X, 1200). In an article in *Le Voltaire*, in June 1880, he dismissed Carolus-Duran's 'facture brillante' as 'un des métiers les plus crânes de l'époque' (*OC*, XII, 1028). The 'côté factice' of his portraits provokes a reaction not unlike his 'haine des intrigues compliquées et mensongères' (*OC*, X, 1307) associated with Romantic fiction. The preferred model (derived from Claude Bernard) of the novelist as examining magistrate allows Zola to praise *La Cousine Bette* as 'le procès-verbal de l'expérience' (*OC*, X, 1179).[14] He admires the contiguous planes of the Goncourts, and Stendhal's *Le Rouge et le Noir*, in so far as 'l'auteur ne cède pas à des idées de symétrie, de progression, d'arrangement quelconque' (*OC*, XI, 79). 'On finira par donner', he wrote in an 1879 review of *Les Sœurs Vatard*, 'de simples études, sans péripéties ni dénouement, l'analyse d'une année d'existence, l'histoire d'une passion, la biographie d'un personnage, les notes prises sur la vie et logiquement classées' (*OC*, X, 1308). In *Le Roman expérimental*, this repudiation of the 'craft of fiction' receives its fullest expression:

> J'ai dit que le roman naturaliste était simplement une enquête sur la nature, les êtres et les choses. Il ne met donc plus son intérêt dans l'ingéniosité d'une fable bien inventée et développée selon certaines règles. L'imagination n'a plus d'emploi, l'intrigue importe peu au romancier, qui ne s'inquiète ni de l'exposition, ni du nœud, ni du dénouement; j'entends qu'il n'intervient pas, pour retrancher ou ajouter à la réalité, qu'il ne fabrique pas une charpente de toutes pièces selon les besoins d'une idée conçue à l'avance [...]. Au lieu d'imaginer une aventure, de la compliquer, de ménager des coups de théâtre qui, de scène en scène, la conduisent à une conclusion finale, on prend simplement dans la vie l'histoire d'un être ou un groupe d'êtres, dont on enregistre les actes fidèlement. L'œuvre devient un procès-verbal (*OC*, X, 1239–40).

Alongside such dogmatic statements, however, there are glimpses of a (perhaps unsurprising) preoccupation with properly artistic transposition and 'the manner of its making'. Zola's 1867 study of Manet, in which he refers to a mastery preceded by an 'apprentissage long et pénible' (*OC*, XII, 827), tries to reconcile episodic veracity with an insistence on form, style and pictorial structure. Art-historians may judge Zola's analysis to be somewhat cursory,[15] but he does inspect the organizations of colour-values and spatial illusion in underlining the 'harmonie' of 'les formes élégantes qui se mêlent' (*OC*, XII, 832). If execution is here subsumed by individuated sensibility,[16] it represents an effort, on Zola's part, to articulate a response still consistent with his oft-cited dictum, subsequently vitiated by polemical pressures, that 'le mot *réaliste* ne signifie rien pour moi, qui déclare subordonner le réel au tempérament' (*OC*, XII, 897). As he mentions Jongkind's craft, his 'métier de peintre', in both 1868 and 1872 (*OC*, XII, 877, 901), so, in less controversial circumstances, in 1875, Zola can point to Manet's 'facture' and the painter's 'nouvelle forme pour le sujet nouveau' (*OC*, XII, 931). And his disenchantment with the Impressionists,[17] in 1879–80, is based, precisely, on the apparent technical insufficiency of work lacking 'une facture largement étudiée' (*OC*, XII, 1015).

It is certainly revealing that, in the very same year as the uncompromising negations of *Le Roman expérimental*, Zola should assert the importance of 'la science de la composition'. His comments on *Le Nabab*,[18] in the summer of 1879, gesture towards 'la fièvre de la réalité' responsible for the modern 'tourment de dresser publiquement des procès-verbaux' (*OC*, XI, 211); but their central thrust is unmistakably at odds with such passivity:

> M. Alphonse Daudet a surtout cette imagination de l'arrangement et de la phrase. De la moindre scène il fait un bijou, par l'art qu'il met à la composer. On lui refuse la science de la composition, comme aux autres romanciers naturalistes d'ailleurs; et je ne connais pas de critique plus injuste, car les œuvres de ces romanciers sont, au contraire, composés avec des raffinements infinis, des intentions très curieuses de poèmes mélodiques ramenant les mêmes effets et enfermant la réalité dans une sorte de châsse symbolique et très ouvragée (*OC*, XI, 212).

As Zola then puts it, 'plus tard, mérite ou défaut, on verra cela'; we too will look at it through a grid of mixed metaphors at least as problematic as Percy Lubbock knew.[19]

A similar ambivalence marks Zola's confrontation with Flaubert. Hemmings has shown that the considered response to *L'Education sentimentale*, in Zola's 1879 study, virtually negates the intuitive appreciation of its qualities he had displayed earlier.[20] The inversion is striking: in 1869, Flaubert's novel was 'une floraison de l'art' (*OC*, X, 919); ten years later, it is 'le modèle du roman naturaliste' (*OC*, XII, 608); what was patently *not* 'la vérité nue' ('c'est toujours la vie interprétée par le poète que vous savez') (*OC*, X, 919) becomes 'la vérité vraie, [...] cette vérité terre à terre, exacte, qui semble être la négation même de l'art du romancier' (*OC*, XII, 608). There is, however, a residual awareness of a craftsmanship not merely applicable to Flaubert. It was 'en homme du métier', Zola admitted, that he had dissected 'la carcasse de l'ouvrage, pour voir "comment c'était fait", pour saisir les oppositions de scènes, les rapprochant, toute cette cuisine de *nos* romans, qu'on *nous* accuse de ne pas composer et dont le plan *nous* donne tant de peine' (*OC*, XII, 607–8; my emphasis).

In foregrounding such contradictions, the intention is not to rehearse a divorce between private and public readings reflected in that between Zola's fictional operations and theoretical pronouncements. It is rather to suggest that assessment of the novelist has long been (and should possibly remain) inseparable from his own attempts to formulate an aesthetic which might coherently accommodate the *vraisemblable* of re-arrangement as well as the unmediated *vrai*. In the intellectual climate in which Zola works, to acknowledge 'craft' as the prerequisite of 'fiction' is to invite its devaluation *as* fictitious; 'higher' or symbolic 'truths' are unacceptably Romantic; the unpalatable 'vérité vraie' is not the domain of Art. For both Zola and his critics, these are the shifting certainties of a conundrum amenable only to ambiguous solutions.

Most of Zola's contemporaries exploited the confusion of categories by subordinating questions of form to those raised by innovatory subject-matter. Initially, the guardians of collective taste had no difficulty in choosing, in the name of Beauty, the high moral ground.[21] From there, physiological and political realities could be attacked under variations on the theme of 'la littérature putride'.[22] This is a critical strain which extends well beyond the signatories of *Le Manifeste des Cinq*, protesting against the crudities of *La Terre* 'au nom de notre culte, de notre amour profond, de notre suprême respect pour l'*Art*!'[23] Less often, it would be reversed by admirers of Zola's courageous portrayal of social injustice and unflinching demystification of human drives. But, as David Baguley writes, there was 'an almost total lack of general assessments of his art'.[24] Intermittent recognition of the poetic and epic power of Zola's fiction seldom went further than unexplained platitudes, which can be seen, in retrospect, as diverting attention from the implications of ideologically sensitive documentation. References to Zola's popular appeal were inherently pejorative or explicitly denounced. As Brunetière put it, 'dans le camp des littérateurs sans littérature, il est à la première place'.[25]

Of those directly anticipating Lubbock's concern with form, none was more bemused than Henry James. In his review of *Nana*, he professed to being shocked less by Zola's choice of subject than by the 'melancholy dryness of his execution'.[26] His distaste, however, for the 'singular foulness of his imagination'[27] is barely disguised. And his reservations about Zola's characters, in their lack of psychological complexity, are familiar ones. His reflections on Zola's craft remain more interesting than most. When in 1903 he looks back at *Les Rougon-Macquart*, James's astonishment prevails over high-mindedness: in *L'Assommoir*, 'the whole handling makes for emphasis and scale'; by a similar process of 'multiplication and accumulation', *Germinal* is a 'finished and rounded book'; *La Débâcle* is 'such a piece of "doing" '.[28] His architectural similes are those developed by Hemmings.[29] Doubting 'if there has ever been a more totally *represented* world', and full of wonder for 'the scale and energy of Zola's assimilations', Henry James outlines the 'mystery' of the 'doing' in a repeated question: 'By what art, inscrutable, immeasurable, indefatigable, did he arrange to make of his documents, in these connections, a use so vivified?'; 'How after all does it so get itself *done*? - the "done" being admirably the sign and crown of it'.[30]

Since that period, Zola criticism has moved in many and varied directions more enlightening than moral strictures or the beating of political drums. His writing has been subjected to the whole gamut of modern approaches: thematic; sociological; psycho-critical; mytho-poetic; archetypal; epistemological.[31] Yet it is not by chance that this remarkable revival of interest had its starting-point in attempts to grapple with Henry James's 'How in the world is it made?' and his implied incredulity, even while retailing them, about the adequacy of Zola's own answers to his question. The latter's reputation as 'ce bon tâcheron des lettres',[32] labouring under the inscription of *nulla dies sine linea* in his study at Medan, had its origins not only in the polemical debate sketched above, but also in Paul Alexis's *Emile Zola: notes d'un ami*.[33] This first authorized biography was seminal in apparently confirming, within Zola's habits of composition, the central importance of his documentation. Not until 1952, with the publication of Guy Robert's magisterial study of *La Terre*,[34] was there a sustained challenge to *Le Roman expérimental*'s 'le plan de l'œuvre leur est apporté par ces documents eux-mêmes' (*OC*, X, 1286). Robert's thesis put this mere *ex post facto* stage of the creative process in its true perspective. By tracing a genesis which did indeed begin, in spite of Zola's denials, with 'une idée' deliberately elaborated into a fictional and poetic structure, Robert opened up the possibility of a new history of Zola's art.

That is ultimately less synonymous with 'craft' than Lubbock suggested. As Hemmings writes, 'the finished work was much more than an admirable specimen of craftsmanship'.[35] Quite apart from the visible gap between plans and textual fabric, there is evidence, even in the midst of conscious crafting, of irruptive imaginative *trouvailles* and associative play. But further investigation of Zola's preparatory *dossiers*, in the footsteps of Robert's pioneering research, has been enormously instructive. For 'they allow us', in Hemmings's words, 'as close a view as we are likely to be granted of a creative imagination at work';[36] and they reveal not merely, but none the less, a 'technician of the novel',[37] and much of the 'fabrique'[38] or 'facture', the 'making' and the 'doing', of Zola's fiction.

In these work-notes, we can find substantiated by intentionality some of Henry James's less hesitant reflections on 'a singleness of mass and a unity of effect',[39] captured earlier in Huysmans's private admiration for 'la charpente, la mécanique si merveilleusement agencée dans un sujet d'une belle simplicité'.[40] That aim is announced in Zola's preliminary thoughts on the *Rougon-Macquart* series as a whole:

> Ecrire le roman par larges chapitres, logiquement construits: c'est-à-dire offrant par leur succession même une idée des phases du livre. Chaque chapitre, chaque masse doit être comme une force distincte qui pousse au dénouement. Voir ainsi un sujet par quelques grands tableaux, quelques grands chapitres (12 ou 15); au lieu de trop multiplier les scènes, en choisir un nombre restreint et les étudier à fond et avec étendue (comme dans *Madeleine Férat*). Au lieu de l'analyse courante de Balzac, établir douze, quinze puissantes masses, où l'analyse pourra ensuite être faite pas à pas, mais toujours de haut. Tout le monde réussit en ce moment l'analyse de détail; il faut réagir par *la construction solide des masses*, des chapitres; par *la logique, la poussée de ces chapitres*, se succédant comme des blocs superposés, se mordant l'un l'autre; par le *souffle de passion* animant le tout, courant d'un bout à l'autre de l'œuvre.[41]

The 'doing' was another matter. As Zola confided to a correspondent, this was often 'une abominable torture',[42] and the repeated revisions of his prose bear witness to an artistic integrity for which we seldom give *this* novelist credit.[43]

If deceptively methodical planning largely conceals the stress of inventive indirections, it is clear that the shape of individual novels was scrupulously organized. Baguley describes this essentially dynamic process as 'the *expansive* accumulation of empirical detail rigorously controlled by the *restrictive* reinforcement of an initial design'.[44] The control is also that dictated by purely narrative considerations. A 'combinatoire romanesque'[45] is precisely calculated[46] in terms of the reading it anticipates. This includes changes of mood and pace: 'Il faut qu'on sente ça dans le récit. Changer la narration'.[47] The outline of *La Terre* provides a space, in the midst of rural savagery, for Fouan's tragic stature: 'Cela doit être un des beaux côtés du livre, bien soigner, bien graduer cette figure.'[48] In all the *Rougon-Macquart*, the distribution of dialogue[49] and description is a particular concern: the financial details of *La Curée* are to be followed by 'une belle page';[50] in *Germinal*, 'comme distribution de la description, il ne faut d'abord qu'une masse presque informe, une vision fantastique de la fosse aperçue dans la nuit'.[51] Prefigurative moments and revelations postponed are to heighten suspense: 'Faire pressentir la situation sans la dire'; 'ne pas encore en montrer le dénouement'; 'laisser un mystère dans l'esprit du lecteur'.[52] The insertion of a 'grande scène d'audace'[53] is as carefully prepared as the structural modulation of beginnings and endings: 'Une simple ouverture annonçant l'œuvre'; 'il ne se dénouera pas par un drame'; 'il faudra arranger l'économie du chapitre pour finir sur un coup de tam-tam ou sur un tableau'; 'Il faudrait un crescendo comme je sais les faire'.[54] With their stage directions motivating the entrances and exits of his characters, such imaginings are consistent with Zola's original 'Notes sur la marche générale de l'œuvre': 'Ne pas oublier qu'un drame prend le public à la gorge'; 'Une continuelle analyse coupée seulement par le drame'

(*RM*, V, 1744–5). The work-notes for his novels embrace a range of devices properly theatrical in conception.[55]

Simply in terms of the months it took him, this planning serves to illuminate Zola's aesthetic preferences: 'C'est l'étude qui fait les œuvres solides' (*OC*, XII, 821); his liking for the perfect finish of the early Manet, as opposed to an 'unfinished' Monet, can be related to his efforts to 'round off' scene, chapter and story. As such, Zola's crafting seems to make of *Le Roman expérimental*'s more extreme denials of novelistic arrangement a grotesquely misleading account of his own practice. What is seldom noticed, however, is that, at a level other than that of the rhetoric of the scientific paradigm, there are significant points of contact between Zola's theoretical pronouncements and textual designs. Synthesizing strategies, deterministic assumptions and deductive logic are common to them both. 'Vous savez', Zola told Alexis, 'que l'affabulation d'une œuvre ne me gêne pas et m'importe peu'.[56] Though a characteristic overstatement, it remains true that, within the interior monologue of his intentions, hesitations and hypotheses are merely the undiscovered or the yet-unconfirmed. 'Quel est le dénouement logique?'[57] invokes an integrated solution. For the Positivist legacy means, as Martin Kanes has written, that Zola 'viewed his novel systems as finite realities of which he was master'.[58] Its totalizing ambitions are registered in the 1866 Preface to his *Nouveaux Contes à Ninon*; 'Tout voir, tout savoir, tout dire' (*OC*, IX, 351). Even in highlighting Daudet's 'science de la composition', Zola talks of symbolic forms *'enfermant* la réalité'. Seeing it whole ('tout voir') finds in his own intentional structuring a means of articulating ('tout dire') an understanding ('tout savoir') of its laws and *order*. Explaining the 'carcasse intime' of his project, in 1868–9, he pointed to dramatization in precisely these terms: 'Chaque épisode, chaque volume contiendra une action dramatique sous laquelle les penseurs pourront retrouver la grande idée de l'ensemble, mais qui aura un intérêt poignant pour tout le monde' (*RM*, V, 1758). Conspectus coincides with technique in so far as the latter translates omniscience into demonstration: 'Pour mieux faire ressortir [...]'; 'A la fin du chapitre il faut que les lecteurs comprennent le drame'.[59] Whether or not, at either end of the communicative exchange, the confidence of this translation always survives its achievement, is another question. But, in the repeated 'Je veux montrer', 'Faire voir' and 'Il faut' of Zola's work-notes, there is an enlightening despot of a novelist compelling our attention. In its programmatic imperatives, at least, his craft of fiction is distinguished by its clarity of outline and coherence of design.

It needs to be repeated, however, that these are the *points of contact* between two ordering activities. They are not exactly superimposed. At that intersection of unifying procedures, the *dossiers* reveal narrative ornamentation and artistic flourishes as deliberately premeditated. Above all, in the '*féconde* dialectique des besoins et des moyens'[60] of the creative process, imaginative choices and underlying principles result in shapes more heterogeneous than 'une construction naturelle et scientifique' (*OC*, X, 1200), and less simple than Zola may have intended. What is certain is that, although separated from their preparatory mechanisms by a dynamic beyond the scope of genetic reconstruction, Zola's novels (in their definitive form) are indelibly marked by the conscious shaping of 'un exceptionnel constructeur littéraire'.[61]

Reference to that crafting has both justified and encouraged commentators of every methodological persuasion in their acknowledgement of its importance. One of the most eclectic (and stimulating) of his modern critics can even assert that 'Zola was nothing if not a superb craftsman, an ingenious and instinctive structuralist'.[62] From analysis of the pictorial[63] and dramatic[64] structures of the parts of his fiction, to rigorous formalist description of the whole,[65] there has been, of course, a retreat from (or interpretative victory over) historical scholarship of the kind exploited by Guy Robert. Self-evident from any point of view, Jacques Dubois's 'Zola est un écrivain de la répétition'[66] could be writ large over numerous studies which have seen in his recurring plots, characters, situations and images 'une prédilection', as Robert Ricatte suggested, 'qui n'est pas celle du technicien'.[67] Kanes rightly insists that to view Zola's procedures as 'a kind of technical handicraft' is to fail to take account of 'deep-seated drives' as operative as intellectual conceptions.[68] The particular shapes of the 'Romantic constructivist'[69] in Zola have been traced back less to his literary apprenticeship than to the speculative location of a personal and collective psyche.[70] Their ideological implications have been explored in Mitterand's correlation of narrative grammar and social vision.[71] Zola's handling of point-of-view has received less attention,[72] not least because of the predominant functionality of his characters; and this consensus about Zola's characterization has itself been reinforced by Philippe Hamon's exhaustive account of the representative agents and actions strategically disseminating the 'savoir' of Zola's explicative venture.[73] But, as well as its design, the very dimensions of Zola's artefact have been precisely measured in recent years, thus documenting Angus Wilson's early insight that 'Zola's obsession with numbers was only a distortion of the strong proportional sense which is the underpin of his whole fictional structure';[74] that this should include a computer-assisted study of lexical permutations[75] could hardly have been envisaged when Lubbock stated the impossibility of a 'really scientific account'.[76] We should not forget that it was Henry James who spoke of Zola's 'multiplication and accumulation', and who (in the Preface to *Roderick Hudson*) defined the craft of fiction as the artist's 'geometry of his own'.

Evaluation of Zola's novels has also focused on his crafting. Recognition of its powerful effects has sometimes been qualified by criticism of its excessive visibility.[77] But 'at his best', as Hemmings was one of the first to note, Zola could 'construct a novel as well as Flaubert'.[78] While his 'Différences entre Balzac et moi' (*RM*, V, 1736–7) indicates in whose gigantic shadow Zola himself felt he was working, it is Flaubert, indeed, who provides the benchmark against which he has been implicitly or explicitly judged. Henry James's reservations, for example, have to be set alongside his declared affinity with the 'fellow-craftsman' he detected in Flaubert, the 'novelist's novelist'.[79] The most remarkable of modern explorations of Zola's fictional design has situated his achievement in a closer relation to Flaubert than ever before, above all in its properly symphonic construction.[80] E.M. Forster had extended Lubbock's analogies in his proposition that 'in music fiction is likely to find its nearest parallel',[81] and no less a craftsman than Valéry noticed in Zola 'le seul "romancier" (que j'aie lu) qui a la composition *musicale*'.[82] It is unlikely that he was aware that Alexis had brought together Zola, Wagner and Flaubert, in his notion of 'le naturalisme musical', and mentioned the endings of the *Rougon-Macquart* in the same terms:

> Dans les livres de ce grand constructeur, livres composés comme une symphonie, avec une symétrie et une science étonnantes, il arrive toujours que tout converge vers l'effet final, le mot de la fin est généralement un trait typique résumant tout, enfonçant une dernière fois l'idée générale dans l'esprit comme un coup de marteau définitif.[83]

Auguste Dezalay has accordingly exploited to the full the novelist's own immodest certainty that 'je suis un poète et que mes œuvres sont bâties comme de grandes symphonies musicales',[84] by detailing his use of harmony and counterpoint, and the extraordinary prevalence of symmetries both inverted and patterned in thematically resonant echoes. The analogies are considerably reinforced by their presence in Zola's work-notes, with their references, as we have seen, to overture, modulated tonality, crescendo and 'un coup de tam-tam'. Long before the review of *Le Nabab* mentioned the 'poèmes mélodiques ramenant les mêmes effets', Zola had consciously organized *La Curée* in terms of the sustained 'double note de l'or et de la chair'.[85] It was in exactly the same year (1869) that he wrote of *L'Education sentimentale* that 'la chair et l'esprit ont leur phrases musicales' (*OC*, X, 919). Allowing a similar indirect authorial commentary to that in the famous *comices agricoles* of *Madame Bovary*, Zola orchestrated, in his own novel, simultaneous scenes with 'la fin comme une phrase musicale revenant'....[86] In *Le Roman expérimental*, he would virtually have to apologize for the interpolated descriptions of Paris in *Une Page d'amour* as 'un caprice d'artiste d'une répétition fatigante' (*OC*, X, 1301). In Zola's fiction, such structures are used to present human experience of a radically different kind, of course, from the mental life of an Emma Bovary. But, in any assessment of his craft, a richly suggestive starting-point is the 1869 study in which Zola developed the metaphorical potential of 'la musique de Gustave Flaubert' (*OC*, X, 917).

If one draws together all these modern descriptions of Zola's work, 'the thing that has been made' is economical in outline, cognitive in its instrumentation, dramatic in conception, visually resplendent, rhythmical in its arrangement and (beyond craft) poetic in its effect. Such complexity refines, rather than invalidates, the architectural model evoked at the beginning of this survey. But the metaphors have to be aligned within the contemporary idiom the modernist in Zola admired. 'Nous devons accepter l'architecture de nos halles et de nos palais d'exposition', he wrote in 1879, 'les boulevards corrects et clairs de nos villes, la puissance géante de nos machines, de nos télégraphes et de nos locomotives' (*OC*, XII, 370). In *L'Œuvre*, Claude's artistic ambitions are his creator's: 'quelque chose d'immense et de fort, de simple et de grand, ce quelque chose qui s'indiquait déjà dans nos gares, dans nos halles, avec la solide élégance de leurs charpentes de fer, mais épuré encore, haussé jusqu'à la beauté, disant la grandeur de nos conquêtes' (*RM*, IV, 138). And, in *Au Bonheur des dames*, the taxonomic emporium reveals 'sous la lumière blanche des vitrages, une architecture légère, une dentelle compliquée où passait le jour, la réalisation moderne d'un palais de rêve, d'une Babel entassant des étages, élargissant des salles, ouvrant des échappées sur d'autres étages et d'autres salles, à l'infini' (*RM*, III, 626). Les Halles themselves, in *Le Ventre de Paris*, are 'tout un manifeste: c'est l'art moderne, le réalisme, le naturalisme' (*RM*, I, 799). All such structures are, in a sense, emblematic of Zola's designs: fashioned from the material of a scientific culture; providing the illusion of natural light through glass; functional, compartmentalized and easily accessible at ground-level; increasingly decorative at the apex; inscribed in endlessly repeated forms. Which leaves at least one of Zola's critics wondering whether his 'glass-house aesthetics' has been '*engineered* precisely to keep at bay a menacing form of literary chaos'.[87]

Lubbock insisted on 'the difficulty that prevents us from ever seeing or describing the shape [of a book] with perfect certainty'.[88] But the geometrical figure which perhaps best accommodates the craft of Zola's fiction is a circle. For the shape corresponds to the 'rounded' quality which struck Henry James, the 'rounding off' so consciously prepared in the work-notes, and the structures of repetition which inform his novels. With its exemplary simplicity, artistically enclosing, finite and complete, it is certainly the shape selected by Zola for an encyclopedic project intended to do the rounds of Knowledge. Circular objects are what the characters of his novel-cycle try to make.[89] And yet there is, of course, a tension. For this ordering activity also speaks of the disorder it masters, the impotence it overcomes,[90] and the points of origin denied by an Eternal Return which simultaneously precludes an ending. In their different ways, the essays in this book explore that creative tension: between Zola's totalizing ambitions and the uncontainable; between the work's spatial organization and narrative dynamic; between generic models and their adulteration; between popular forms and their assimilation; between the synthesizing patterns of Zola's craft and the fictions generated by its circles.

Notes

1. Percy Lubbock, *The Craft of Fiction* (London, Jonathan Cape, 1965), p. 272.
2. *Ibid.*, p. 22.
3. *Emile Zola*, 2nd ed. (Oxford University Press, 1966; paperback ed., 1970), p. 68.
4. *The Craft of Fiction*, p. v.
5. *Ibid.*: 'I claim for this book, written more than thirty years ago, a happy title, and since the title is all that I can read of the book, I incline to dwell upon its happiness'.
6. *Ibid.*, p. 22: 'I have often wished that the modern novel had been invented a hundred years sooner, so that it might have fallen into the hands of the critical schoolmen of the seventeenth century. As the production of an age of romance, or of the eve of such an age, it missed the advantage of the dry light of academic judgement, and I think it still has reason to regret the loss. The critic has, at any rate; his language, even now, is unsettled and unformed'.
7. In the course of the Clark lectures delivered at Trinity College, Cambridge, in the spring of 1927, and published as *Aspects of the Novel*; cited from the Pelican ed. (Middlesex, Harmondsworth, 1962), pp. 85–6. See also René Wellek and Austin Warren, *Theory of Literature*, 3rd ed. (Middlesex, Harmondsworth, 1963), p.

223; *and* Wayne C. Booth, *The Rhetoric of Fiction* (University of Chicago Press, 1961), pp. 8, 24, and 272, for an assessment of Lubbock's influence.

8. Notably in the corrective to 'point-of-view' offered by the distinction between 'focalization' (the consciousness that *takes in* the narrative) from 'voice' (the discourse that *tells* the narrative); see Gérard Genette's 'Discours du récit' in *Figures III* (Seuil, 1972), and Peter Brooks, *Reading for the Plot. Design and intention in narrative* (Oxford University Press, 1984), who writes of 'the once influential *Aspects of the Novel*' (p. 5) and puts Forster in context (p. 339, n.1).

9. 'How they are made is the only question I shall ask' (*The Craft of Fiction*, p. 12).

10. See Hemmings, *Emile Zola*, p. 63; and his 'The Elaboration of Character in the *Ebauches* of Zola's *Rougon-Macquart* Novels', *PMLA*, LXXXI (1966), 286.

11. Most of them are in the Cabinet des Manuscrits of the Bibliothèque Nationale (Paris); significant sections have been reproduced by Henri Mitterand in his annotation for the Pléiade edition of the *Rougon-Macquart* (*RM*).

12. *The Craft of Fiction*, p. 6.

13. See R. Butler, 'Zola's 'Art Criticism (1865–1868)', *Forum for Modern Language Studies*, X (1974), 334–47; and my 'Zola, Manet and *Thérèse Raquin*', *French Studies*, XXXIV (1980), 278–99 (pp. 293–94).

14. 'Nous sommes les juges d'instruction des hommes et de leurs passions' (*OC*, X, 1180). The 'procès-verbal' is a recurrent analogy; see *OC*, X, 1240, 1296, 1332, and XI, 211. Its implications are explored below; see pp. 3–4.

15. See Richard Shiff, *Cézanne and the End of Impressionism* (University of Chicago Press, 1984), pp. 93-7.

16. 'Toute la personnalité de l'artiste consiste dans la manière dont son œil est organisé: il voit blond, et il voit pas masses' (*OC*, XII, 831).

17. See F.W.J. Hemmings, 'Zola, Manet, and the Impressionists', *PMLA*, LXXIII (1958), 407–17.

18. In *La Réforme* of 15 June and 15 July 1879; the article had originally appeared in March 1878 in *Vestnik Evropy* - for a Russian audience far from the polemical fray; this may well serve as an explanation for what otherwise might seem to be Zola's arbitrary (as well as careless) critical stance.

19. 'They are words usurped from other arts, words that suppose a visible and measurable object, painted or carved. For criticizing the craft of fiction we have no other language than that which has been devised for the material arts; and though we may feel that to talk of the colours and values and perspective of a novel is natural and legitimate, yet these are only metaphors, after all, that cannot be closely pressed' (*The Craft of Fiction,* pp. 10–11).

20. 'Zola and *L'Education sentimentale*', *Romanic Review*, L (1959), 35–40.

21. See my 'L'accueil critique à l'œuvre de Zola avant *L'Assommoir*', *Les Cahiers naturalistes*, LIV (1980), 214–23.

22. The title of Louis Ulbach's review of *Thérèse Racquin*, in *Le Figaro* of 28 January 1868.

23. Cited by Henri Mitterand (*RM*, IV, 1529).

24. In the Introduction (p. 4) to his edition of *Critical Essays on Emile Zola* (Boston, G.K. Hall, 1986), which provides an excellent synopsis of the contemporary response; see also the opening chapter of Auguste Dezalay, *Lectures de Zola* (Armand Colin, 1973).

25. *Revue des deux mondes*, 15 February 1880, p. 938.

26. In *The House of Fiction: essays on the novel*, ed. Leon Edel (London, Rupert Hart-Davis, 1957), p. 280.

27. *Ibid.*, p. 276; and the novel's 'monstruous uncleanness' (p. 275).

28. *Ibid.*, p. 230, p. 244, and p. 279.

29. See above, p. 1

30. *The House of Fiction*, p. 243.

31. See F.W.J. Hemmings, 'The Present Position in Zola Studies', *French Studies*, X (1956), 97–122, followed by my 'Twenty Years of Zola Studies (1956–1975)', *French Studies*, XXXI (1977), 281–93. With its 27 references to his own work, the sequel provided by Patrick Brady's 'A Decade of Zola Studies, 1976–1985', *L'Esprit créateur*, XXV (1985), 3–16, needs to be treated with caution. The essential reference-work is David Baguley, *Bibliographie de la critique sur Emile Zola, 1864–1970* (University of Toronto Press, 1976), and his supplementary volume (1982) for the period 1971–80.

32. Henri Mitterand, 'Le Regard d'Emile Zola', *Europe*, 468–9 (1968), 182–99 (193).

33. Charpentier, 1882. The friendship extended to 'Zola going over the proofs of the book'; see Alexis's letters of November and December 1881, in, B.H. Bakker, *'Naturalisme pas mort': lettres inédites de Paul Alexis à Emile Zola, 1871-1900* (University of Toronto Press, 1971), pp. 215–20. The 'offical' biography explaining the novelist's work-habits is to be situated in the same context as Zola's own declarations on the subject.

34. *'La Terre' d'Emile Zola: étude historique et critique* (Les Belles Lettres, 1952). *Emile Zola: principes et caractères généraux de son œuvre* (Les Belles Lettres, 1952), in which Robert went on from his study of *La Terre* to make more general remarks on Zola's work, is also important in this respect. The debt is acknowledged in *Les Critiques de notre temps et Zola*, ed. Colette Becker (Garnier, 1972), p. 14, and by Dezalay, *Lectures de Zola*, pp. 93–5.

35. *Emile Zola*, p. 67; and, in any case, 'though it might seem that Zola, with his stage-by-stage approach to the business of writing a novel, aimed to reduce the craft of fiction to an almost mechanical technique, it yet remains obvious that this technique would have availed him nothing had it not been that he possessed, to the degree he did possess them, the gifts of imagination, vision, and a sense of artistic balance and direction, and employed them at all stages of the work' (p. 68).

36. *Ibid.*, p. 63.

37. *Ibid.*, p. 67.

38. To echo the title of Colette Becker's *Emile Zola: la fabrique de 'Germinal': dossier préparatoire de l'œuvre* (SEDES, 1986).

39. *The House of Fiction*, p. 226.

40. In a letter to Zola of 16 April 1882 (about *Pot-Bouille*); cited in *RM*, III, 1633–4.

41. 'Notes générales sur la nature de l'œuvre' (*RM*, V, 1743; Zola's emphases).

42. In a letter to Jan Van Santen Kolff of 26 January 1892; cited in *RM*, V, 1417.

43. As Henri Mitterand puts it: 'On peut récuser la légende selon laquelle il ne se relisait jamais'; see his 'Remarques d'introduction à l'étude des techniques de la composition et du style chez Emile Zola', *Les Cahiers naturalistes*, XXIV–XXV (1963), 79–81 (80), and John C. Lapp, 'On Zola's Habits of Revision', *Modern Language Notes*, LXXIII (1958), 603–11. This is particularly true of early novels. The text of *La Curée*, for example, was revised on at least five, and possibly six, separate occasions.

44. 'Event and Structure: the Plot of *L'Assommoir*', *PMLA*, XC (1975), 823–33 (823).

45. Chantal Jennings, *Espaces romanesques: Zola* (Sherbrooke, Naaman, 1987), p. 9.

46. One of the most characteristic of Zola's reminders to himself, in the *dossiers*, is 'tout cela reste à calculer'.

47. Work-notes for *La Bête humaine* (B.N., N.a.f., Ms. 10274, fol. 167).

48. B.N., N.a.f., Ms. 10329, fol. 440.

49. Particularly admired by Gide; see his Journal entry of 22 July 1932, cited by Dezalay, *Lectures de Zola*, p. 68.

50. B.N., N.a.f., Ms. 10282, fol. 241.
51. B.N., N.a.f., Ms. 10307, fol. 13; and then, later (fol. 14) 'reprise de la description'.
52. Respectively, work-notes for *La Curée* (Ms. 10282, fol. 225 and fol. 210) and *La Bête humaine* (Ms. 10274, fol. 27).
53. In *La Curée* (Ms. 10282, fol. 309).
54. Respectively, work-notes for *La Curée* (Ms. 10282, fol. 212), *Son Excellence Eugène Rougon* (Ms. 10291, fol. 118), *La Curée* (Ms. 10282, fol. 360), and *Nana* (Ms. 10313, fol. 207).
55. See Henri Mitterand, 'Quelques aspects de la création littéraire dans l'œuvre d'Emile Zola', *Les Cahiers naturalistes*, XXIV–XXV (1963), 9–20.
56. Alexis, *op. cit.*, p. 124.
57. Work-notes for *La Curée* (Ms. 10282, fol. 298).
58. *Zola's* La Bête humaine: *a study in literary creation* (University of California Press, 1962), p. 102.
59. Work-notes for *La Curée* (Ms. 10282, fol. 303 and fol. 317).
60. Mitterand (*loc. cit.*; see n. 55 above), p. 16.
61. Alexis, in a review of *Au Bonheur des dames* (*Le Reveil*, 4 March 1883); cited in Bakker, *op. cit.*, p. 477.
62. Naomi Schor, *Zola's Crowds* (Baltimore, Johns Hopkins University Press, 1978), p. 35.
63. See Philippe Hamon, 'A propos de l'impressionisme de Zola', *Les Cahiers naturalistes*, XXXIV (1967), 139–47.
64. See Janine Godenne, 'Le Tableau chez Zola: une forme, un microcosme', *Les Cahiers naturalistes*, XL (1970), 135–43.
65. See Neide de Faira, *Structures et unité dans* Les Rougon-Macquart *(la poétique du cycle)* (Nizet, 1977).
66. *L'Assommoir de Zola: société, discours, idéologie* (Larousse, 1973), p. 180.
67. 'Zola conteur', *Europe*, 468–9 (1968), 217.
68. *Op. cit.*, pp. 102–3 (and n. 17).
69. To borrow Ima Ebin's description of Claude Lantier in *L'Œuvre*; see 'Manet et Zola', *Gazette des beaux-arts*, XXVII (1945), 45–6. On this character as a partial self-portrait, see Robert J. Niess, 'Lantier-Zola', in *Zola, Cézanne, and Manet: a study of* L'Œuvre (Ann Arbor, University of Michigan Press, 1968), pp. 151–69.
70. See, especially, Jean Borie, *Zola et les mythes, ou de la nausée au salut* (Seuil, 1977).
71. See his articles collected in *Le Discours du roman* (Presses universitaires de France, 1980).
72. Except in *L'Assommoir*: see Joy Newton and Basil Jackson, 'Gervaise Macquart's Vision: a closer look at Zola's use of "point of view" in *L'Assommoir*', *Nineteenth Century French Studies*, XI (1983), 313–19.
73. *Le Personnel du roman: le système des personnages dans* Les Rougon-Macquart *d'Emile Zola* (Geneva, Droz, 1983).
74. *Emile Zola: an introductory study of his novels* (London, Mercury Books, 1965), p. 65; this was first published in 1952. See Auguste Dezalay, 'Pour déchiffrer Zola: du goût des symétries à l'obsession des nombres'. *Travaux de linguistique et de littérature*, VII (1969), 157–66; and Jacques Allard, *Zola, le chiffre du texte: lecture de 'L'Assommoir'* (Presses universitaires de Grenoble, 1978).
75. Etienne Brunet, *Le Vocabulaire de Zola* (Geneva, Slatkine, 1985).
76. *The Craft of Fiction*, p. 11.
77. In his edition of *La Curée* (Garnier-Flammarion, 1970), Claude Duchet remarks that 'le métier [...] se devine parfois un peu trop' (p. 28); even as sympathetic a reader of *Pot-Bouille* as Henri Céard did not hesitate to tell Zola that he found in it

'une mécanique dont la précision savante ne se dissimule pas assez' (letter of 19 April 1882, cited in *RM*, III, 1634–5).

78. *Emile Zola*, p. 114.

79. *The House of Fiction*, pp. 187–219; Lubbock adopts the same view (unsurprisingly, in view of his acknowledged debt to James).

80. See Auguste Dezalay, *L'Opéra des* Rougon-Macquart: *essai de rythmologie romanesque* (Klincksieck, 1983), pp. 334–43.

81. *Aspects of the Novel*, p. 169.

82. *Cahiers* (Gallimard, 'Bibliothèque de la Pléiade', 1974), II, 1221; see Dezalay, *loc. cit.*, p. 10.

83. Review of *La Joie de vivre*, in *Le Réveil* of 17 February 1884 (in Bakker, *op. cit.*, p. 484); his reflections on 'Le Naturalisme en musique' were published in *Le Cri du peuple* on 11 March of the same year (*ibid.*, pp. 186–7).

84. In a letter to Guiseppe Giacosa of 28 December 1882 (*Corr.*, IV, 357).

85. B.N., N.a.f., Ms. 10282, fol. 327. Confirmed by Alexis, as Zola's spokesman, in *La Cloche* of 24 October 1872: 'L'or et la chair, comme le romancier l'a voulu, y chantent à chaque page. Ces deux thèmes s'enroulent l'une à l'autre, se confondent, se soutiennent, se quittent pour s'enlacer bientôt plus étroitement encore, et cette phrase mélodique dure tout le long du livre, produisant une musique à part' (in Bakker, *op. cit.*, p. 455). Alexis was not the only reader to develop the analogy: see Ginisty on the 'symphonie merveilleuse' of *La Faute de l'Abbé Mouret* (cited in *RM*, IV, 1862); and Céard, on the affinity with the Wagnerian leitmotif, in the *Revue illustrée* in 1887 (cited in *Corr.*, IV, 358, n. 5).

86. Work-notes for *La Curée* (Ms. 10282, fol. 227).

87. Naomi Schor, in her review of Hamon (see above, n. 73), *L'Esprit créateur*, XXV (1985), 115–16 (my emphasis).

88. *The Craft of Fiction*, p. 14.

89. See Auguste Dezalay, 'L'Exigence de totalité chez un romancier expérimental: Zola face aux philosophes et aux classificateurs', *Cahiers de l'Association Internationale des Etudes Françaises*, XXIV (1972), 167–84 (181).

90. The psychiatrist who interviewed Zola in 1896 noted his 'perpétuelle crainte de ne pouvoir faire sa tâche journalière, d'être incapable de terminer un livre, de ne pas achever un discours', as well as 'son besoin de mettre de l'ordre partout, *même où il n'y en a pas*' (my emphasis); see Edouard Toulouse, *Enquête médico-psychologique sur la supériorité intellectuelle: Emile Zola* (Flammarion, 1896), p. 250

1

ZOLA, THE NOVELIST(S)

David Baguley

The novel is a form, type or mode notoriously impervious to generic definition. A number of the contributors to a fairly recent anthology of studies drawn from the American journal *Novel* and tentatively entitled *Towards a Poetics of Fiction* emphatically make this point, especially Walter L. Reed, who argues that 'a poetics proper of the novel proper is a highly problematic undertaking, attempting, as it must, to systematize the antisystematic and to canonize the anticanonical'; indeed, 'the novel characteristically opposes itself to the view of literature that a poetic implies'.[1] In the same work, Robert Scholes looks wistfully back to a confident Aristotelian era in this 'age of suspicion', and Malcolm Bradbury suggests that 'the novel is not a traditional literary genre, like tragedy or comedy' and that 'any attempt at generic classification is likely to end up with some splendid monstrosity of definition, like Henry Fielding's "comic epic poem in prose" '.[2]

The novel, then, is a form with such vague contours, as Gide argued some considerable time ago, that it 'cannot aspire to perfection'; for so eclectic a form, as others have argued since then, the notion of purity is irrelevant and the 'demands that theoretical criticism be appropriately flexible are so considerable as almost to inhibit theory altogether'.[3] Certainly, Aristotelian methods of categorization, with their tendency towards essentialist notions, seem thoroughly inappropriate to the novel, which demands a more Ramistic approach, working from the particular to the general and recognizing the perpetual modification that particulars bring to the latter. It is undoubtedly the case that our 'ideology of modernism', as Frederic Jameson points out, with its emphasis on uniqueness and innovation, values to which the new and hybrid form of the novel is remarkably well suited, resists in any case classification in terms of traditional kinds.[4]

In view of this indeterminacy, when not boldly asserting that the novel is simply *post-generic*, critics tend to define the form in all possible ways other than as a distinct literary genre. By virtue of its complexity, its openness, its capaciousness, certain critics, like Malcolm Bradbury, present it as a kind of *hypergenre*, 'open to a great variety of schemes, orders, and typologies' and capable of drawing on 'a wide range of modes of selection and explanation', enjoying the status of other comprehensive kinds of literature like poetry and drama.[5] Others see the novel as constantly evolving in a critical relationship to prevailing conventions, as a kind of *anti-genre*, in opposition to the canonical forms of literature, parodying the literary in the name of the real: fiction that is perpetually repudiating fictions. 'Literary paradigms', writes Walter Reed, 'are not simply modified in the novel, they are opposed by paradigms from other areas of culture'. The novel is thus always a 'nouveau roman', for, from the time of *Don Quixote*, it has 'adopted an antagonistic stance both toward the literary canon and toward its own precursors - even in novels like *Joseph Andrews*, written in mock-Neoclassical "imitation" of *Don Quixote*'.[6] For Aron Kibédi Varga, 'le roman est un anti-roman', relentlessly questioning, renewing, regenerating its forms. Hence the tendency of the novel, particularly in modern times, to become its own subject matter, whether in the guise of what David Lodge calls the 'problematic novel', which builds into the form its own self-questioning tendencies, or in the shape(lessness) of what Alastair Fowler calls the *poioumenon*, the work-in-progress novel, which dwells upon its own fabrication.[7]

But the usual tendency is to consider the novel to be somehow a-generic, a *non-genre*, literature situated at the outer reaches of literariness. This may be because it maintains a special relationship with the reality that it is most commonly supposed to represent, for, to quote Malcolm Bradbury again, 'there is something inherent in it which is at odds with the needs of form or art. This dross is contingency or reality, the over-bulk of reality: the unformed looseness of event, the shapelessness of life and of persons.'[8] Thus it tends to be defined either in relation to the literary kinds that it no longer is: as the epic of an unheroic age (for Lukacs) - or in relation to forms that it should aspire to be: as drama (for Lubbock) - or in relation to what it is not: as in the commonplace opposition between novel and romance. Inevitably, therefore, its boundaries become indeterminate and its matter unsubstantial. For E.M. Forster it is a 'spongy tract' bounded by two opposing mountainous ranges, represented as a vague, dotted line, moving tentatively between a gauntlet of firmly established genre sets, 'satire–romance', 'picaresque–tragedy', 'comedy–sentiment', in the direction of history.[9] For most poeticians the novel is subsumed under the more general categories of 'narrative' or 'fiction', as it is to some degree in the four general orientations of prose genres (romance, confession, novel, anatomy) of Northrop Frye, who dismisses 'novel' as a 'catch-all term', then links the characteristics of the form, 'whatever they are', to the comedy of manners.[10] But when poeticians venture to provide a minimal definition, they seem obliged either to construe the form in too limited a way thematically,[11] or to proffer a purely formal delineation, emptied of specific thematic determinants.[12] Yet the view is also seriously and not unconvincingly argued that the novel is not so much a subgenre, but a *supergenre*, assimilating all varieties of discourse, canonizing non-literary types and marginally literary forms, 'heteroglossic', 'heterogeneric', predatory even as it absorbs all other genres, 'that cannibal, the novel', as Virginia Woolf characterized it, 'which has devoured so many kinds of art'.[13]

However elusive, then, a definition of the novel may be, the fact remains that there *are* distinctive novel types that are readily identifiable: picaresque, historical, pastoral, didactic, epistolary, psychological, detective, adventure *novels.* The solution is perhaps to consider the novel, as both Frederic Jameson and Gérard Genette tend to do, however different their approaches and terminology, as a mode or form, flexible but with certain constant features, admitting a seemingly limitless variety of subjects. As Genette trenchantly observes:

> Il y a des modes, exemple: le récit; il y a des genres, exemple: le roman; la relation des genres aux modes est complexe, et sans doute n'est-elle pas, comme le suggère Aristote, de simple inclusion. Les genres peuvent traverser les modes (Oedipe raconté reste tragique), peut-être différemment: mais nous savons bien qu'un roman n'est pas seulement un récit, et donc qu'il n'est pas une espèce du récit, ni même une espèce de récit.[14]

The novel is thus a form of limitless *semantic* possibilities and of considerable *syntactic* variability, a substantive without a given structure, a form that is often idiosyncratic but always 'idocratic', yet capable of restraining its seemingly boundless mutability to take on the configurations of such distinctive types as those listed above or even to lapse into the formulaic moulds of the popular novel. In the face of this prodigious adaptability of the novel genre, novelists, I would suggest, tend themselves to belong to one of three possible types. There are those who exploit an established model of the genre, usually one that is currently enjoying public favour and brings some degree of commercial success. Then there are those who stamp their own form on the genre, with a similar consistency, but with a more lasting fame in view, addressing themselves, as far as their public is concerned, to a happier few, even to a later age. As F.W.J. Hemmings writes of the obvious case in point:

> the corpus of Stendhal's fictional work presents a superficial appearance of the wildest confusion: a tangle of false starts and loose ends above which tower two acknowledged masterpieces. In reality the work is astonishingly homogeneous; one can talk about the Stendhalian novel with more assurance than one can about the Flaubertian novel or even the Jamesian novel. From the start Stendhal instinctively adopted a basic form or pattern from which he rarely deviated, and never with any success (in the sense that he never succeeded in pushing very far a work which was conceived according to a different pattern).[15]

Within this category would fit the novelist whose works transform generic conventions, even establish a new type of novel, if, indeed, such a feat is possible, as Todorov, for example, would have us believe:

> transgresser une règle de genre, c'est suivre une voie déjà virtuellement présente dans le système littéraire synchronique (mais sans y être réalisée); en revanche, la transgression typologique atteint ce système lui-même. Un roman comme *Ulysse* n'enfreint pas seulement les règles du roman préexistant, mais découvre de nouvelles possibilités pour l'écriture romanesque.[16]

My third category of novelists embraces those protean souls who, successfully or not, avail themselves of different novel types, whose potentialities they seek to exploit in different works, like Paul Adam in Zola's age or Anthony Burgess in our own. Clearly certain novelists, with Balzac the obvious example, could be placed in all three categories. As far as Zola is concerned, he has tended to be assigned to one of the first two; resolutely to the first by his detractors, the more frequently to the second by his admirers and by critics of the naturalist novel. I wish to present the case for a transfer to division three.

An overriding tendency of Zola criticism, particularly in its more traditional forms, has been to subsume the diverse and complex nature of his corpus of novels into a uniform model, usually according to some notion of what constitutes a naturalist novel, then to attribute the residual elements to some other generic category or period concept. This tendency is most evident in the literary manuals, for example in Lagarde and Michard, where Zola's novels are presented as sociological enquiries with scientific pretensions, yet a 'souffle romantique', which links the novelist to Victor Hugo, is (paradoxically) said to be the way in which 'Zola, écrivain naturaliste, a dégagé son originalité et enrichi le roman de pages puissamment épiques'.[17] Critics unsympathetic to Zola's works tend, as one would expect, to be similarly or more reductive. If, for Jules Lemaître, according to his famous definition, Zola's novels are 'une épopée pessimiste de l'animalité humaine', for Lukacs the problem is that they are not epic enough, for the author lost sight of 'the comprehensive vision and omniscience of the old epic narrators'; he has retreated into 'a kind of description' which is 'the writer's substitute for the epic significance that has been lost'; he merely paints 'the outer trappings of modern life'.[18] Zola, the describer, then, 'as soon as he departs from the monotony of naturalism', is, according to Lukacs, who remarkably falls in with the standard view, 'immediately transmuted into a decorative picturesque romanticist, who treads in the footsteps of Victor Hugo with his bombastic monumentalism'.[19] At the other extreme on the ideological spectrum, Brunetière likewise dismisses Zola's novels as exercises in nugatory description, with their mass of 'remarques patiemment accumulées', with their 'foule d'observations prises' and their 'fatras de notes recueillies', unredeemed by any of the human, moral or ideal elements that are the hallmarks of the true (naturalist) novel.[20] Zola is thus a depicter of the externals of life, 'worshipping the offal of experience', as Beckett once graphically wrote of Proust's view of naturalist writers, 'prostrate before the epidermis and the swift epilepsy, and content to transcribe the surface, the façade, behind which the Idea is prisoner'.[21] Within such hostile perspectives Zola's works are summarily dismissed from the novelistic canon as lacking what are considered to be its essential features: social significance, moral responsibility, psychological complexity. His is a rudimentary handiwork that never measures up to the crafts of fiction.

More sympathetic, better-informed and more modern Zola critics, however, have not substantially altered this view, but they have still tended to situate Zola's novels, usually, of course, in a more constructive manner, beyond the pale of the genre. If we are to believe Guy Robert in his study of the principles and general characteristics of Zola's work, the novelist's art is essentially mythical and epic. Its human dramas no longer take place at a human level (the province of the novel), for Zola is not 'un grand créateur d'âmes' (an essential requirement for the novelist).[22] His plots are rigorously formulaic, lacking the openness and unpredictability of the novel, which mirrors life's uncertainties.[23] His essential procedures - accumulation, repetition, expansiveness - belong to the epic. Indeed, the art of the *Rougon-Macquart* transports us *beyond* the realm of the novel into more cosmic and ethereal regions which it is not the usual business of the novel - after all, a somewhat prosaic and down-to-earth genre - to explore. 'De plus en plus', Robert writes,

> l'aspect proprement romanesque s'est effacé et la fidélité de la traduction a cédé à la hardiesse de la création. Au-delà même des groupes humains et des choses dont le poète évoque la vie singulière, se lève tout le cortège des forces élémentaires. La lutte éternelle et silencieuse des puissances contraires mais complémentaires, la victoire toujours compromise de la Vie et de l'Espérance sur les décompositions et les désastres, œuvre de la Mort, nous mènent au cœur même du drame essentiel de l'univers.[24]

Zola's novels have habitually been judged other than as novels - and no more so than by their author himself! 'Le *roman* naturaliste - celui de Zola comme celui des autres - et le *discours* naturaliste ne sont pas homologues', as Henri Mitterand has recently written. 'Et le roman naturaliste réunit des traits littéraires que *Le Roman expérimental* ne permet pas à lui seul de cerner, et dont ni Zola ni ses amis n'ont tenté l'analyse'.[25] In fact, in his theoretical writings, we find Zola adopting a number of the problematic positions in regard to the novel that I have outlined above. He is significantly ill at ease with the term 'roman', and its necessary generic connotations: 'Ce mot entraîne une idée de conte, d'affabulation, de fantaisie, qui jure singulièrement avec les procès-verbaux que nous dressons' (*OC*, X, 1297). For the author of *Le Roman expérimental*, the ideal novel is both a non-generic and an omni-generic form. It is, on the one hand, a 'procès-verbal', 'une tranche de vie', 'un lambeau d'existence', consisting of 'de simples études, sans péripéties ni dénouement', 'notes prises sur la vie et logiquement classées' (*OC*, X, 1308), which capture, on the model of *L'Education sentimentale*, 'cette vérité terre à terre, exacte, qui semble être la négation même de l'art du romancier' (*OC*, XI, 608).[26] On the other hand, the novel knows no limits:

> il a envahi et dépossédé les autres genres. Comme la science, il est maître du monde. Il aborde tous les sujets, écrit l'histoire, traite de physiologie et de psychologie, monte jusqu'à la poésie la plus haute, étudie les questions les plus diverses, la politique, l'économie sociale, la religion, les mœurs. La nature entière est son domaine. Il s'y meut librement, adoptant la forme qu'il lui plaît, prenant le ton qu'il juge le meilleur, n'étant plus borné par aucune limite (*OC*, X, 1240).

Zola's concept of the novel is both totalizing and totalitarian, allied to the fundamental scientific project (with its profound ideological implications) as defined by Claude Bernard and approvingly quoted by the author of *Le Roman expérimental*: 'asservir la nature', 'régler la vie, régler la société', 'nous rendre maîtres de la nature' (*OC*, X, 1188-9). It evinces that 'rationality of domination', with its strategies based on analytic knowledge, that characterizes, as Habermas has argued,[27] the ideology of science and of its 'systems of purposive–rational action'. Inevitably it leads to a thoroughly univocal concept of the novel, which deprives it of its 'literariness', its specifically literary 'genericness', and of (what interests us here) its inherent diversity, for the novel is surely, to employ the terms that Habermas applies to the alternative systems, a genre of 'symbolic interaction'.

'Il faut défendre Emile Zola contre lui-même aussi bien que contre ses critiques', writes Henri Mitterand, for, when it comes to works like *L'Assommoir* or *Germinal*, 'leur univers mimétique, narratif et symbolique ne souffre aucun déchiffrement univoque'.[28] A poetics of the Zola novel, which is still to be written, but to which the various studies in this volume make an important contribution, would have to take into account its usually unacknowledged diversity, at different levels of analysis. There is, of course, at the most obvious level, a standard model for the Zola novel, inherited from Balzac: roughly, the study of a passion or a conflict of passions in a given milieu (as Robbe-Grillet describes the Balzacian type),[29] out of which, consciously - as we see in his 'Différences entre Balzac et moi' (*RM*, V, 1736-7) - or unconsciously, Zola fashioned his own characteristic design. Then, within this general framework, there would be a need to define, on the one hand, the generic complexity of individual texts or groups of texts, and, on the other hand - as I wish to show - to identify the characteristics (formal, modal, thematic) of various novel types (traditional, emergent, constant) which individual novels take up, and, more significantly, modify.

To take a few examples, firstly by reference to older forms, *Une Page d'amour*, as Brian Nelson has shown in a rare study of this work,[30] is the result of a conscious attempt by Zola to write a 'psychological novel' and, in its modest way, confounds the view that Zola is not a depicter of internal states. F.W.J. Hemmings (in another rare study) draws comparisons with *La Princesse de Clèves* and remarks upon the novel's neo-classicism in inspiration and design.[31] In the *Ebauche* of *Au Bonheur des Dames*, to turn to a similar case in point, Zola summarizes the essential ingredients of his future work: on the one hand, 'le côté financier et commercial, la création du monstre, donné par la rivalité des deux magasins'; on the other hand, 'le côté passion, l'amour, donné par une intrigue de femme, une petite ouvrière pauvre dont je raconte l'histoire et qui conquiert Octave peu à peu. *Tout le roman est là*, décidément' (*RM*, III, 1682). Thus, within the very contemporary context of the bustling *grand magasin*, there is an epic of modern commercialism, of commodity fetishism, but also a work with a fundamentally novelistic component, drawing upon a well-tried format: the eighteenth-century 'sentimental novel', in which the humble Denise, a reincarnation of Richardson's Pamela, overcomes her inferior state and by her virtue, turns to her advancement the advances of her master, 'conquis par une femme, qui n'y a mis aucun calcul, qui l'a conquis par sa force de femme' (*RM*, III, 1682). Thirdly, let us take an example of what is perhaps in France a novel type most particularly associated with the age of Balzac and Stendhal. 'Existe-t-il une variété du roman qu'on pourrait appeler le roman politique?', asks Henri Mitterand. 'Si oui', he adds, '*Son Excellence Eugène Rougon* est peut-être le meilleur modèle du genre. Ou le moins mauvais'.[32] Indeed, more than just a novel about politics, it is a novel which plunges the reader into the essential dynamics of the political. Drawing upon the polar tendencies of the type, history and satire, without lapsing into the chronicle or the polemical, the novel politicizes the requisite love intrigue through Eugène and Clorinde's peculiar relationship and, above all, its plot captures the fundamentally conflictual, uncertain, kinetic movement of political life: the ups and downs of the fortunes of this Rougon, the victories and the humiliations, the dialectic of ostentatious public occasions and secret schemes, of elaborate rhetoric and effective deed, of sexual restraint and orgies of power, the reciprocal dependency of the powerful and their supporters, of the strong and the weak, the whole 'ballet des pouvoirs et des honneurs'.[33] In Zola's *Rougon-Macquart* series, we can also point to works which exemplify and contribute to the development of new, emerging, even future novel types. There is in *La Bête humaine*, for example, something of the 'murder mystery', more murder than mystery, of course, but there is a police inquiry, Denizet's brilliant deductions, 'un chef-d'œuvre de fine analyse', 'une reconstitution logique de la vérité', 'une création véritable' (*OC*, VI, 277), which Zola, interestingly, totally deconstructs. Then there is *Germinal*, generically one of Zola's most complex creations[34] and also a work of undeniable generic innovation. As a novel, it is representative much less of the 'roman naturaliste' than of an embryonic kind, the 'roman populiste', which will develop in a later age, in the works of Barbusse and Guilloux for example, into the type of novel that not only portrays the conditions of working-class life, but also problematizes the attitudes of the reader to those conditions through the conscience of an intellectual, bourgeois hero or narrator. In fact, in the earliest stages of what Colette Becker has called 'la fabrique de *Germinal*', the work was intended to be a much more naturalist novel, centring upon the plight of Catherine, her struggles, her fall, her degeneration, her destitution, and according, no doubt, to the model of *L'Assommoir*.[35] It is Zola's earlier novel, his simple life of Gervaise Macquart, that embodies the form, a quintessential naturalist novel, which refines (if that is the appropriate term) the Goncourtian prototype of *Germinie Lacerteux*, rigorously submitting the newest and humblest avatar of the tragic fate to the fundamental naturalist experience of social, moral, linguistic, physical and, above all, ontological disintegration.

The last novel in the 'Macquart cycle', the epic of national disaster, *La Débâcle*, constitutes a significant contribution to a type of novel that is more constant, yet inevitably in transition, and no more so than through Zola's text. This historical novel not only renounces the privileged, authoritative perspectives and discursive voice of the traditional historical narrative, but locates the action at the level of the blind indeterminacy, unpredictability and problematic narrativity of the workings of history itself.[36] Other novels of Zola's series - to complete our troika of examples in this third category - take on the natural tendency of fiction, which the novel normally resists, to interest itself in intellectual matters, even to structure itself accordingly. The obvious case in point is *La Joie de vivre*, a work in which the characters' actions as much as their words debate the current issues of Schopenhauerism, the meaning of life, and whether or not it is worth the effort - 'a true novel of ideas'.[37] The text which has the closest affinity in kind with *La Joie de vivre* (and which, incidentally, Zola originally intended to set by a symbolic sea) is the equally didactic *La Faute de l'abbé Mouret*, a work that can be read, despite its evident lyricism, biblicism and botany, as a novelized 'conte philosophique', as certain indications in the *Ebauche* confirm. Serge, then, would be a representative of humanity, a priest of problematic candidness by virtue of his position; frère Archangias, of course, the vicar of Old Testament lore/law; Jeanbernat, the eighteenth-century 'philosophe', 'un athée ridicule', who cultivates his garden; Désirée, the noble savage; Pascal Rougon, the agent of modern science; with Albine as 'le naturalisme qui va dans le sens libre de l'instinct et de la passion', from whom Serge 'fatalement' turns away.[38]

It is only from such cursory comments in notes and plans that the reader can find in Zola's writings any indication of this generic diversity, for the novelist made no attempt to theorize about it or even to recognize it in his own or other novels. Quoting from *Le Roman expérimental*, Lukacs strenuously objects to the way in which Zola ignores the complexity of Balzac's *La Cousine Bette*, a novel of the 'old realism', by reducing it to the Tainian model of the new naturalism. But, by taking at its face value Zola's description of his own naturalist method expounded in the same work, Lukacs operates the same reductive process.[39] He cites a passage from *Le Roman expérimental* which purports to describe the genesis of a naturalist novel on the theatre, a future *Nana*, a novel which will, as it were, write itself out of the accumulated documentation gathered by the experimental novelist, who 'n'aura qu'à distribuer logiquement les faits' (*OC*, X, 1286). Ironically, the enormous gap between what Zola prescribed and what he achieved with the novel form is best illustrated by this same 'roman sur le monde des théâtres', which is as far removed as any of Zola's works from the linear, demonstrative, documentary design of the experimental novel.

Theatre is not only the setting of certain scenes in *Nana*, it is the very essence of the world that the novel depicts. Nana's life is a series of performances, both in and out of her bed. She not only makes her way in the world of the theatre, but transforms the world into theatre. 'Elle n'a qu'à paraître' (*OC*, IV, 24), declares Borderave, for the whole show to begin. The opening scene of *Nana* is startlingly programmatic: the empty theatre, the darkened stage, suddenly illuminated and bursting with life in the frenzied bustle of activity of the show under the great crystal chandelier, 'le grand lustre de cristal d'un ruissellement de feux jaunes et roses, qui se brisaient du cintre au parterre en une pluie de clarté'. But the dazzling splendour, the 'richesse de palais fabuleux', is all illusion, masking 'la pauvreté du cadre, où les lézardes montraient le plâtre sous la dorure' (*OC*, IV, 27). With its ostentation, its illusory surfaces, its garish displays, its cracks, decay, corruption beneath the lavish exteriors, its frantic animation, all snuffed out with the lights, the theatre represents an elaborate metaphor of Nana herself, her life, her society and the régime that she comes to symbolize. Each scene of the novel is a separate tableau, switched on and off, 'allumé' like the inflamed passions of the men in the theatre. It is the novel of the lust beneath the lustre. The tenor of the theatre scene, like that of the novel as a whole, is captured by the rhythm of the prose, fast, furious, frenzied, fragmented, showing flashes of flesh, 'froissements d'étoffe, un défilé de jupes et de coiffures', 'frisons', 'fard' (*OC*, IV, 27), all the feminine 'froufrou', 'La même fatigue et la même fièvre' (*OC*, IV, 28) in the men too, Fauchery, La Faloise, Muffat, immense explosions of energy fuelled by fantasy and fizzling out in the final 'fouterie'.

'Ce monde du théâtre', the narrator notes, as a count and a prince sip champagne in Nana's dressing room, 'prolongeait le monde réel, dans une farce grave, sous la buée ardente de gaz' (OC, IV, 121). In this 'monde singulièrement mêlé, fait de tous les génies, gâté par tous les vices' (OC, IV, 28), society is at once an immense theatre, devoted to the display of Nana's body, an immense bordello, given over to promiscuous exchanges, an immense temple, dedicated to the religion of her sexuality: 'le *cul* sur un autel et tous sacrifiant devant', as Zola starkly puts it in his preparatory notes. Nana is 'la *chair* centrale', the novel is 'le poème du *cul*' - as the author quaintly insists - 'et la moralité sera le *cul* faisant tout tourner' (RM, II, 1673). It is indeed Nana's 'love' that makes this world go round. In chapter III, for example, set in the Muffat salon, all the comings and goings, all the confused and animated conversations, all lead to a final rendez-vous: 'A demain, chez Nana' (OC, IV, 81), for Nana is the magnetic force towards which all the action gravitates. Or, in more astronomical terms, Nana is at once a gaping black hole, consuming men and their fortunes, and a solar presence from which emanates light: 'et, dans cette transparence, dans cette eau de source, traversée d'un large rayon électrique, elle semblait un soleil, avec sa peau et ses cheveux de flamme. Paris la verrait toujours comme ça, allumée au milieu du cristal, en l'air, ainsi qu'un bon Dieu' (OC, IV, 340).

A novel of theatre, *Nana* is also a kaleidoscope, made up of snatches of Nana's body seen from every angle and from a multiplicity of points of view. As the reader peeps into dressing rooms backstage in the life of the theatre and in the theatre of life, 'on apercevait des coins de nudité, des blancheurs de peau, des pâleurs de linge' (OC, IV, 132). The novel is one long, frenzied, vertiginous peep show, a veritable orgy of voyeurism. As Janet L. Beizer remarks, *Nana* may be defined 'as a prolonged *strip-tease*', in which 'the courtesan's unveiling is more *tease* - promise and process - than disclosure and fait accompli, or *strip*' - an illusion, then, of revelation that is fundamentally a revelation of illusion.[40] In a key, symbolic scene, Muffat, fascinated, transfixed, watches Nana in the mirror of illusion construct her image, create her mythical self, the parodic Venus of the vaudeville. The whole novel is a seemingly endless sequence of disconnected acts, beginning in the appropriately named 'Théâtre des Variétés' and, by the force of Nana's inexhaustible energy and capricious will, progressively transforming society itself into an elaborate Palace of Varieties. It is a work remarkable for the seriality of its plot, fuelled by Nana's insatiable appetites, as a constant procession of men (and women) wait for their 'turns' to parade in and out of her life, men of all varieties, stations, ages, creeds, nations, professions. In total opposition to the naturalist scheme of gradual degeneration, Nana remains indestructible, as if unaffected by time, even in the last stages of the work, as the disasters pile up around her: 'Elle restait grosse, elle restait grasse, d'une belle santé, d'une belle gaieté. Tout ça ne comptait plus, son hôtel lui semblait idiot, trop petit, plein de meubles qui la gênaient. Une misère, simplement histoire de commencer' (OC, IV, 335). Nana's is indeed a story that is constantly beginning again, a serial perpetually 'to be continued'. In the final chapter, what is more, when she disappears from Paris, she literally becomes story (*récit*), a source of endless narratives, a kind of carnal Scheherazade, her name alone generating a thousand and one tales:

> Lorsque son nom revenait, parmi ces messieurs et ces dames, les plus étranges histoires circulaient, chacun donnait des renseignements opposés et prodigieux. Elle avait fait la conquête du vice-roi, elle régnait au fond d'un palais, sur deux cents esclaves dont elle coupait les têtes, pour rire un peu. Pas du tout, elle s'était ruinée avec un grand nègre, une sale passion qui la laissait sans une chemise, dans la débauche crapuleuse du Caire. Quinze jours plus tard, ce fut un étonnement, quelqu'un jurait l'avoir rencontrée en Russie. Une légende se formait, elle était la maîtresse d'un prince, on parlait de ses diamants. Dans le recul de ces contrées lointaines, elle prenait le rayonnement mystérieux d'une idole chargée de pierreries (*OC*, IV, 336).

Just as Nana's insatiable (female) appetites feed upon the (male) possessions that she consumes in exchange for her favours, so the (male) discourse of narrative feeds inexhaustibly upon her sexuality in exchange for the limitless fantasies that it provokes. Such is the essential trade in the bazaar of Zola's courtesan: fiction for fantasy, boundless illusion for the price of admission to Nana's bed. It is not only to Nana's bed that the centripetal direction of the plot is constantly drawn and the seriality of the action invariably leads, but the prodigious creation of her boudoir, her sanctuary and her shrine, comes to figure all the ostentation and lavishness of this extraordinary extravaganza:

> Dans son luxe royal, la nouvelle chambre resplendissait. Des capitons d'argent semaient d'étoiles vives le velours rose thé de la tenture, de ce rose de chair que le ciel prend par les beaux soirs, lorsque Vénus s'allume à l'horizon, sur le fond clair du jour qui se meurt [...]. Puis, en face, c'était le lit d'or et d'argent qui rayonnait avec l'éclat neuf de ses ciselures, un trône assez large pour que Nana pût y étendre la royauté de ses membres nus, un autel d'une richesse byzantine, digne de la toute-puissance de son sexe, et où elle l'étalait à cette heure même, découvert, dans une religieuse impudeur d'idole redoutée (*OC*, IV, 328).

From what aesthetic, then, does Zola's remarkable creation derive? Certainly not from the model of the experimental novel: human documents logically classified. With its theatricality, its constant play upon appearances and illusions, its fragmentary order, its antitheses and inexhaustible elaborate effects contained within a pattern of alternating divergence and convergence, its ostentatiousness, its monumentality, its relentless seriality, *Nana* can only be defined as a *baroque* novel. 'Sur tous les tons, sur tous les modes', writes Claude-Gilbert Dubois, 'une métaphore parcourt la période baroque: *la vie est un théâtre*'.[41] The baroque is an aesthetic of illusion, an art of appearances, creating a world of shifting forms and distinctions. The unity of the baroque work, as we have seen *Nana* to be, is defined by Dubois as an 'unité de convergence', which effects a 'confusion égalitaire des catégories. La truculence et l'afféterie, l'érotisme et le mysticisme voisinent dans la création d'un univers mêlé, où toute chose n'a de sens que comme composante non privilégiée dans le bouquet bigarré du monde'.[42] The privileged figures of the baroque are asyndeton and hyperbole; its figureheads, as Jean Rousset has shown in a famous study, Circe, the magician, or Proteus, god of metamorphosis, and the Peacock, symbol of ostentation.[43] It relishes displays of glory, power, the grandiose and the monumental. Its mythical hero is Don Juan, whether in the guise of Tirso de Molina's 'burlador de Sevilla'[44] or, to span the ages and the sexes, Nana herself through her inexhaustible conquests, for the baroque spirit, as Genette has characterized it, is 'syncrétisme, son ordre est ouverture, son propre est de n'avoir rien en propre et de pousser à leur extrême des caractères qui sont, erratiquement, de tous les lieux et de tous les temps'.[45]

What, then, of the ending of Nana, her eventual defeat and her death, her sudden transformation into 'un charnier, un tas d'humeur et de sang, une pelletée de chair corrompue, jetée là, sur un coussin' (OC, IV, 347–8)? Has the naturalist novel, with its fundamental biological fatality, with its allegory of Nana as the 'mouche d'or', yielding here to her own contamination, finally caught up with the baroque narrative which has, as it were, held it in suspense until now? We should note, however, that Nana's extravagant adventures serve to mask, or are even fuelled by, her fear of death. She always wears 'une médaille de la Vierge', which she devoutly kisses, 'comme une conjuration contre la mort, dont l'idée l'emplissait d'une horreur froide' (OC, IV, 286). This is the familiar dialectic of Don Juan or of Tirso's seducer, who presents 'el haz y el envés de una medalla acuñada por Dios para la eternidad: el goce sensual y el terror de la ultratomba'.[46] Is not Zola's deathbed scene, this final view of Nana's body, in its excessive, antithetical, ghastly splendour, 'ce masque horrible et grotesque du néant, les cheveux, les beaux cheveux, gardant leur flambée de soleil, qui coulaient en un ruissellement d'or' (OC, IV, 348), the character's last show, the ultimate baroque spectacle of this work?

Zola's novel, therefore, brings about an extraordinary reversal of aesthetic values, transforming naturalist reality into illusion and illusion into reality. The lesson of Nana - to return to our main argument - is that the interpreter of Zola's novels must maintain open definitions and resist the temptation to foreclose freer interpretations than those prescribed by Zola himself, by his contemporary critics and by many more modern expositors of his works. Though Zola inherited a standard novelistic form, the Balzacian model, and modified it, theorized in relation to it, to develop his own characteristic arrangement, his novels retain the vitality, the plurality and the receptiveness of the genre. They reinforce the problematics of the form, both conforming to its inherited patterns and departing from them, but undeniably adding to the inexhaustible potentialities of the most capacious of genres.

Notes

1. 'The Problem with a Poetics of the Novel', in *Towards a Poetics of Fiction*, ed. Mark Spilka (Bloomington and London, Indiana University Press, 1977), p. 67.
2. *Ibid.*, pp. 41, 6.
3. Philip Stevick (ed.), *The Theory of the Novel* (New York, The Free Press; London, Collier-Macmillan, 1967), p. 2.
4. 'Magical Narratives: romance as genre', *New Literary History*, VII (1975), 135.
5. *Possibilities: essays on the state of the novel* (Oxford University Press, 1973), p. 11.

6. In *Towards a Poetics of Fiction*, pp. 64–5.
7. See David Lodge, *The Novelist at the Crossroads* (Ark, 1971), pp. 22–4; Alastair Fowler, *Kinds of Literature: an introduction to the theory of genres and modes* (Cambridge, Mass., Harvard University Press, 1982), pp. 123–6.
8. *Possibilities ...*, p. 4.
9. E.M. Forster, *Aspects of the Novel* (London, Edward Arnold, 1927), p. 15. Scholes's familiar diagram is reproduced in *Towards a Poetics of Fiction*, p. 48.
10. *Anatomy of Criticism* (Princeton University Press, 1957), p. 304.
11. As does Maurice Z. Shroder in an article 'The Novel as a Genre' (*The Massachusetts Review*, IV (1963), 291–308), in which the 'matter' of the novel is considered to be a record of 'the passage from a stage of innocence to a state of experience' (p. 292); but so too, one could object, are works belonging to other genres.
12. Cf. N.W. Visser ('The Generic Identity of the Novel', *Novel*, XI (1978), 104): 'the novel is a written, developmental, fictional prose narrative which projects a largely or wholly invented world in which characters - one or more of whom are endowed with interiority - act in minutely discriminated time and space.'
13. In 'The Narrow Bridge of Art', from *Collected Essays*, vol. 2 (London, 1966); quoted by Alastair Fowler, *op. cit.*, p. 122. For the notion of 'heteroglossia', see *The Dialectic Imagination: four essays by M.M. Bakhtin*, ed. Michael Holquist (Austin and London, University of Texas Press, 1981): 'The novel can be defined as a diversity of social speech types (sometimes even diversity of languages) and a diversity of individual voices, artistically organized. Authorial speech, the speeches of narrators, inserted genres, the speech of characters are merely those fundamental compositional unities with whose help heteroglossia can enter the novel; each of them permits a multiplicity of social voices and a wide variety of their links and interrelationships (always more or less dialogized)' (pp. 262–3).
14. *Introduction à l'architecte* (Seuil), pp. 75–6. Cf. Jameson's comments, in 'Magical Narratives', cited above (note 4), that the nature of genre could be defined as: that literary phenomenon which may be articulated *either* in terms of a fixed form *or* in terms of a mode, and which *must* be susceptible of expression in *either* of these critical codes optionally. The advantage of a definition like this consists not only in its exposure of false problems (thus, it would no longer make any sense to wonder whether the novel *as such* can be considered a genre, inasmuch as one cannot imagine any determinate literary mode which would correspond to such a 'form'); but also in its capacity to generate new lines of research, for example, to raise the question of the nature of the *mode* to which such a fixed form as the historical novel may be said to correspond, or that of the *fixed form* of which a familiar mode like that of romance may be said to be the expression (pp. 137–8).
15. *Stendhal: a study of his novels* (Oxford, The Clarendon Press, 1964), p. 33.
16. Tzvetan Todorov, 'Genres littéraires', in, O. Ducrot and T. Todorov, *Dictionnaire encyclopédique des sciences du langage* (Seuil, 1972), p. 196. I suspect that *Ulysses* does not belong to a different category of novel, but presents a particular case of complex generic combinations and transgressions.
17. In the Bordas edition, 1969, pp. 484–5, where the emphasis appears.
18. 'Narrate or Describe?', in *Writer and Critic, and Other Essays*, ed. and tr. A.D. Kahn (New York, The Merlin Press, 1970), pp. 133, 127; and 'The Zola Centenary', *Studies in European Realism* (New York, Grosset & Dunlap, 1964), p. 92.
19. *Ibid.*, p. 93.
20. *Le Roman naturaliste* (Calmann-Lévy, 1896 edition), p. 138.
21. *Proust* (Calder & Boyars, 1965 edition), pp. 78–9.

22. *Emile Zola: principes et caractères généraux de son œuvre* (Les Belles Lettres, 1952), pp. 113, 133, 114.
23. 'La plupart des romans de la série ont entre eux un air de parenté qui vient d'abord des caractères les plus généraux de leur structure et du déroulement de leur intrigue. Jamais Zola n'abandonne celle-ci à elle-même, il ne laisse plus les événements s'engendrer eux-mêmes que les caractères se développer en vertu d'une loi qui leur soit propre. Chaque roman est consacré à l'étude d'un milieu particulier; l'action y est strictement une; tous ses nœuds se défont parfaitement à la fin de l'œuvre. Il est peu de formule aussi rigoureuse: Zola ne tolère ni interférence des milieux, ni enchevêtrement des faits hétérogènes' (*ibid.*, p. 119).
24. *Ibid.*, pp. 134–5.
25. *Zola et le naturalisme* (Presses Universitaires de France, 1986), p. 19.
26. On Zola's interpretations of Flaubert's novel, see F.W.J. Hemmings, 'Zola and *L'Education sentimentale*', *The Romanic Review*, L (1959), pp. 35–40.
27. See Jurgen Habermas, 'Technology and Science as "Ideology" ', in *Towards a Rational Society* (Boston, Beacon Press, 1970), pp. 91–4.
28. *Le Regard et le signe* (Presses Universitaires de France, 1987), pp. 55, 7.
29. *Pour un nouveau roman* (Gallimard, 1963), p. 17.
30. See *Zola and the Bourgeoisie: a study of themes and techniques in* Les Rougon-Macquart (London, Macmillan, 1983), pp. 96–128.
31. *Emile Zola* (2nd edition, Oxford, The Clarendon Press, 1966), pp. 129–31.
32. *Le Regard et le signe*, p. 191.
33. *Ibid.*, p. 202.
34. See D. Baguley, '*Germinal* et les genres: parcours transtextuels', *Europe*, LXIII, (1985), 42–53.
35. See Colette Becker (ed.), *Emile Zola: la fabrique de* Germinal (SEDES, 1986): an edition of the whole preparatory dossier of the novel. Cf. p. 266: 'Etudier le personnage de Catherine, de façon à le faire central et intéressant. Il faut qu'il emplisse le livre, si je veux obtenir beaucoup d'intérêt' (*Ebauche*, fol. 436).
36. On this point, see D. Baguley, 'Le Récit de guerre: narration et focalisation dans *La Débâcle* ', *Littérature*, no. 50 (1983), 77–90.
37. See F.W.J. Hemmings, *Emile Zola*, p. 183.
38. B.N., N.a.f., Ms. 10294, fol. 9 and fol. 4.
39. See 'The Zola Centenary', *op. cit.*, pp. 89–91.
40. 'Uncovering *Nana*: the courtesan's new clothes', *L'Esprit créateur*, XXV (1985), 47. On the voyeurism of this novel, see also Chantal Jennings, 'Les Trois visages de *Nana*', *The French Review*, XLIV, (1971), 121.
41. *Le Baroque: profondeurs de l'apparence* (Larousse, 1973), p. 179.
42. *Ibid.*, p. 61.
43. See Jean Rousset, *La Littérature de l'âge baroque en France: Circé et le Paon* (José Corti, 1954).
44. On *El Burlador de Sevilla y convidado de piedra* (1630) and the baroque spirit, see Guillermo Diaz-Plaja, *El Espiritu del barroco* (Barcelona, Editorial Critica, 1980), chapter 10.
45. 'D'un récit baroque', in *Figures II* (Seuil, 1969), p. 222.
46. Guillermo Diaz-Plaja, *op. cit.*, p. 156.

2

ZOLA AND THE ART OF CONTAINING THE UNCONTAINABLE

Philip Walker

Many of the main characteristics of Zola's fiction largely resulted from his commitment to two partly incompatible sets of artistic goals. It is impossible to form a clear notion of the problems that Zola faced as a craftsman or to grasp the overall structure of his works without taking this dichotomy and how he coped with it into account.

One of these two sets of goals consisted of unity, order, harmony, coherence, clarity, simplicity, solidity - all those widely shared, if not universal, artistic values that can be described as exclusively constructive, ordering, delimiting, and centripetal.[1] In 1860, at the very outset of his career, he counselled Cézanne to 'travailler le dessin fort et firme - *unguibus et rostro*'.[2] He wrote in a letter to Baille that same year: 'Dieu me garde d'être bégueule, tu sais combien je désire la liberté dans l'art, combien je suis romantique, mais avant tout je suis poète et j'aime l'harmonie des idées et des images'.[3] Outlining his poetic ambitions in *Le Journal populaire de Lille* on 16 April 1864, he affirmed that poets and scientists alike 'essaient de donner dans leurs œuvres une idée de l'harmonie universelle' (*OC*, X, 312). Artistic geniuses may portray reality in any colour they wish and represent circles by squares and straight lines by broken lines, he stated in a letter addressed to Valabrègue that August, 'pourvu que les images reproduites aient l'harmonie et la splendeur de la beauté'. He insisted that all the great general rules common to geniuses 'se réduisent au simple usage du bon sens et de l'harmonie innée'.[4] 'Rien ne ravit l'esprit,' he remarked in *L'Echo du Nord* a few months later, 'comme l'unité dans la grandeur' (*OC*, X, 325). In another letter to Valabrègue, he represented the artist as a demiurge creating order out of chaos, light out of darkness.[5] He confessed that what drew him to realism was partly its extraordinary 'solidité'.[6]

Ever faithful to the same group of artistic ideals, he observed in *Le Figaro* of 9 November 1880 that one of the advantages of always speaking the truth was that it assures that everything one says will be consistent: 'aucune incohérence, aucune contradiction à redouter' (*OC*, XIV, 470). In 1896, sixteen years later, he exclaimed:

> Ah!, la clarté, la limpidité, la simplicité! imaginez-vous que j'en meurs! [...] Ah! pas
> septentrional pour deux sous, latin dans le cœur et dans le cerveau, amant fou des

belles architectures symétriques, constructeur de pyramides sous le brûlant ciel bleu. Tel est mon état, je n'en comprends pas d'autre. Je voudrais la phrase de cristal, clair et si simple que les yeux ingénus des enfants pussent la pénétrer de part en part [...]. Je voudrais l'idée si vraie, si nue, qu'elle apparût transparente elle-même, et d'une solidité de diamant dans le cristal de la phrase (OC XIV, 725).

As he jotted down his plans for Les Rougon-Macquart in the winter of 1868–9, he was strongly motivated, particularly at the outset, by the same centripetal artistic aims. He began with the intention of making this new project as unified, harmonious, clear, simple, and solid as possible. Comparing it with La Comédie humaine, he told himself that he must react to Balzac's running analysis 'par la construction solide des masses, des chapitres' (RM, V, 1743). 'Mon roman,' he insisted, 'doit être simple' (RM, V, 1740). He specified that he must limit it to a small cast of characters (RM, V, 1744), include hardly any descriptions (RM, V, 1745) and keep his subject within strict bounds. 'Je ne veux pas peindre la société contemporaine,' he noted, 'mais une seule famille [...]. Si j'accepte un cadre historique, c'est uniquement pour avoir un milieu qui réagisse' (RM, V, 1737). Whereas Balzac was not only a scholar, but also a political thinker, philosopher and moralist, he, Emile Zola, must, he insisted, be simply a naturalist, simply a physiologist (RM, V, 1737). He envisaged his major scholarly subjects - heredity and the Second Empire - as the two faces of a single coin. Each novel, he wrote, sounding like Taine, was to be deduced 'mathématiquement' from a single 'fait générateur' (RM, V, 1742). Granting that it is impossible to avoid having some philosophy or other, he told himself, 'Prendre avant tout une tendance philosophique, non pour l'étaler, mais pour donner une unité à mes livres' (RM, V, 1744).

He customarily began his preliminary sketch of a novel by summing up its central theme in a nutshell, writing, for example, in the 'Ebauche' of La Conquête de Plassans, 'ce roman est la province sous l'empire',[7] or in the 'Ebauche' of L'Assommoir, 'En un mot, un tableau très exact de la vie du peuple avec ses ordures, sa vie lâché, son langage grossier' (RM, II, 1543). He would then 'deduce' the plots from these initial definitions, striving to hold the flood of his imagination safely within the channels carved by his invariably rigorous logic.[8]

Yet hard as Zola laboured to attain unity, order, harmony, clarity, simplicity, consistency, and solidity, he was also, it would seem, at least equally committed to the other set of goals which I have mentioned - goals which compelled him to move away from, or even dispense with, a centre.

One of them was surely his ideal of the modern novel as a form with room for every traditional literary form but bound to none. 'Depuis le dix-huitième siècle,' he wrote in 1878, 'le roman chez nous a brisé le cadre étroit où il était enfermé; il est devenu l'histoire et la critique, je prouverais même aisément qu'il est devenu la poésie. Avec Balzac, il a absorbé tous les genres.' Montaigne's Essais was, in his opinion, 'un roman'. So also were Pantagruel, Les Provinciales, Les Lettres persanes, and all other 'études humaines' (OC, X, 1340).

Another of Zola's centrifugal aims was to try, like Montaigne, to incarnate himself in his works - his whole vast, complex self, with all its contradictions.

He deplored the inability of human beings to communicate or to see each other as they really are. He wanted to tear away all masks, including his own, and cursed Heaven 'de nous avoir faits ainsi, d'avoir permis le mensonge éternel en cachant l'être sous le paraître'.[9] He also loathed not only the regimentation but also the specialization of modern society. 'L'homme n'est plus un entier, il n'est plus libre,' he complained after quitting in disgust his first job, a clerkship on the Paris docks. Any truly free spirit, he said, 'aimera mieux se laisser briser que se soumettre à devenir une partie, lui qui est un tout'.[10] 'Je suis artiste,' he proclaimed in a well-known early manifesto,

> et je vous donne ma chair et mon sang, mon cœur et ma pensée. [...] Je ne puis vous donner autre chose, puisque je me donne entier, dans ma violence ou dans ma douceur, tel que Dieu m'a créé. [...] Si vous me demandez ce que je viens faire en ce monde, moi artiste, je vous répondrai: 'Je viens vivre tout haut'.[11]

Still another of Zola's centrifugal goals - one that he shared with many other members of his generation - was omniscience.[12] 'On mesure le génie,' he wrote in 1880, 'aux vérités qu'il apporte sur l'homme et la nature' (*OC*, XII, 509). As numerous critics have noted, he wanted to portray the whole of reality.[13] At the outset of his career, he had, as one knows, stubbornly, but vainly, tried to embrace all creation past, present and future in a single poem. His subsequent writings were largely motivated by the same urge to comprehend and portray the great whole. 'Je voudrais être un nouveau Lucrèce et écrire en beaux vers la philosophie de nos connaissances, plus étendues et plus certaines que celles de l'ancienne Rome,' he confessed in April 1864 (*OC*, X, 313). Later that same year, he divulged another reason why he liked the realists: their craving to paint nature 'dans son ensemble, sans exclusion aucune'. 'L'œuvre d'art,' he stated, '[...] doit embrasser l'horizon entier'.[14] His failure to do so tormented him. 'Ah! Ninon, je n'ai rien fait encore,' he sighed in his preface to *Nouveaux Contes à Ninon* (1866):

> Je pleure sur cette montagne de papier noirci; je me désole à penser que je n'ai pu étancher ma soif du vrai, que la grande nature échappe à mes bras trop courts. C'est l'âpre désir, prendre la terre, la posséder dans une étreinte, tout voir, tout savoir, tout dire. Je voudrais coucher l'humanité sur une page blanche, tous les êtres, toutes les choses; une œuvre qui serait l'arche immense (*OC*, IX, 351).

In *L'Œuvre*, his *alter ego* Sandoz voices the same intention, the same anguish, the same stubbornness, and Claude, Zola's other principal *alter ego* in that novel, 'se brisait à cette besogne impossible de faire tenir toute la nature sur une toile' (*OC*, V, 636). As Zola approached the end of the *Rougon-Macquart* series, he remained as attached as ever to this painful, yet to him infinitely desirable object. 'L'enfantement d'un livre est pour moi une abominable torture,' he confessed in 1892, while struggling to complete *La Débâcle*, 'parce qu'il ne saurait contenter mon besoin impérieux d'universalité et de totalité' (*RM*, V, 1417).

Like thousands of his thoughtful contemporaries, he had taken refuge from the extreme metaphysical confusion of the times in little, firm empirical facts and scientific certainties. But these were hardly enough to satisfy his appetite for absolute knowledge. No less than Littré, Taine or Renan, and other contemporary positivists (Madame Ackermann, for example), could he resist the temptation to venture beyond the limits of empirical observation and scientific law. He longed for 'cette Vérité une et entière,' as he once put it, 'qui seule guérirait mon esprit malade' (*OC*, IX, 182). Unfortunately, the Grail-like ultimate Truth eluded him no matter how hard he tried to grasp it. 'Il n'est peut-être pas deux hommes qui aient le même dogme, la même foi,' he lamented. 'Chacun apporte un léger changement à la pensée du voisin. La vérité n'est donc pas de ce monde, puisqu'elle n'est point universelle, absolue' (*OC*, X, 139).

What was he to do, then, this would-be painter of the totality of all that was, is, and ever shall be? If he could not embrace everything, he could at least come as close to doing so as possible. He could record in apparently exhaustive detail what he did see, creating through the sheer mass and variety of his finite observations the illusion of reality in all its infinitude. Moreover, if he could not compel the angel of truth to reveal his name, he could at least leave behind in his writings the traces of his Jacob-like struggle with him. (The image is, of course, Zola's: the image at the heart of *L'Œuvre*.) He could communicate, if nothing more, the imperfect, unsystematic, yet none the less precious knowledge about it that he was gaining from their confrontation. He could pass on, if not the Ultimate Truth itself, the many disparate, largely cloudy philosophical and religious intuitions, hypotheses, reveries, nightmares, and visions competing for predominance in his head. He was, moreover, compelled to do so not only to achieve his goal of baring to the public his whole heart and mind, but also because there was always the chance that some of his ideas just might be right.

He obviously devoted enormous energy and skill to the formidable task of achieving all three of these centrifugal, highly disruptive goals. *Les Rougon-Macquart* in particular is an exceedingly complex mixture of naturalistic, realistic, romantic, classical, and other contrasting literary ingredients. It includes, along with other fictional or poetic genres or subgenres, the historical novel, the psychological novel, the philosophical novel, the *roman à clef*, the *roman à idées*, the crime thriller, the fairy tale, science fiction, satire, melodrama, allegory, farce, comedy, tragedy, the lyric, the epic and the Greek tale. Their tense interplay is further complicated by the admixture of those non-fictional forms that one associates with Zola - above all physiological and sociological treatises, history, autobiography, and prophecy. It would be futile to identify *Les Rougon-Macquart* exclusively with any one of these different sorts of writing. Even the term *epic*, often applied to Zola's works, may strike one as inadequate, perhaps even misleading (especially if one has in mind Mikhail Bakhtin's well-known definition of this genre). Zola's *magnum opus* transcends all genres, like life itself; but at the same time, it reflects his urge to exploit the whole universe of literary conventions.[15]

Zola's propensity to complicate the generic structure of his fiction, thereby sometimes straining its formal unity to the breaking point, is already apparent in the series' overture. *La Fortune des Rougon* combines the realistic novel of money, bourgeois greed, and social climbing, laced with satire and vulgar farce, with the humanitarian epic and what Zola referred to as 'les anciens contes grecs', 'l'éternelle idylle que chaque époque reprend, depuis *Daphnis et*

Chloé (*OC*, XII, 665).[16] *La Curée*, the second novel in the series, seeks to fuse together Balzac, Petronius, Longus, Euripides and Racine. The third, *Le Ventre de Paris*, is an explosive mixture of naturalistic and romantic forms, a Zolaesque variation on *Notre-Dame de Paris*. Volume IV, *La Conquête de Plassans*, relatively sober and classical, attests to its author's lingering admiration for Molière. *Germinal* itself, Zola's masterpiece, is at least as generically incongruous as any of Zola's other works, largely patterned as it is, in this respect, on *La Fortune des Rougon*. Moreover, when one stands back and views *Les Rougon-Macquart*, *Les Trois Villes* and *Les Quatre Evangiles* as a whole, one can perceive, embedded in it, a vast, shadowy medieval mystery play including numerous biblical stories and characters in modern dress - not to mention the traditional stations, the Eden of *La Faute de l'abbé Mouret*, the demons and tortured souls of *L'Assommoir* and *Germinal*, and the New Jerusalems of *Les Quatre Evangiles*.

The more familiar one becomes with Zola's work, the more one may also be struck by his commitment to his second centrifugal goal: embodying himself in his works - his whole self. He never abandoned this objective. He devoted to it enormous energy and skill. He not only populated his fiction with part-time or full-time mouthpieces, avatars, *alter egos*, realistic or idealized veiled self-portraits - Pascal Rougon, Lazare Chanteau, Pauline Quenu, Etienne Lantier, Sandoz, Claude Lantier, Pierre Lantier, Madame Caroline and all the rest. He imparted to the narratives in which many of these characters appear a strongly autobiographical quality. While many writers content themselves with only one or two such works - usually their maiden efforts - he kept on producing them, year after year, decade after decade. *La Joie de vivre*, *L'Œuvre* and *Le Docteur Pascal* reflect Zola's life no less than *La Confession de Claude*. All three massive volumes of *Les Trois Villes* revolve around another of Zola's major *alter egos*, the confused, spiritually questing Abbé Pierre Froment. *Fécondité*, *Travail* and *Vérité*, with their messianic heroes, Mathieu, Marc and Luc, are all imaginary autobiographies. But, of course, Zola did not stop there in his efforts to project himself into his writings. He did it quite consciously through his style,[17] his constant exploitation of his own obsessions and myths. He did it through the scientific, political, oneiric, prophetic and other uses to which he put his fiction. He did it through his endless celebration of his supreme values, his cults of nature, life, love, work, truth, power, science, humanity, history, justice, progress, France, Paris, the nineteenth century.

Both his work and his personality continually frustrate critical assimilation. Most of the early critics who thought that they had taken Zola's measure - Brunetière, Faguet, Croce, Ortega y Gasset, among others - as one can see now, were wrong. One is constantly discovering new and surprising traits. Nor is there any fixed centre in him. Zola is impossible to pin down, as the Goncourt brothers remarked after their first meeting with him.[18] What defines him are, above all, his very human contradictions, the multiple heterogeneous personae constantly competing in him for full self-expression: the arrogant Zola and the humble Zola, the dogmatist and the self-doubter, the pious son and the Oedipal monster, the hateful, vengeful Zola, and the apostle of brotherly love, the crude Zola and the delicate Zola, the chaste moralist and the voluptuary, the optimist and the pessimist, the male and the female, the scientist and the shaman, the positivist and the idealist, the committed man of action and the detached observer, the realist and the romantic, the enemy of Christianity and the Christian despite himself, the serious seeker after truth and the dreamer, the 'grand primaire' and the subtle, profound thinker.

Zola also never ceased labouring to attain those centrifugal goals engendered by his desire to depict the whole of reality. As Harry Levin has remarked, no comparable man of letters, except Poe, has tried so hard to grasp the scientific imagination.[19] However, far from limiting himself to the purely scientific vision of reality, itself unstable and constantly expanding,[20] Zola also poured into his novels the often contradictory results of his unending quest for angelic knowledge. In work after work, his characters, actions, settings and narrative style - the entire form and content of his fiction - reflect not only the infinitely aspiring scientist, but also the equally ambitious philosopher and would-be prophet. A literary realist without any fixed centre (as Mircea Eliade would have said) around which to organize a unified vision of reality, he does indeed pass on to us, for want of anything better, the disparate, largely warring elements of his thought about it: his mountainous accumulations of direct, empirical observations; his folders bulging with scientific notes; his positivism à la Littré or Bernard; his scientism à la Michelet, Lucas, Taine or Renan; his murky, shifting scepticism reminiscent now of Montaigne, now of Voltaire, now of Jouffroy; his pessimism, recalling now Pascal, now Musset, now Sainte-Beuve, now Darwin, now Schopenhauer; his materialism; his idealistic 'new faith' based on geology, with its Cuvier-like catastrophism and its unquestioning trust in eternal progress; his evolutionism; his apocalyptic humanitarianism; his myth of eternal return; his 'new religions' of work, love and life.[21] Their very mass does indeed create an illusion of omniscience.

The artistic problems that arose from the conflicts between the two sets of goals with which I am concerned here were for the most part awesome. To solve them, the young Zola, groping for the right form for his *magnum opus*, had to make a truly enormous creative effort, especially since what he once called 'mon amour de l'absolu' made him abhor halfway measures (*OC*, IX, 349). How, in the same work, could he exemplify a genre whose nature was to devour all genres, embody his entire protean self, and convey his whole chaotic vision of reality while sacrificing no more unity, harmony, simplicity, clarity and solidity than was absolutely necessary?

One of the things which any craftsman hoping to cope with these problems would have to do would be to start out by giving himself plenty of room, and this, of course, is what Zola did. To be sure, he had other motives for choosing a large canvas - for example, his desire to impose himself on the public, if only through sheer size and weight. But his need to deal successfully with the tensions between his centripetal and centrifugal objectives was in itself sufficient reason, and one wonders if without it the ultimate size of *Les Rougon-Macquart* would have had to be quite as large.

A craftsman with the same centripetal and centrifugal goals as Zola's would also be well advised not to attempt to inject his entire self into just one or two characters, but, instead, to distribute different aspects of it among a large number of them. He could thus portray as many of his own different traits as he pleased without making any of his dramatis personae overly complex or incoherent. This too Zola did. Each of his mouthpieces, *alter egos*, and the like is no more complicated than many other fictional creations. As a group, however, they come much closer to reflecting the man in all his complexity and roundness than any one of them does individually.

Another procedure that would help such a craftsman reconcile his centripetal and centrifugal goals would be to adopt an extremely complex, composite, compartmentalized structure, dividing and subdividing his subject-matter, story and recital into numerous parts, multiplying voices, points of view and narrative sections. It would thus be possible to achieve within individual parts, chapters, episodes and so on something of the simple harmony and clarity that the work could never possess when considered in its entirety. At the same time, there would be no end to the pleasing symphonic patterns that could be created through an ordered play of contrasts, rhythmic alternations, contrapuntal elaborations.

It would be particularly to this craftsman's advantage, in this respect, to adopt an outright serial form, splitting up his massive 'roman' into separate volumes each of which could be read and appreciated either as an independent novel or as only a part of the larger artistic whole. Those readers who chose to approach this or that volume as a separate work could appreciate its inner unity, simplicity, solidity and clarity in so far as it possessed them, without being disturbed by the complexities and incoherences discernible in the whole *opus*. On the other hand, when one contemplated the entire *opus* as a single work, those aspects of it which were grounded in Zola's centrifugal aspirations would become apparent.

It is not surprising, therefore, that Zola did indeed organize *Les Rougon-Macquart* in this fashion. Here, too, he had other reasons for doing so, but, given the two sets of goals with which one is concerned here, he really had no alternative. As for the precise ways, many of which have already been identified by Auguste Dezalay, Neide de Faria and others, in which he organized the series, there is not enough space here to enumerate them all.[22] But one may note in passing how, for example, he seems to have favoured primarily his centripetal aims in some novels. In *La Conquête de Plassans*, for instance, or *Une Page d'amour* or *Le Rêve*, he confines himself to simpler, more coherent thematic, generic and narrative structures; he limits himself to smaller casts of characters and prefers a simpler, more homogeneous style than he generally does elsewhere; he maintains a more consistent mood; he shows fewer sides of himself and his view of nature; he has a plainer, more coherent message. On the other hand, in other volumes - for instance, *La Bête humaine*,[23] not to mention *Germinal* - he gives greater freedom to one or more of his centrifugal urges. I have already mentioned the complex generic structure of the latter novel, but one might also recall its many levels of meaning, huge cast of characters, collective hero, sweeping horizons, alternation between cinematic, dramatic and historical narrative modes, mirage-like reflections of all the chief clashing elements of Zola's personality and all the main persistent elements of his chaotic vision of God, man, nature and history.

Moreover, each of the different *Rougon-Macquart* novels can be treated as a separate, self-contained entity. It is not at all necessary, in order to enjoy one, to have read any of the others. Just as the series as a whole has its central themes, each volume has its own. Each volume has its own self-contained plot, central cast, special setting. Each has its own distinctive structural traits: for example, the sinister thirteen chapters and arching narrative line of *L'Assommoir*, patterned on the curve of the sea at Saint-Aubin-sur-mer; or *Une Page d'amour*, with its five parts, each ending with a lyrical description of Paris. Although Zola is a master of the art of arousing curiosity, he makes little use of it to force his readers to go on from one novel to the next. The volume whose final pages engender the most suspense is, paradoxically, the last one, *Le Docteur Pascal*. (Is Pascal and Clotilde's baby boy, 'l'enfant inconnu', truly the New Messiah for which all the world is waiting?)

Yet these devices hardly sufficed, if Zola was to solve all the problems engendered by the tensions between his centripetal and centrifugal goals. He also had to seek an overall form which, again paradoxically, would at once restrain his urge to expand and give it free rein. He had to find a way of appearing to narrow his focus without really doing so, of seeming to portray only a corner of infinite nature while actually trying to convey his vision of it all. This, too, is exactly what he did - and, one may suppose, very deliberately. For he was surely sharing with us something of his own experience when he related in *L'Œuvre* how Sandoz, after vainly attempting a gigantic project reminiscent of *La Genèse* or *La Chaîne des êtres*, had set out to discover a more limited (as well as human) setting for this ambitious plan, 'un cadre plus resserré, plus humain, où il ferait tenir pourtant sa vaste ambition' (*OC*, V, 466–7).

Part of the solution was, needless to say, to treat his uncontainable theme figuratively, using synecdoche, metonymy and metaphor, making what he could depict directly into a symbol of his true subject-matter. He himself employed the common technical terms 'cadre' (as in the passage just cited) to describe those elements of fiction through which one shows - or at least points at - something bigger and/or farther away and, in other respects also, perhaps less artistically manageable. But he might also have used the word 'lens' or 'mirror' or, like the Saint James version of Paul's first epistle to the Corinthians, 'glass'. Or even the phrase 'glass bottle' or 'glass bowl', for when one enters a narrative consisting of such elements, one finds oneself within, so to speak, a more or less transparent container from which, like a goldfish or trapped fly, one can survey the outside world. Yet the word 'cadre' is marvellously apt. One can imagine the young Zola, brush in hand, trying to capture all of Nature directly on a canvas. His gigantic subject, incompletely and dimly revealed, mostly swathed in churning clouds and shifting shadows, is as much a figment of his imagination as not, and, what is worse, what he thinks he sees keeps changing. The portrait, constantly scraped and repainted, lacks order, harmony, clarity, simplicity and solidity. Try as he may, he cannot crowd all of what he sees or suspects he sees on to it. The design has no central focus, no clear organizing principle. He rips the canvas up in despair. Then, suddenly, he has an idea. He pours all his art into fashioning an empty frame and holds it up at such an angle that passers-by can glimpse through it his vast, elusive model, and, as they do so, he helps them to try to understand what they are seeing by sharing with them his own tentative observations.

But what he actually produced in *Les Rougon-Macquart* is far more elaborate than just a single frame. It is, instead, an enormously complex optical structure involving multiple series of frames, each frame larger than the one through which it is reached as the eye travels from one to the other towards its infinitely distant goal. The history of the Rougons and Macquarts is a fictional frame through which one perceives the history of an age, through which one sees the history of humanity, through which one's vision is focused on the whole of creation. Les Halles in *Le Ventre de Paris* are not only, as Zola puts it in his working notes, 'le ventre; - le ventre de Paris [...] le ventre de l'humanité, et, par extension, la bourgeoisie [...] le ventre de l'Empire'.[24] They are also a frame through which he invites his readers to contemplate the eternal struggle between the fat and the lean. The stories of Etienne, the Maheus, the Grégoires, and other leading individual characters of *Germinal* are frames through which one sees the whole fictional community of Montsou, through which one sees a whole typical mining community, through which one sees the whole mid-nineteenth-century French working class and its struggle for economic justice, through which one sees the whole worldwide, still-unfolding conflict between capital and labour, through which one dimly perceives something perhaps resembling (one cannot be sure) Darwin's struggle for survival or Zola's myth of life's eternal recommencement or the march of Humanity towards Utopia or perhaps something more like Cuvier's catastrophism. The real subject of *La Terre*, glimpsed through the lives of its fictional peasants, is not old Fouan's King Lear-like story or Jean's unhappy tale, or peasants in general. Nor is it La Beauce or its rich soil. For these are only still other frames for the great, unbounded theme on which all the multitudinous frames of *Les Rougon-Macquart* are centred, like batteries of telescopes fixed on the same shimmering, evasive galaxy.[25]

Again, no inventory of the principal means employed by Zola to achieve his two sets of goals would be complete that did not mention ambiguity. Without exploiting this device to the hilt, no writer with Zola's temperament and view of reality could possibly hope to incarnate them in a single novel and at the same time placate his love of unity, simplicity, harmony, clarity and solidity. Through ambiguity, on the other hand, it would be possible to write a work open to multiple interpretations, each of which could be internally unified, simple, harmonious, clear and solid, but which, taken together, would evoke his temperament and thought in all their complexity and incoherence. To re-read *Les Rougon-Macquart* is to become aware that this is also surely one of the things that Zola was consciously or unconsciously trying to do in it.

One thinks above all of the apparently inexhaustible capacity of *Germinal* to give birth to one different interpretation after another, most of them justifiable as far as they go. Not even *La Faute de l'abbé Mouret*, *L'Assommoir*, *La Joie de vivre* or *L'Œuvre* would appear upon reflection to be so richly, violently ambiguous. I say again 'upon reflection' because Zola's ambiguity, like numerous other aspects of his art, is not immediately apparent. Probably most readers, including many highly intelligent ones, have read *Germinal* all the way through without suspecting it. When, for example, André Wurmser declares that the truth conveyed to us by *Germinal* conforms to his own Marxist views, he does so with utter conviction. He vigorously rejects any contradictory interpretation.[26] On the other hand, Jules Lemaître, surely one of Zola's most brilliant contemporary critics, was unaware of anything in this novel that did not fit in with his conception of *Les Rougon-Macquart* as 'une épopée pessimiste de l'animalité humaine'. 'Les hommes apparaissant,' he wrote of *Germinal*, 'semblables à des flots, sur une mer de ténèbres et d'inconscience: voilà la vision philosophique, très simple, dans laquelle ce drame se résout'.[27]

Yet as soon as one becomes aware of the ambiguity of *Germinal* and starts looking for it, one finds it everywhere - and not just in the old debate as to whether this novel is a product of Zola's pessimism or Zola's optimism or in the numerous different possible readings of its celebrated ending. What is the allegorical significance, if any, of Etienne's and Négrel's brotherly embrace? Is *Germinal* a pantheistic novel, and, if so, what sort of pantheism does it reflect? Is it a deterministic work, and, if so, what kind of determinism does it express - scientific, Tainian, pantheistic? Is its time geological time or some other kind of time - the circular time of the myth of eternal return or a time more in accordance with apocalyptic romantic humanitarianism? These are only a few of the many questions which a close reading suggests and which admit two or more conflicting answers.[28]

After probing *Germinal* and Zola's other most ambiguous novels deeply, one also becomes aware of the complex craft, the rich assemblage of devices, whereby their ubiquitous psychological and philosophical ambiguity is produced: the mask of impersonality and impassibility; the studied dearth of direct, unveiled authorial commentary; the free indirect discourse; the metaphors, similes and personifications which may or may not be just figures of speech; the vast array of untagged possible symbols or symbolic patterns (like those which psychoanalysts hunt for in apparently realistic dreams), some of which support one interpretation, others alternative interpretations. (One begins to understand Mallarmé's remark that if he had been a novelist he would have written like Zola.)

The complex frame structures of many *Rougon-Macquart* novels, not to mention that of the series taken as a whole, are themselves vehicles of ambiguity; for one's interpretation of these texts largely depends on which of their successive frames one perceives, if any, and which one takes to be the final, most distant one. If, for example, one regards the story of the Monsou miners' strike as merely a frame for a general socio-historical study of modern economic class warfare, one will interpret *Germinal*'s message one way. But if one sees both the strike story and the socio-historical study as frames for a metaphysical vision, one will interpret the novel in another way, shedding light on a different side of Zola.

Zola's use of a serial form in *Les Rougon-Macquart* also contributes to the ambiguity of its novels. By dividing the series up into volumes each of which can be enjoyed as a distinct work of art, Zola further weakened its overall unity. This had the advantage of multiplying indefinitely the number of contexts in which each of the works can be read. It is understandable that the major explicators of *Germinal* have come up with such different glosses. And it is not surprising that almost all of them have merit as far as they go. They do not invalidate one another. Rather, their differences are due to their scholarly authors' having viewed the novel through lenses of different colours. Added up, they provide, however, a truer, more complete view of the man embodied in the text than each of them does alone. In their ensemble, they go a long way towards capturing most of Zola's bewildering complexity and incoherence, his clashing traits and roles, his discordant reveries and nightmares, his competing intuitions regarding the nature of God, man, nature and history. Yet taken separately, each of these different interpretations does indeed seem, if not as 'simple' as Lemaître's, quite unified, clear, harmonious and solid.

Finally, still another recourse was available to Zola in his struggle to work out the problems arising from the tensions between his centripetal and centrifugal goals. Besides giving himself plenty of room, multiplying mouthpieces, establishing Renan-like dialogues, employing frames and cultivating ambiguity, he could utilize the art of compensation. He could try to make up for the enormous generic, psychological and philosophical incoherences and nebulosities in his fiction by ensuring that it would be manifestly circumscribed, solid and harmonious in other respects. This, also, Zola's artistic genius led him to do. The confusion, elusiveness and infinite expansiveness of his philosophical vision is aesthetically balanced to a great extent by the extraordinary concreteness, consistency and clarity of his portrayal of empirical reality. It is also partly compensated for by the rigid, exposed scaffoldings, the striking geometrical figures, the strong colour patterns and other formal features characteristic of Zola's fiction, comparable in these respects to Cézanne, Van Gogh or Seurat.

Needless to say, Zola's efforts to serve both his centripetal and centrifugal objectives met with considerable, if not complete success. It would, of course, have been astonishing if he had made little or no headway at all, for, as I intimated at the beginning of this essay, these objectives are not wholly at odds with each other. It is quite possible to expand and complicate a work of art within certain broad limits and thereby actually gain in clarity, for example. Like a rubber band, each of the centripetal elements that I have been concerned with here can be stretched up to a point without breaking. Who would disagree with the young Zola that nothing so ravishes the spirit as 'l'unité dans la grandeur'? Few harmonies are as satisfying as those which join the most diverse elements. It is difficult to imagine any significant act of artistic creation that does not involve an attempt to resolve tensions between centripetal and centrifugal forces. One is tempted to recall the very old, seductive Hindu tradition according to which the universe itself springs, in the hands of Brahma, from the interplay between *sattva*, the cohesive force, personified by Vishnu, the Preserver, and its opposite, *tamas*, personified by Shiva, the Destroyer.

Zola's determination to expand the physiological and socio-historical studies underlying *Les Rougon-Macquart* until they were complete, perfect, cyclopedic enhanced the overall geometrical structure of the series. It graced it with the simplicity of the circle and the sphere. Moreover, most of the contrapuntal relationships that he set up between various conflicting elements of his philosophical and religious thought are aesthetically satisfying. Recall, for example, the sustained opposition that he establishes in *La Joie de vivre* between his pessimistic rejection of life, represented by Lazare, and his acceptance of life 'malgré toutes ses horreurs', represented by Pauline.

Yet even where Zola's centripetal and centrifugal goals do conflict, he still copes with them, it seems to me, with superb artistry. I do not mean to imply, however, that he reconciles them perfectly. I doubt that he ever really wanted to. Indeed, I am increasingly convinced that the relationship between them in his mind was lopsided. His urge to expand and elaborate, surpass limits, lay bare his divided heart and soul, embrace the infinite, do everything, speak the whole truth, and share with us his whole confused thought is usually paramount. One can see this in his remarks about art and about himself as an artist, remarks which, as one knows, tend to stress far more frequently than mere formal perfection (in the usual sense) the importance of a work of art's truth-content, living qualities, and reflections of its creator's temperament. As a young man, he even went so far as to proclaim (in the preface to *Mes Haines*), 'Je n'ai guère souci de beauté ni de perfection. Je me moque des grands siècles. Je n'ai souci que de vie, de lutte, de fièvre' (*OC*, X, 27).

It is above all through an examination of Zola's fiction and work-notes that one perceives the predominantly centrifugal movement of his art. His best works are open-ended, permitting infinite vistas. They initiate an expansive movement of the mind, a flight from the small to the large and from the specific and concrete to the general and abstract. His ultimate objective is obviously not so much to unify, reduce, simplify, harmonize, clarify, solidify (although he can be very good at that), as it is to expand, complicate, disrupt, obfuscate, gasify. In the course of creating *Les Rougon-Macquart*, he found it impossible to abide within the bounds that he had at first imposed on himself under the influence of his centripetal goals. From the initial planning stage of the series on, his centrifugal tendencies are relentlessly at work. The number of projected *Rougon-Macquart* volumes, which he had at first limited to ten, doubles. The small number of dramatis personae to which he had originally hoped to restrict the series swells into a cast of thousands. Most of his characters, instead of being predominantly exceptional, as he originally intended, explode into general types. The hero of *Germinal* is a social class, of *La Débâcle* a nation. Despite Zola's initial intention to write primarily a physiological study of a family,[29] the historical and sociological themes end up by becoming just as important or even more so. He enlarges the family tree. Descriptive passages, which he had meant to hold to a minimum, multiply. His style, which he had hoped to keep simple, grows complex, compound, elaborate. Indeed, he strays so far from his original formal ideal that, by the time he starts planning the twelfth volume, *La Joie de vivre*, he is constrained to specify:

Pas ma symphonie habituelle. Un simple récit allant au but [...] les descriptions réduites aux strictes indications. Et le style carré, correct, fort, sans aucun panache romantique. La langue classique que je rêve. En un mot, pas d'emballage.[30]

Moreover, despite his original resolve to be just a naturalist, just a physiologist, he ends up making at least as much room for the political thinker, philosopher and moralist - not to mention the dreamer, mythopoet, prophet and would-be New Messiah. He pours into *Les Rougon-Macquart* his republican indignations, Oedipal conflicts, loves and hates, hopes and fears. In short, it would be absurd to characterize the series, as he does in his preparatory notes, as nothing but 'de simples procès-verbaux' (*RM*, V, 1744). He also fails utterly, of course, to limit himself to just one 'tendance philosophique' - the vague materialism that he specifies in his early preparatory notes.

When, furthermore, *Les Rougon-Macquart* is contemplated in the context of Zola's complete works, it is seen to be part of a still larger pattern including *Les Trois Villes* and the unfinished *Les Quatre Evangiles*. Together, the three series echo *La Chaîne des êtres*, with its tripartite division: past, present and future. Zola's fiction, like the French language, is fundamentally agglutinative. It all ends without any final conclusion, any last word, like a long, uncompleted - and no doubt uncompleteable - sentence. Nor must one overlook the extraordinary massiveness of his last three novels or their immense time frame, embracing the whole mythical twentieth century, portraying the rise and fall of cities, the spread of civilization, the transformation of the planet, the redemption of mankind.

After one's knowledge of *Les Rougon-Macquart* has reached a certain point, it begins to seem less coherent than it once did. What at first appeared, with each new probe, more solid, harmonious and clear, now starts, as one goes on studying it, to develop cracks, to emit discordant notes, to grow more obscure, to dissolve into a cloud. Sooner or later, the attentive critic who penetrates the incongruous assemblage of literary genres in this or that novel, becomes aware of their jarrings. For example, the marriage that Zola effectuates in *La Curée* between Phaedra and Trimalchio is surely one of the strangest, most generically cacophonous in all literature. Goujet as a literary creation has more in common with George Sand's idealized peasants than he does with Gervaise, Coupeau, Lantier and the other, more realistic characters of *L'Assommoir*. *Le Rêve* is an indigestible mélange of the naturalist novel, medieval legend and fairy tale. The generic differences between individual *Rougon-Macquart* novels - for instance, *La Faute de l'abbé Mouret* and *Pot-Bouille* or *La Joie de vivre* - are equally hard to reconcile.

The harder one looks for a consistent view of reality underlying *Les Rougon-Macquart*, the more one is struck by its radical philosophical instability and incoherences. It is impossible to reconcile philosophically *La Faute de l'abbé Mouret* and *La Joie de vivre*, for example, or *Le Rêve* and *Le Docteur Pascal*. The *Quatre Evangiles* also broadcast conflicting messages - each with its different New Messiah, different prophetic vision of the future, different path to social and individual salvation. In *Les Trois Villes*, Zola even goes so far as to lead his readers directly into the tempestuous crater of his own and his contemporaries' thought, making it a central theme of the whole trilogy.[31]

In short, Zola's fiction in both form and content is predominantly explosive, chaotic. Here, too, the centre does not hold. However, it would be absurd to see in all of this a failure of Zola's craft. What his works lack in unity, harmony, simplicity, clarity and solidity they make up for in vitality and autobiographical value. Their incoherences, contradictions and ambiguities mirror Zola's. The form of his writings fits his obsession with catastrophe, upheavals, the perilous, fiery forces of creation. It fits his conception of what the art of his age should be: an explosive, liberating agent. Recall his characterization of himself and his fellow writers in *Mes Haines* as demolishers of the old world in order to prepare the ground for the new (*OC*, X, 27). Or Claude's cry in *L'Œuvre*: 'Ah! tout voir et tout peindre! [...] Des fresques hautes comme le Panthéon! Une sacrée suite de toiles à faire éclater le Louvre!' (*OC*, V, 467). The form of Zola's works, its predominant centrifugality, also fits his vision of the explosive nature of truth and of his self-appointed role to 'hâter l'explosion de la vérité et de la justice'.[32] It reflects better than any other form would have the hot disorder of his thought. It suits the essentially volcanic nature of his poetry, described by Ferreira de Castro:

> Fréquemment, il nous est apparu comme un démiurge qui tente d'ordonner le chaos, en lutte avec les éléments que lui-même a déchaînés; et, alors, de ses amples compositions jaillit toute une poésie épique, volcanique, qui illumine le ciel et la terre, l'âme et le corps.[33]

The predominantly centrifugal, volcanic, eruptive character of Zola's fiction suits not only Zola's own thought but also the intellectual life of his age - that 'long torrent de lave', as his contemporary Charles Fuster aptly put it[34] - and indeed, one might well add, the violent, explosive nature of the whole modern era. As such Zola would seem to help confirm Carl Jung's remark:

> The development of modern art with its seemingly nihilistic trend toward disintegration must be understood as the symptom and symbol of a mood of world destruction and world renewal that has set its mark on our age [...]. We are living in what the Greeks called the 'right time' for a metamorphosis of the gods - that is, of the fundamental principles and symbols.[35]

Furthermore, the supremely artful yet self-exploding structure of Zola's fiction as I have analysed it here would seem to be in accordance with the veiled cult of Vulcan which one suspects in Zola, especially the Zola of 'Le Forgeron' and the Goujet episodes of *L'Assommoir* - Vulcan, the binder and the unbinder, the supreme craftsman, the magician of the forge, the Lord of Fire (the fire that constructs and the fire that destroys), Vulcan, or, as Michel Serres has put it, 'Héphaïstos, dieu de la Gueule d'Or, dieu souterrain des mines germinantes'.[36]

Finally, it must be noted that, in Zola's very failure to attain omniscience, to pin down the whole truth, symptomized in the fissures, contradictions and ambiguities of his writings, there lies a marvellous paradox. If nothing else, Zola seizes and makes palpable the unseizable, eternally elusive character of his divine opponent. The full blast of Reality in all its overwhelming vitality and fearful infinitude invades Zola's best works with the force of a roaring wind rushing through a broken windowpane.

Notes

1. The manner in which such goals tend, like the force of gravity, to pull everything that goes into a work towards a single centre, thereby delimiting and controlling the creative process, may be seen, for example, in Igor Stravinski's account of his compositional method: 'Composer, pour moi, c'est mettre en ordre un certain nombre de ces sons selon certains rapports d'intervalle. Cet exercice conduit à chercher le centre où doit converger la série de sons qui se trouve engagée dans mon entreprise. Je suis donc amené, un centre étant donné, à trouver une combinaison qui le joigne, ou bien, une combinaison étant établie qui n'est encore ordonnée à rien, à déterminer le centre vers lequel il doit tendre, la découverte de ce centre me suggère la solution' (*La Poétique musicale* , Plon, 1962, p. 28).

2. *Corr.*, I, 141.

3. *Corr.*, I, 207.

4. *Corr.*, I, 376.

5. *Corr.*, I, 385).

6. *Corr.*, I, 379.

7. B.N., N.a.f., Ms. 10280, fol. 18.

8. Concerning Zola's creative logic, see, for example, P.D. Walker, 'The "Ebauche" of *Germinal*', *PMLA*, 80 (Dec. 1965), 571–83.

9. *Corr.*, I, 275.

10. *Corr.*, I, 186.

11. 'Proudhon et Courbet', *OC*, X, 38–9.

12. 'Puis, quel enthousiasme et quel espoir étaient les nôtres! Tout savoir, tout pouvoir, tout conquérir!' (*OC*, XII, 678).

13. Colette Becker, Auguste Dezalay, Roger Ripolli, Chantal Bertrand-Jennings, *et al.* See Bertrand-Jennings, *Espaces romanesques: Zola* (Québec: Editions Naaman, 1987), p.12, n.10.

14. *Corr.*, I, 380.

15. Cf. Janice Best. Noting that Zola's realism depended on two contradictory factors, Best remarks: 'la liberté du roman permettait à l'écrivain de ne plus se conformer aux règles d'une convention spécifique, mais sa visée totalisante l'engageait à ne laisser de côté aucun détail et à prendre en considération l'ensemble des conventions. Les romans de Zola sont ainsi faits d'un mouvement de synthèse à la fois formel et narratif' (*Expérimentation et adaptation: essai sur la méthode naturaliste*, Corti, 1986, p. 206).

16. There can be little doubt that in *La Fortune*, as elsewhere, Zola was quite consciously mixing genres: 'Le souffle d'épopée qui emportait Miette et Silvère [...] traversait avec une générosité sainte les honteuses comédies des Macquart et des Rougon. [...] Et la farce vulgaire, la farce ignoble, tournait au grand drame de l'histoire' (*RM*, I, 162). Cf. 'Les jeunes gens [...] avaient vécu une de ces naïves idylles qui naissent au milieu de la classe ouvrière, parmi ces déshérités [...] chez lesquels on retrouve encore parfois les amours primitives des anciens contes grecs' (*RM*, I, 170).

17. 'Nous faisons du style et de l'art avec notre chair et notre âme; nous sommes amants de la vie, nous vous donnons chaque jour un peu de notre existence' (*OC*, X, 39).

18. E. and J. de Goncourt, *Journal: mémoires de la vie littéraire*, ed. R. Ricatte (Monaco, L'Imprimerie Nationale, 1956), VIII, 155.

19. *The Gates of Horn: a study of five French realists* (New York, Oxford University Press, 1963), p. 309.

20. Aimé Guedj, 'Diderot et Zola: essai de redéfinition du naturalisme', *Europe*, XLVI (1954): 'Il reste que le naturalisme bouleverse la base substantielle de l'art; c'est une vision du monde à la recherche d'elle-même et qui doit à l'approfondissement et à l'élargissement continus de sa matière la révolution permanente de ses formes' (pp. 291–2).

21. For a general introduction to Zola's philosophical and religious thought, see, P.D. Walker, *'Germinal' and Zola's Philosophical and Religious Thought*, (Amsterdam/Philadelphia, John Benjamins, 1984, 'Purdue University Monographs in Romance Languages).

22. Neide de Faria, *Structures et unité dans 'Les Rougon-Macquart' (La poétique du cycle)* (Nizet, 1977); August Dezalay, *L'Opéra des 'Rougon-Macquart': essai de rythmologie romanesque* (Klincksieck, 1983).

23. See Robert Lethbridge's essay, 'Zola and the Limits of Craft', in this volume.

24. B.N., N.a.f., Ms. 10338, fol. 47.

25. Cf. Zola's own, precious, frequently cited definition of his personal optics in his letter of 22 March 1885 to Henry Céard: 'J'aurais aimé seulement vous voir démonter le mécanisme de mon œil. [...] je mens [...] dans le sens de la vérité. J'ai l'hypertrophie du détail vrai, le saut dans les étoiles sur le tremplin de l'observation exacte. La vérité monte d'un coup d'aile jusqu'au symbole' (*OC*, XIV, 1440).

26. See Wurmser's preface to the Gallimard edition of *Germinal* (1978), pp. 16–17 and *passim*.

27. *Les Contemporains*, première série (Boivin, 1903), pp. 281, 284.

28. See P.D. Walker, *'Germinal' and Zola's Philosophical and Religious Thought*, pp. 94–5.

29. Cf. F.W.J. Hemmings, 'Intention et réalisation dans *Les Rougon-Macquart*', *Les Cahiers naturalistes*, no. 42 (1971), 93–108.

30. B.N., N.a.f., Ms. 10311, fol. 366.

31. Zola's tendency to provide his fictions with multiple possible morals is already apparent in his youthful tale, 'Aventures du grand Sidoine et du petit Médéric': 'Bonnes gens qui m'avez lu [...] je ne puis vous détailler ici les quinze ou vingt morales de ce récit. Il y en a pour tous les âges, pour toutes les conditions. Il suffit de vous recueillir et de bien interpréter mes paroles' (*OC*, IX, 182).

32. 'Et l'acte que j'accomplis ici n'est qu'un moyen révolutionnaire pour hâter l'explosion de la vérité et de la justice' (*OC*, XIV, 931).

33. *Essais de critique*, 2nd edition (E. Giraud, 1886), p. 68.

34. 'Le "Phénomène" Zola', *Présence de Zola* (essays by various hands) (Fasquelle, 1953), p. 37.

35. 'God, the Devil, and the Human Soul', *Atlantic Monthly*, 200 (1957), 63.

36. The full extent to which both the blacksmith of 'Le Forgeron' and Goujet are Vulcanic figures has too rarely been pointed out. Note, in addition to the obvious resemblances, their fecundating, revitalizing, reinvigorating, restorative, healing functions, and the phallic symbolism associated with Goujet in particular. See, Marie Delcourt, *Héphaïstos ou la légende du magicien* (Les Belles Lettres, 1982).

3

L'ATTENTE DE LA FICTION

Alain Pagès

Synopsis

One aspect of Zola's art of fiction is the manner in which, in writing, he adopts the standpoint of his reader, experiencing for himself the processes of waiting, expectation and repetition involved in reading. His novels are conceived as parts of a series, organized in relation to a dossier and published in serialized form. In each case, it is as much the logic of the reader as that of the writer that is developed.

The principle of the series is the deep-rooted one of continuity, and, in Zola's case, is prior to the novels proper. The unifying theme of the family allows him to make transitions from one volume to another in each of his three series of novels, and even to link the series themselves. Within the Rougon-Macquart *there are short cycles of novels and Zola constantly thinks in terms of sequences of events interlinking characters. But while the writer finally completes the series or dies in the attempt, the reader continues to ask for more.*

The presence of the reader can even be detected in Zola's dossiers and work-notes. They are compiled from a 'neutral' point of view; that is, from the reader's viewpoint. They anticipate the novel's reception, though Zola sometimes goes beyond this. He drafted, corrected and re-wrote at length, yet encouraged others to think that no such labour was involved, establishing a mysterious gap between dossier and completed text and giving the dossier a certain autonomy for the reader.

The serialization of novels was common in the nineteenth century, but had obvious disadvantages for the writer. On the other hand, it can maximize the pleasure gained from some features of the reading process and it prolonged the publicity generated by the publication of Zola's novels.

The eminently readable quality of the Rougon-Macquart *novels is not a feature of his later series, although these enjoyed great popularity at the time. It is as if in the later novels Zola has made much less progress beyond the* dossier *stage, which perhaps gave them greater documentary interest for his contemporaries, but means that we must plunge into the historical background in order to appreciate them.*

The importance of the reader has been recognized in relation to Zola's narrative structures, but insufficiently noted in connection with the genesis of the novels. There is a cyclical movement whereby the reception of the completed novel returns to and completes what was foreseen in its origins.

'Art': invention, technique ou artisanat? Il est difficile de le décider. Faut-il partir du thème du romancier *travailleur*, traçant chaque jour son sillon, enfoncé dans la solitude de son cabinet de travail - *nulla dies sine linea*? Nous connaissons trop bien cette image mythique du solitaire de Médan: essayons plutôt de la renverser et, en quelque sorte, de retourner la carte - comme dans ces jeux de cartes où les personnages représentés ont deux têtes. La carte du romancier, renversée, laisse apparaître la figure du lecteur. Le lecteur qui est là, et qui *attend*: situé dans cet 'horizon d'attente' où on le décrit depuis quelques années à la suite de Jauss et des théoriciens de l'Ecole de Constance. Le lecteur, *double* de l'écrivain, double 'hypocrite' pour reprendre une formule célèbre, masque possible, donc ...

Le romancier face à son double, le lecteur? Il faut imaginer un romancier *lecteur*, non pas seulement lecteur de son œuvre ou de l'œuvre des autres, mais pensant son existence de romancier - son art/artisanat, précisément - à la manière d'un lecteur; c'est-à-dire construisant la fiction qu'il élabore dans l'attente de ce qui va venir, et dans l'attente de ce qui est déjà advenu, et donc dans la répétition d'un déjà dit - dans cet étrange plaisir qu'apporte la pulsion de répétition. Ainsi Zola, dans *l'attente de la fiction*: Zola *romancier* empruntant la figure du *lecteur* (puisque la lecture est une 'hypocrisie', un masque que l'on peut revêtir), et vivant cette attente qui caractérise la lecture.

Observons-le d'abord au moment où la fiction est en train de naître, dans l'étape de la genèse. Ne nous demandons pas comment il progresse dans son travail d'écrivain, mais plutôt comment son travail se situe dans la perspective de la lecture, inclut dans son mouvement les principes d'attente et de répétition qui sont ceux de la lecture.

Au moment de concevoir son œuvre, Zola rencontre et utilise ce que l'on pourrait appeler des *schèmes opérateurs*, que la tradition lui offre et qu'il s'efforce de perfectionner. Ces schèmes sont au moins au nombre de trois. Ce sont la *série*, pour imaginer l'œuvre; le *dossier*, pour l'organiser; et le *feuilleton*, pour la publier. Chacun de ces schèmes est développé autant dans la logique du lecteur que dans celle du producteur ou du créateur.

Commençons par la série. Sa loi impose d'enchaîner les romans les uns après les autres, et surtout, de ne pas s'arrêter. Que la machine ne s'arrête pas, et qu'elle roule toute seule, sans fin, échappant à la loi de l'entropie: c'est le rêve de toute une époque, que Michel Serres a si bien décrit.[1] Très tôt, Zola a médité cette *règle* de la série, dès ses premières expériences de journaliste: le journalisme, asservi au quotidien, s'exerce dans l'ordre de la répétition sérielle. Et il a probablement vécu, au cours de sa jeunesse misérable, le *fantasme* biologique de la série: redouter par dessus tout de ne pouvoir, un jour, continuer; de manquer, un jour, de travail, de pain; et que ce manque conduise à l'arrêt définitif, à la mort. La série, c'est donc un principe de vie. Elle est *a priori*, posée *avant* l'écriture, alors que la série balzacienne, elle, est conçue *a posteriori*. Pour Balzac, la série suit l'œuvre, c'est une justification; pour Zola, elle la précède, c'est un *prétexte* - avec tout ce que ce mot comporte: *antériorité* de l'avant-texte théorique; *aléatoire* de la théorie que l'on appliquera plus ou moins, que l'on ne réalisera jamais entièrement.

En cela, il suit la tradition romanesque du XIXe siècle (que les peintres impressionnistes connaissent aussi). La plupart des romans de cette époque sont conçus à l'intérieur de cadres généraux qui impliquent l'idée d'une répétition et d'une continuité. Le plus souvent, il s'agit de séries ouvertes, peu contraignantes. Les titres le disent clairement: il suffit de les lire jusqu'au bout (ce que d'ailleurs on oublie de faire aujourd'hui). Tel roman a pour sous-titre:

Mœurs contemporaines; tel autre: *Mœurs parisiennes*, *Roman parisien*, etc. Tous jouent sur une double appellation, générique (la série)/spécifique (le drame particulier). Mais alors que la plupart des romanciers indiquent le drame et mentionnent ensuite, de façon imprécise, la série, Zola fait l'inverse: il pose d'abord la série des *Rougon-Macquart*. La contrainte est avancée *a priori*: c'est tout ce qui différencie un Zola d'un Daudet; comparez, par exemple, *Sapho - Mœurs parisiennes*, et *Les Rougon-Macquart: histoire d'une famille sous le Second Empire - Nana*. S'il fallait trouver un point commun aux écrivains naturalistes, c'est là qu'il faudrait le trouver: chacun pris dans sa ou ses séries, Goncourt, Daudet, Zola ou Maupassant; et chacun l'organisant à sa manière. On ne peut décrire le naturalisme dans son ensemble qu'en retrouvant la logique de ces parallélismes.

Puisque la série représente la dynamique de la vie, il ne faut surtout pas créer de rupture, casser le fil; et donc trouver une continuité, une poursuite, non seulement à l'intérieur de la série, mais au moment crucial où celle-ci doit s'achever. Comment nier ou contourner la nécessité de la clôture?

Le premier problème à résoudre est celui de la *transition*: c'est ce qui impose le thème unificateur de la famille dans *Les Rougon-Macquart*, dans *Les Trois Villes* et dans *Les Quatre Evangiles*. Lien dans la série, et même entre les séries: entre les *Les Trois Villes* et *Les Quatre Evangiles* où il s'agit de la même famille; et entre *Les Rougon-Macquart* et *Les Trois Villes*, symboliquement, avec cette scène de non-clôture du *Docteur Pascal* où naît l'enfant des futurs 'Evangiles'.

En outre, Zola imagine, dans la série, la structure du *cycle*:[2] dynamique différente, qui implique le retour et le rappel, et permet une lisibilité plus grande, fragmentant la longue durée de la série. D'où les micro-cycles à l'intérieur des *Rougon-Macquart* (par exemple, *L'Assommoir/Nana/ Germinal*, ou *La Curée/L'Argent*). D'où également les micro-cycles des dernières œuvres, qui annoncent dès l'entrée une suite limitée, trois puis quatre romans.

Le romancier du cycle pense par *enchaînements*. Le voilà tout entier pris dans cette mécanique. Voyez comment il va s'intéresser à l'Affaire Dreyfus. Absorbé par le cycle des *Trois Villes*, il ne peut pas entendre Bernard-Lazare qui vient lui parler, en novembre 1896, du condamné de l'île du Diable.[3] Mais à l'automne 1897, alors qu'il a terminé *Paris*, il devient libre tout d'un coup - et presque dans cette angoisse du vide que suscite le moment de la transition. C'est alors qu'il perçoit dans l'Affaire un 'drame' possible, c'est-à-dire un *enchaînement* d'événements et de personnages; comme il l'écrit, 'une trilogie de types':

> Le condamné innocent, là-bas, avec la tempête dans son crâne; le coupable libre ici, avec ce qui se passait en lui, tandis qu'un autre expiait son crime; et le faiseur de vérité Scheurer-Kestner, silencieux et agissant.[4]

Toute l'Affaire se déroulera de la sorte avec la logique que supposent ces rôles thématiques, l'innocence condamnée, le crime en liberté, et la vérité en marche.[5]

Reste qu'il existe une fatalité de la série: malgré qu'on en ait, la fatalité de son achèvement. L'idéal serait de faire coïncider la fin de la vie du romancier et la fin de la série, ou au moins de l'un de ses cycles. Car la série épuise, et conduit par son entraînement infini à la mort. Le destin du romancier de la série est de laisser de l'inachevé.[6] Zola meurt quelques semaines après avoir achevé *Vérité*, dont la publication sera posthume. Mais il manque *Justice*, représentée dans son inachèvement même par quelques notes. Comme Proust, qui demandera à l'existence de lui laisser finir *La Recherche*, et aura un peu plus de chances que Zola avec *Le Temps retrouvé*, mais guère plus: *La Recherche* comporte aussi une part importante d'inachevé.[7]

On voit bien que cette logique de la série relève plus d'une logique du lecteur que d'une logique du créateur. Puisque ce dernier s'y épuise, et manque son achèvement; puisque, malgré son dynamisme vital, la série conduit à la mort. Le lecteur, au contraire, en demande toujours plus, et souhaite indéfiniment que ça continue.

Le dossier, les notes de travail personnelles et secrètes (jusqu'à un certain point) du créateur semblent exclure tout à fait le point de vue du lecteur. Pourtant, à regarder les choses de près, la figure du lecteur s'y dessine aussi, insistante. Recueil de documents, le dossier n'est dans sa plus grande partie que le résumé de ce que pense et croit le lecteur. Il se situe précisément dans son horizon d'attente. Quand Zola constitue son dossier préparatoire, il se nie en tant qu'individu sachant et connaissant. Il s'efforce d'atteindre cet état difficile qui est celui de la 'neutralité'.[8] Il apprend ce que les autres savent; en un mot, il se fait lecteur.

Le dossier imagine le lecteur futur, il en construit la réception. Mais, pour ce faire, il part du lecteur présent, déjà là. On observe alors un court-circuit étonnant: le dossier contient déjà la réception de l'œuvre, avant que celle-ci ne surgisse. Voyez *Germinal*. Le dossier du roman contient un certain nombre d'articles de journaux (sur la condition des mineurs, sur la grève, etc) qui sont presque exactement, presque mot pour mot (dans leur façon d'argumenter et présenter les choses) les articles écrits en mars 1885, au moment où paraît le roman.[9] La réception retourne ironiquement vers la genèse.

Asservi au dossier - c'est-à-dire finalement au point de vue du lecteur - le romancier prend le risque, constant, de s'écarter de ce point de vue: c'est là où il nous intéresse, quand il dépasse ses contemporains; mais c'est là aussi où ses contemporains l'arrêtent et lui reprochent son *incompétence* - quand justement il n'a pas su rester un simple lecteur.[10] Le critique-lecteur suspectera toujours l'imagination du créateur, n'ayant de cesse qu'il ne l'ait réduite à sa propre vision. Toute l'histoire de la réception des *Rougon-Macquart* se résume dans ce rappel à l'ordre prononcé par le critique - au nom des droits du lecteur.

Placé avant l'écriture, le dossier participe d'une autre logique qu'elle. Il serait faux de croire qu'il prépare directement l'écriture: il la repousse plutôt dans le temps. Tout au plus annonce-t-il le *saut* de l'écriture, mais il y aura toujours ce saut, ce passage au texte achevé que le dossier ne dit pas et n'explique pas. Tous les commentateurs des dossiers préparatoires ont noté l'écart qui sépare l'ébauche, les plans détaillés et la rédaction définitive.[11]

Il existe donc comme un impensé de l'écriture. Faut-il le renvoyer au hasard de la création et à sa démarche géniale? Peut-être. Mais il est sans doute plus intéressant de remarquer la volonté qui anime Zola de ne pas laisser à la postérité les traces de son écriture. Il laisse les ébauches, les plans, etc, tous les documents lointains, mais non les documents immédiats, les différents états de la page écrite. Il voudrait donner aux autres l'idée d'une écriture du premier jet, sans ratures ou avec le moins de ratures possibles: c'est ce que ses commentateurs disent, et il accepte cette version des faits.[12] Or cela est faux, de toute évidence. Il suffit d'observer le rythme temporel de sa composition romanesque, il suffit de suivre mois après mois la réalisation d'un roman (comme la *Correspondance* permet de le faire) pour s'en rendre compte. Zola récrivait et recopiait; il ne conservait pas les brouillons issus de ce travail de réécriture. Il voulait laisser de lui l'image d'un lecteur - d'un organisateur ou d'un interprète - et non d'un homme aux prises avec le hasard des mots: l'incertitude ou les angoisses du style, il les abandonne aux romantiques. Visible, évidente, la trace du dossier l'est sans doute un peu trop: laissée là - comme dans les histoires policières - pour effacer d'autres traces qui doivent demeurer cachées.

En somme, le dossier est une *décision*, c'est-à-dire: un *projet* (le projet de décrire telle ou telle partie de la société); mais aussi, par là même, une *coupure* ('décision' étymologiquement veut dire 'coupure'): une coupure avec la réalité de l'écriture - puisqu'il appartient à l'ordre de la lecture, et non à celui de l'écriture.[13]

Alors que les règles méthodologiques de la série et du dossier sont depuis longtemps étudiées par les commentateurs de Zola, le principe du feuilleton l'est très peu. On le comprend aisément. Pratique impure, le feuilleton dégrade la forme de l'œuvre à venir. Pourtant son omniprésence dans la littérature du XIXe siècle mérite quelque attention.

Faut-il brûler les feuilletons? Sur ce point, les avis sont partagés au XIXe siècle. Pour le romancier, quand il s'exprime en tant que créateur, le feuilleton est insupportable. Il interrompt brutalement le texte, en réduit la perspective, empêche de saisir une unité - sans parler des coupures imprévisibles de la censure qui sont toujours possibles dans les journaux. Ainsi Céard à Zola, en disciple fidèle partageant le point de vue de son maître, alors que *Germinal* paraît en feuilleton dans le *Gil Blas*: 'Je lis *Germinal*, haché menu comme chair à pâté dans les feuilletons du *Gil Blas*: vous vous doutez bien, n'est-ce pas, que je n'ai aucune impression de l'ensemble.'[14] Mais pour le lecteur naïf, le feuilleton possède un certain charme. Il donne à la lecture une durée imprescriptible, il en prolonge la consommation, il en matérialise le plaisir. Plaisir multiplié par les feuillets, et l'effeuillage du sens. Pour le lecteur plus intellectuel même, le feuilleton n'est pas sans intérêt. Il ménage l'attente, apporte une découverte progressive, et permet de vivre une œuvre dans son présent, dans sa signification immédiate. C'est la situation dans laquelle Péguy lit *Fécondité* en 1899, au moment où l'Affaire Dreyfus bat son plein:

Nous avons lu *Fécondité* en feuilletons dans *L'Aurore*. Par une harmonie merveilleuse, comme l'auteur avait écrit au loin, s'interrompant pour lire les journaux de France, ainsi nous avons lu au loin, nous interrompant pour lire les nouvelles de Rennes. Et, sans vouloir en faire un moyen d'art, les ajournements successifs du feuilleton donnèrent aux recommencements successifs du roman une singulière perspective, agrandie encore par l'importance des événements réels intercalaires. Quand nous arrivâmes à la fin, il y avait vraiment de très longs jours et de très longues années que Mathieu Froment s'était installé avec sa femme dans le petit pavillon à la lisière des bois.[15]

Le feuilleton correspond aux attentes du lecteur. On ne le brûlera donc pas. Et, malgré ses défauts, on l'utilisera pleinement. Zola, mieux que quiconque, saura jouer de ses pouvoirs. C'est que le feuilleton démultiplie la durée de la réception: alors qu'un livre publié tient trois semaines au plus dans l'opinion publique, le feuilleton fait durer l'œuvre beaucoup plus, près de quatre mois, ce qui est considérable - sans compter l'écho publicitaire que le journal en donne avant même le début de la publication.

Soit l'exemple de *Germinal*. La réception du roman ne se limite pas aux quelques semaines qui suivent la publication en librairie, le 2 mars 1865. Mais par le jeu du feuilleton, elle a commencé bien avant: elle a commencé en février 1884, quand Alexis a livré avec une indiscrétion soigneusement calculée le titre du prochain roman de Zola; elle s'est poursuivie avec les échos du voyage à Anzin; et elle a pris de l'ampleur dans le courant de l'automne 1884, avec le début des feuilletons dans le *Gil Blas*.[16] Ainsi se succèdent *deux* réceptions: avant la parution en librairie, une réception que l'on peut appeler 'génétique' - moment où l'œuvre est encore mal connue, moment instable des échos, des rumeurs et des polémiques naissantes; et après la publication du livre, une réception plus complète, disons, 'usuelle', puisque l'ouvrage est alors dans toutes les mains: l'œuvre peut alors être analysée, discutée, évaluée pour la postérité. Mais grâce au feuilleton, elle est restée dans l'actualité pendant plus d'une année.

Après l'attente qui précède la fiction, voici l'attente inscrite dans la fiction, l'attente (structurelle) qui correspond au déroulement de l'intrigue, au dévoilement du sens.

Cet aspect de l'œuvre de Zola est bien connu. Il a été largement développé par les études conduites au cours de ces dernières années, notamment par toutes les recherches qui ont porté sur le récit et sur les personnages et ont insisté sur le caractère éminemment 'lisible' du texte naturaliste. Comme l'écrit P. Hamon:

> Le personnage zolien, posons-le ici tout de suite, sera un *personnage lisible* et délégué à la lisibilité: lui-même d'une part, sera un personnage entièrement élucidé [...]: par lui, d'autre part, par son savoir, par ses actions, ses paroles, ses regards, il élucidera tout ce qui l'entoure, y compris les autres personnages. Lieu et objet d'une lisibilité, il sera *aussi* sujet et opérateur de lisibilité.[17]

L'œuvre zolienne est donc construite en fonction du lecteur. La technique en est parfaitement au point dans *Les Rougon-Macquart*. Mais remarquons que seul ce corpus, pratiquement, a été étudié dans cette perspective. Que se passe-t-il après, avec *Les Trois Villes* et *Les Quatre Evangiles*? On ne le sait pas vraiment. De toute évidence, l'art de la fiction s'est modifié. Et le sentiment de réussite - de plaisir à la lecture - qui caractérisait l'époque précédente semble avoir disparu. Faut-il risquer une explication? Zola abandonne-t-il les procédés qu'il a pratiqués avec *Les Rougon-Macquart* pour en essayer d'autres, et lesquels? Ou, plus simplement, se met-il à écrire vite, mal, niant et refusant, en quelque sorte, son habileté ancienne?

Il faut noter au préalable que si les derniers romans de Zola nous intéressent moins que ceux du cycle des *Rougon-Macquart*, la chose n'est pas vraie pour les lecteurs de la fin du XIXe siècle qui ont beaucoup apprécié, discuté *Les Trois Villes* et *Les Quatre Evangiles*: les tirages de ces romans en sont la preuve.[18]

Aussi est-il possible d'avancer l'hypothèse suivante: la poétique du lecteur, dans ces œuvres, ne se modifie pas ni ne se dégrade, mais elle se poursuit, au contraire, et va jusqu'au bout de sa logique; et ce qui disparaît, c'est plutôt la poétique 'insciente' du créateur - cette sorte d'équilibre entre la poétique du lecteur et la poétique du créateur qui caractérisait la période précédente. L'inconnu de la création, le 'saut dans les étoiles' de la création[19] - le travail final *après* le dossier - tout cela s'appauvrit ou paraît tout d'un coup moins utile. Et il ne reste que le dossier, les documents rassemblés pour le lecteur. En quelque sorte, après 1893, et surtout après 1898, Zola n'écrit plus que des *Carnets d'enquête*. D'où l'intérêt que ce dossier romanesque suscite pour le lecteur contemporain, proche de la matière politique et sociale qui est traitée; et la difficulté que nous avons aujourd'hui à y prendre de l'intérêt.

Sauf à *remotiver* cet intérêt par une plongée dans l'histoire de l'époque. *Vérité*, par exemple, est insupportable, si l'on n'a qu'une vague idée de l'Affaire Dreyfus; mais devient, au contraire, un roman passionnant si l'on connaît de près les événements des années 1898-9. Car on suit alors, pas à pas, la reprise des épisodes de l'Affaire, l'accusation, la machination contre l'innocent, le premier procès, le second procès, etc; et surtout on prend plaisir à cette attente narrative étonnante, qui consiste à donner l'Affaire, sans la donner, mais en la transposant dans le monde de l'école laïque et des congrégations. *Vérité* est un roman réussi. Mais pas pour nous: pour le lecteur de 1900. Pour l'apprécier, il fallait connaître *le dossier*!

Dans sa naissance comme dans son élaboration, l'œuvre zolienne manifeste la présence du lecteur. La poétique du lecteur, caractéristique de l'écriture naturaliste, est précédée par une *génétique du lecteur*. Les conséquences de cette présence du lecteur sont essentielles. Bien des recherches les ont analysées dans le domaine des structures narratives. Mais on n'a peut-être pas encore mesuré suffisamment l'importance de ces conséquences dans le domaine de la genèse. On voit que la réception, quand elle surgit, ne s'oppose pas à ce qui précède, mais qu'elle retrouve et complète ce qui a déjà été prévu, puisqu'il est possible, dans certaines conditions, que la genèse, sous l'emprise du lecteur, anticipe le mouvement de l'œuvre, ou que la réception régresse vers la genèse et accompagne le surgissement de l'œuvre. La naissance et l'achèvement sont liés, indissociables. L'art de la fiction se résume - pourquoi s'en étonner? - dans la figure du cycle.

Notes

1. M. Serres, *Feux et signaux de brume. Zola* (Grasset, 1975).
2. Voir A. Dezalay, *L'Opéra des 'Rougon-Macquart'. Essai de rythmologie romanesque* (Klincksieck, 1983); voir 3e partie, ch. I, 'Le Problème des cycles'.

3. Voir sur ce point N. Wilson, *Bernard-Lazare* (Albin Michel, 1985), ch. 9; et J. Reinach, *Histoire de l'Affaire Dreyfus. III: la crise* (Fasquelle, 1903), pp. 66–7 - citant cette parole de Zola: 'Si j'avais été dans un livre, je ne sais pas ce que j'aurais fait', avec ce commentaire: 'C'est ce qu'il m'a dit à plusieurs reprises, avec une touchante sincérité' (p. 67).

4. *Impressions d'audience* (OC, XIV, 1109).

5. Pour les acteurs de l'Affaire, la difficulté consistera à bien savoir lire les événements, et à choisir entre les différents types d'interprétation qui leur seront proposés, soit l'épopée magnifiante des allégories, soit les retournements hasardeux du roman-feuilleton. Sur ce sujet, voir mon article, 'L'Affaire Dreyfus comme roman-feuilleton', *Actes du colloque de Naples*, 'Il terzo Zola' (mai, 1987).

6. Sur cette idée, voir, L. Hay *et al.*, *Le Manuscrit inachevé* (Eds du CNRS, 1986); notamment l'article de J.Y. Tadié, 'Proust et l'inachèvement'.

7. Ce parallèle Proust–Zola mériterait d'ailleurs d'être développé: l'un et l'autre sont des romanciers de la série *a priori*; l'un comme l'autre puisent cette idée dans la pratique du journalisme; et on observe chez eux un effort continuel pour comprendre et saisir le déroulement, la continuité - aboutissant d'un côté à une philosophie du 'temps retrouvé', de l'autre à une philosophie du 'temps prophétisé'.

8. Selon la formule proposée par A. Fernandez-Zoïla ('Zola, le naturalisme, le neutre', *Exercices de la patience, Effets de neutre*, I (1985).

9. Voir, dans le dossier du roman publié par C. Becker, la série des articles de journaux sur la grève d'Anzin de 1884 (*La Fabrique de 'Germinal'*, Sedes, 1986: pp. 443 sq).

10. Sur l'argument de l'incompétence dans le discours critique de l'époque, voir ma thèse de doctorat: 'Figures du discours critique: la réception du naturalisme à l'époque de "Germinal"' (Atelier National de Reproduction des Thèses, Université de Lille III, 1987, 1030 pp.).

11. Voir notamment les travaux d'Henri Mitterand (édition de la Pléiade des *Rougon-Macquart*) et de Colette Becker (édition de *Germinal*, Garnier, 1979). Cet écart semble cependant se réduire dans les derniers romans, au moins à partir de *Fécondité* (voir D. Baguley, *'Fécondité' d'Emile Zola*, University of Toronto Press, 1973).

12. Ainsi le Dr Toulouse, dans son *Enquête médico-psychologique* (Flammarion, 1896; pp. 273–5), ne relève que les corrections stylistiques de surface et non le travail en profondeur de l'écriture.

13. Dernière preuve de cette autonomie du dossier, l'utilisation qu'on peut en faire à l'heure actuelle, où on ne se contente plus d'en faire la matière de recherches érudites, mais où on se met à le considérer dans son intérêt propre et à l'éditer: témoins les *Carnets d'enquête* procurés par Henri Mitterand (Plon, 1986, coll. 'Terre humaine'), ou, pour Flaubert, les *Carnets de travail* donnés par Pierre-Marc de Biasi (Ballard, 1988) - textes publiés l'un et l'autre non dans des collections universitaires, mais dans des collections de grande diffusion. Ultime avatar de ces notes de lecteur: on les conservait jadis dans les marges ou les notes du texte; aujourd'hui on les *découvre*, à côté de l'œuvre achevée, et différentes.

14. H. Céard, *Lettres inédites à Emile Zola* , ed. C.A. Burns (Nizet, 1958), p. 267.

15. C. Péguy, 'Les récentes œuvres de Zola', *Le Mouvement socialiste*, 1 et 15 novembre 1899, repris dans *Œuvres en prose complètes* (Gallimard, 1987, 'Bibliothèque de la Pléiade'), I, 247.

16. Pour plus de détails, voir ma thèse, *op. cit.*

17. P. Hamon, *Le Personnel du roman: le système des personnages dans les 'Rougon-Macquart' d'Emile Zola* (Droz, 1983), p. 38.

18. Quelques chiffres: *Fécondité* et *Travail* se sont vendus, l'année de leur parution, à 70,000 exemplaires; en 1902, à la mort de Zola, *Fécondité* atteignait 94,000 exemplaires, et *Travail* 77,000.

19. L'expression est de Zola, comme on le sait: voir *Corr.*, V, 249 (lettre à Céard du 22 mars 1885).

4

ZOLA ET LE MÉLODRAME

Colette Becker

Synopsis

Zola was a keen theatregoer from his adolescence onwards. He mixed with dramatists, directors and critics, making a number of attempts at writing for the theatre before completing his fist major play, Madeleine Férat. *It deals with problems that he was experiencing at the time, but borrowed both characters and scenes from contemporary melodrama, as well as following the same formula as his first great novel,* Thérèse Raquin: *drama, passion, violence.*

The melodramatic repertoire of the theatres he frequented influenced him both directly and through the popular novels that it inspired. The influence was apparent when he had occasion to suggest ways of adapting his novels for the stage, but it also marked his novels themselves. He always starts from stock situations and characters, transforming these by endowing them with his own obsessions and fantasies.

Melodrama is a mechanism calculated to stimulate the spectator's curiosity and emotions through extravagant scenes of violence and pathos, but one that also appeals to our sense of justice by showing virtue triumphant in the end. It frequently involves highly spectacular events and effects, and it matched particularly well Zola's view of man and society, according to which men are governed by hidden forces that sometimes erupt in violence and society is the battleground where the eternal struggle between life and death takes place.

Zola's aesthetic in the Rougon-Macquart *was strongly influenced by melodrama, and the dossiers show the extent to which he conceived his novels as sequences or dramatic scenes. He chose traditional scenes with a strong visual impact and emotional charge, and every novel has as least one extravagantly moving or terrifying set-piece. Similarly, with regard to character, Zola not only took stereotypes from melodrama as his starting-point, but also set them in opposition in the Manichean manner characteristic of melodrama.*

Yet Zola breathes new life into these conventions by introducing his personal obsessions or fantasies into his novels, as well as giving them a mythical dimension. Thérèse Raquin *constitutes a special example of this process, for while his stated aim of writing a scientific novel is subverted by the influence of the traditions of the melodrama, these ultimately serve as a springboard for his own imaginative powers. Thus the paralysis and aphasia of Madame Raquin produces a kind of dramatic effect common in melodrama, but is also used to illustrate Zola's preoccupation with the all-powerful nature of the gaze and related themes - themes echoed by other elements in the novel.*

La tentation du théâtre a été - malgré les échecs - une des plus fortes et des plus tenaces de Zola. En même temps qu'il essayait, à ses débuts, dans la voie du journalisme et dans celle du roman, il écrivait pour la scène. Près d'achever *Les Rougon-Macquart*, il rêve encore de se tourner vers le théâtre, il le confie dans plusieurs interviews en 1890 et 1891.[1]

Comme on le sait, le théâtre connut, au XIXe siècle, une vogue considérable. Sous Napoléon III, en particulier, il fait partie de la 'fête impériale'. On s'y rend pour s'y montrer, comme on va au Bois de Boulogne, tout récemment ouvert aux promeneurs. Les très nombreuses salles de Paris ou de province n'accueillent pas la seule société élégante. Un large public s'y presse. Les journaux ont une 'Revue des théâtres' et le feuilleton dramatique y tient une place importante. Emile Augier, Sardou, les Dumas et autres obtiennent des succès retentissants et enviables, mais la scène attire aussi George Sand, Goncourt, Flaubert, dont la correspondance révèle l'intérêt qu'ils y ont porté. Comme Zola l'expliquera plus tard, le théâtre, qui répondait à une demande d'un public vaste et diversifié, était, dans la société de l'époque, un moyen plus rapide que le roman de gagner de l'argent et de se faire un nom.[2]

Toutefois, le besoin d'argent n'est pas sa seule motivation. Ce goût pour le théâtre remonte à son adolescence. Il le partageait avec ses deux amis, Baille et Cézanne. Tous trois savaient par cœur et déclamaient les drames de Victor Hugo, ils fréquentaient assidûment le théâtre d'Aix, ils écrivaient. Baille composa les *Chandelles autrichiennes*, pièce que nous ne connaissons que par la mention qu'en fait Zola dans une lettre du 4 juillet 1860.[3] Cézanne annonçait, le 9 juillet 1858, qu'il avait 'conçu l'idée d'un drame en cinq actes', *Henry VIII d'Angleterre*, qu'il souhaitait écrire avec Zola pendant les vacances.[4] Quant à celui-ci, il avait fait plusieurs essais: une comédie, 'mille et quelques vers', commencée à Aix, continuée à Paris, en 1858, *Enfonce le pion!*; une tragédie dont nous ne conservons que le plan, *Annibal à Capoue*; un 'gros drame', resté probablement à l'état de projet, que nous ne connaissons que par Paul Alexis, *Rollon l'archer*;[5] un proverbe en un acte, *Perrette*, achevé en mars 1860; à quoi il faut ajouter un autre proverbe en un acte mentionné par ses biographes mais perdu, *Il faut hurler avec les loups*, écrit, selon Paul Alexis, au lycée.[6]

En 1865, Zola achève une comédie, *La Laide*, qu'il a probablement commencée en 1860–1, abandonnée puis reprise au moins deux fois - nous conservons les différents états du texte.[7] Il compose aussi un drame en trois actes, *Madeleine*, qu'il ne peut pas faire jouer et dont, en 1868, il tire *Madeleine Férat*.

Non seulement il écrit, mais il s'intéresse de près à la production de son époque. Il est lié, depuis 1860, avec un auteur dramatique, Pagès du Tarn, dont il commente l'œuvre à ses amis.[8] Il va au théâtre. Il est attiré par les pièces à succès.[9] Il s'est fait des relations parmi les auteurs dramatiques ou les critiques, qui lui donnent des billets et s'offrent même à l'introduire auprès des directeurs de salles: ainsi Adolphe Belot, Charles Deulin,[10] Alexandre de Lavergne. Ce dernier, en particulier, l'invite plusieurs fois et lui propose, le 5 septembre 1865, d'assister à sa place aux premières: il partait en voyage pour deux ou trois semaines, et, comme il souhaitait assurer sa chronique, il demandait à Zola de lui envoyer ses impressions.[11] Zola joua ainsi, en 1865, auprès d'Alexandre de Lavergne, le rôle que Céard tint pour lui, des années plus tard. Invité par les Goncourt, qui veulent le remercier de l'article chaleureux qu'il a consacré à *Germinie Lacerteux*, il assiste à la première d'*Henriette Maréchal*, le 5 décembre 1865. Enfin, il tente, sinon d'obtenir une chronique dramatique dans un journal, du moins de faire publier une ou des études, probablement consacrées à la pièce des Goncourt, qui l'a enthousiasmé.

Si j'ai énuméré toutes ces œuvres et ces projets, et rappelé ces activités, c'est pour souligner que Zola s'est d'abord tourné vers le théâtre. *Madeleine* - le dernier des essais que j'ai traité et sa première grande pièce - a été conçu et écrit en même temps que *La Confession de Claude*, le premier roman, avec lequel elle entretient des liens étroits. Or ce drame, dans lequel Zola projette les problèmes existentiels qu'il affronte alors, frôle souvent le mélodrame auquel il emprunte personnages et scènes. Retenons simplement la rencontre de Laurence, en haillons, et de Madeleine dans une chambre de l'auberge où le couple est descendu, scène que Sarcey estimera, en 1889, lorsque la pièce sera enfin jouée, 'd'un grand effet mélodramatique',[12] ou encore la mort de l'héroïne, qui dispute à son mari un flacon de strychnine et s'empoisonne sous ses yeux, 'dénouement tout au plus acceptable sur une scène de mélodrame', selon le directeur du Gymnase, A. Lemoine-Montigny, qui a refusé la pièce en 1866.

La manière dont Zola présente l'œuvre aux lecteurs du *Figaro*, en mai 1889, est, pour nous, très riche d'enseignements. 'C'est un drame', explique-t-il, 'dans la formule de *Thérèse Raquin*, passionné, violent, et, je ne m'en défends pas, romantique. Du théâtre à coups de poings, en un mot.' *Thérèse Raquin* est devenu pour lui une sorte de référence, il en fait mention plusieurs fois, à la même époque, dans l'*Ebauche* de *La Bête humaine*.

Théâtre ou roman, la 'formule' est la même. Le 13 septembre 1867, Zola a déjà défini ce premier grand roman en termes presque identiques: 'L'œuvre est très dramatique, très poignante, et je compte sur un succès d'horreur'.[13]

C'est que, comme l'ont été des générations, avant et après lui, il a été fortement marqué par un certain théâtre, le répertoire du Gymnase, de l'Ambigu et de la Porte-Saint-Martin. Influence doublement subie: à travers le roman populaire et à travers les pièces elles-mêmes. Du roman populaire, en effet, qui doit beaucoup au roman noir et, surtout, au mélodrame,[14] il s'est nourri dans son adolescence, et il a continué à en lire les œuvres marquantes comme chroniqueur littéraire, pour sa revue des 'Livres d'aujourd'hui et de demain' de *L'Evénement*, par exemple, en 1866.[15] Par ailleurs, se rappelant les soirées passées, avec passion, au théâtre d'Aix, il commente, dans un de ses articles, qu'il recueillit dans *Le Naturalisme au théâtre*, 'Les Jeunes':

Le théâtre jouait trois fois par semaine, et j'en avais la passion. Je ne dînais pas pour être le premier à la porte, avant l'ouverture des bureaux. C'est là, dans cette salle étroite, que pendant cinq ou six ans, j'ai vu défiler tout le répertoire du Gymnase et de la Porte-Saint-Martin. Education déplorable et dont je sens toujours en moi l'empreinte ineffaçable. Maudite petite salle! J'y ai appris comment un personnage doit entrer et sortir; j'y ai appris la symétrie des coups de scènes, la nécessité des rôles sympathiques et moraux, tous les escamotages de la vérité, grâce à un geste ou à une tirade; j'y ai appris ce code compliqué de la convention, cet arsenal des ficelles qui a fini par constituer chez nous ce que la critique appelle de ce mot absolu 'le théâtre'. J'étais sans défense alors, et j'emmagasinais vraiment de jolies choses dans ma cervelle.

On ne saurait croire l'impression énorme que produit le théâtre sur une intelligence de collégien échappé. On est tout neuf, on se façonne là comme une cire molle.[16]

Empreinte ineffaçable d'une tradition, constate l'écrivain, qui a conscience de la façon dont certaines impressions d'enfance peuvent irrémédiablement former - ou déformer - la sensibilité et l'imagination. Cette imprégnation marque, évidemment, le travail de Zola dramaturge. Nous l'avons vu avec *Madeleine*, écrit en 1865. Elle est toujours pleinement visible, des années plus tard; ainsi, dans la lettre qu'il envoya, le 19 août 1877, à William Busnach, pour lui expliquer ses idées sur la manière de tirer une pièce de *L'Assommoir*, le roman dont il a souhaité faire 'un tableau très exact de la vie du peuple'. C'est lui qui imagine de donner un rôle essentiel à Virginie, dont il fait le traître de la pièce, 'un traître de mélodrame', écrit-il. C'est lui qui en fait - malgré les réticences de Busnach - la responsable de la chute de Coupeau: poussée par la haine et le désir de se venger, elle dénoue les cordes de l'échafaudage sur lequel il travaille et pose une planche en bascule. C'est lui qui a l'idée du dénouement par lequel Poisson poignarde Virginie et Lantier.[17] Il serait facile de multiplier les exemples de ce type.[18]

Plus intéressant, cette imprégnation est aussi sensible dans les romans. Zola part toujours de ce matériel - situations et personnages - qui lui est familier, matériel banal et usé. Il ne cherche pas à inventer, à innover. Sa recherche se situe ailleurs: dans l'exploration de ces stéréotypes, dans des expérimentations qu'il fait à partir d'eux, dans la manière dont il les transforme, les revivifie, les investit, de toutes parts, de ses obsessions et ses fantasmes, dans la liberté laissée, finalement, à l'imagination et aux mots.

Définir le mélodrame serait une entreprise périlleuse tant les formes que ce genre, d'une extrême fertilité, a prises, depuis les débuts du XIXᵉ siècle, sont diverses. Jean-Marie Thomasseau répertorie, quant à lui, le mélodrame classique (1800–23), le mélodrame romantique (1823–48), le mélodrame diversifié (1848–1914), rubrique sous laquelle il classe 'le mélodrame militaire patriotique et historique, le mélodrame de mœurs et naturaliste, le mélodrame d'aventures et d'exploration, le mélodrame policier et judiciaire', enfin, 'D'autres auteurs'. Cette lecture de la table des matières de son 'Que sais-je' est suffisamment éloquente.[19] Toutefois, comme le suggère Peter Brooks,[20] il est possible de se mettre d'accord sur un certain nombre de caractéristiques du genre et, pour ma part, je partirai de deux essais de définition, qui viennent recouper les affirmations de Zola que j'ai citées plus haut. Le premier est le compte rendu fait par Paul de Saint-Victor des *Deux orphelines*, drame en cinq actes et 8 tableaux, célèbre entre tous, de Dennery et Cormon, au lendemain de la première, en 1874, au théâtre de la Porte-Saint-Martin, et que reprirent à leur compte Noël et Stoullig, lorsqu'on joua à nouveau la pièce en 1892:

M. d'Ennery et M. Cormon [...] viennent de nous donner avec *Les Deux Orphelines*, le drame le mieux fait et le plus touchant qu'ils aient produit peut-être dans toute leur carrière. Ce n'est pas que les situations en soient neuves, mais elles sont remaniées et rajustées de main d'ouvrier. L'intrigue, terriblement compliquée, se déroule avec une clarté parfaite; ses péripéties se tiennent et s'enchaînent, il y a de l'ordre dans son mouvement et de la liaison dans les mille fils entremêlés de sa trame. L'intérêt monte de scène en scène sans jamais faillir jusqu'à son point culminant. [...]. Ajoutez à ce métier consommé une action poignante qui vise au cœur et qui le frappe à tout coup. Les auteurs jouent des cordes sensibles du public, comme un virtuose des touches d'un clavier. Ils savent quelle note d'angoisse ou de pitié, d'attendrissement ou d'effroi sortira de ce sentiment plus ou moins pressé. Nous avons rarement vu ce qu'il faudrait appeler *la pompe aux larmes* fonctionner, au théâtre, avec autant de vigueur et d'adresse.[21]

Ma seconde définition, je l'emprunterai à Jules Lemaître commentant, en 1890, une reprise de *Marie-Jeanne ou le femme du peuple*, du même Dennery:

Je calculais que ce genre humble et puissant a trois propriétés fondamentales car, premièrement, il excite en nous l'étonnement et la plus grossière mais la plus impérieuse curiosité, par des combinaisons extraordinaires d'événements, et il prête une surprenante intelligence au Hasard, ce 'dieu inconnu', ce dieu de tout le monde, au fond le premier des dieux et le seul qui n'ait pas un athée; deuxièmement, il nous remue par le spectacle de souffrances très violentes et très peu compliquées, et troisièmement, il contente toujours et pleinement, notre naïf besoin de justice distributive, et, baptisant pour une heure le Hasard Providence, flatte un de nos désirs les plus mémorables et les plus longs à mourir.[22]

Résumons: le mélodrame, c'est, d'abord, un engrenage, un mécanisme parfaitement monté qui doit captiver le spectateur, en aiguisant, en particulier, constamment, sa curiosité. Peter Brooks, reprenant l'idée de Jules Lemaître, parle d'"esthétique de l'étonnement'.[23]

C'est, aussi, une machine à émotion. Le mélodrame doit émouvoir violemment, en provoquant des émotions simples, primaires, sans complication. Combat manichéen du Bien et du Mal, le mélodrame donne à voir, *in fine*, le triomphe de la Vertu, enfin reconnue. Il touche ainsi notre invincible besoin de justice, après avoir laissé libre cours à tous les excès de la violence, du pathétique et de l'extravagance.[24]

Ajoutons une troisième caractéristique: le mélodrame est entièrement voué au spectaculaire. Th. Gautier le définissait comme un spectacle 'oculaire'.[25] Certains des 'clous' de mise en scène, orage, incendie, inondation, éruption de volcan, accident de chemin de fer, firent époque: ainsi une avalanche dans la *Cabane de Montainard* de Frédéric Dupetit-Méré, ou l'éboulement final dans *La Citerne* de Pixérécourt, ou encore une éruption volcanique dans *Tête de mort* du même Pixérécourt.

Si Zola est particulièrement attiré par ce langage théâtral, c'est, probablement, qu'il est plus en accord avec son type d'imagination, qu'il lui paraît plus apte qu'un autre à exprimer sa conception de l'homme et de la société - d'un homme travaillé souterrainement par des forces obscures, secrètes, qui se libèrent parfois avec violence - ce 'drame mystérieux et poignant' dont il parle plusieurs fois dans l'*Ebauche* de *La Bête humaine*,[26] mais aussi dans celle d'*Une Page d'amour*[27] et ailleurs - d'une société qu'il voit comme le lieu de terribles affrontements, du grand combat pour la Vie, qui, par delà, anime l'univers entier, de la lutte éternelle entre la Vie et la Mort.

L'invention mélodramatique s'adapte probablement mieux qu'une autre à l'esthétique qu'il expose, au moment où il réfléchit aux futurs *Rougon-Macquart*, dans ses *Notes générales sur la nature de l'œuvre*, esthétique issue de sa vision de l'homme et de la société, et, à l'évidence, fortement influencée par le mélodrame. On notera le choix et l'accumulation des images qu'il utilise alors, visant, non sans quelque incohérence, à donner vie à l'abstrait, aux mots. Les romans, prévoit-il, seront organisés par 'larges masses', 'se succédant comme des blocs superposés, se mordant l'un l'autre, [...] le *souffle de la passion* animant le tout, courant d'un bout à l'autre de l'œuvre', les 'études' ne devant 'guère sortir de l'exception'. Zola rappelle encore, après avoir pris pour exemple *Thérèse Raquin*, qu'un drame 'prend le public à la gorge. Il se fâche, mais n'oublie plus. Lui donner toujours, sinon des cauchemars, du moins des livres excessifs qui restent dans sa mémoire'.[28]

Sur le plan de la pratique, cette influence d'un certain théâtre se révèle, tout d'abord, dans les dossiers préparatoires, par la façon dont il procède. Il imagine, d'emblée, il *voit* serait plus juste, le récit par 'tableaux' ou par 'scènes'. Il emploie constamment, souvent sans différence nette, ces deux termes désignant deux unités de découpage du texte dramatique. S'il lui arrive d'utiliser 'tableau' dans le sens de 'peinture', 'description' (ainsi dans les premières lignes de l'*Ebauche* de *L'Assommoir*, lorsqu'il réfléchit à ce que sera son roman: 'En un mot, un tableau très exact de la vie du peuple'),[29] il désigne, essentiellement, par ce terme, une unité spatiale, avec son décor, son atmosphère, son action, c'est-à-dire qu'il prend le mot dans son acception dramatique.

Les premiers feuillets de l'*Ebauche* de *Germinal* donnent un bon exemple de ce type de découpage proprement théâtral:

> Une scène dans la mine, une scène dans un intérieur d'ouvrier. Une scène chez le patron. La grève éclate dans la grande mine, scène. La peur du patron que la grève ne gagne son puits, nouvelle scène dans la mine, détails du travail. La grève éclate aussi là. Nouvelle scène chez le patron, nouvelle scène chez l'ouvrier.[30]

L'important, que Martin Kanes souligne avec raison, c'est que Zola prévoit les scènes avant même d'en imaginer le contenu précis.[31]

Il a toujours admiré l'habileté et l'efficacité des engrenages mis en place par les feuilletonistes ou les auteurs de mélodrame. Il en a compris la leçon, qui est celle, aussi, des grands auteurs classiques. Il sait qu'une scène tire une grande partie de sa force de la place qu'elle occupe dans l'économie du récit. Dans ce début de l'*Ebauche* de *Germinal*, nous le voyons explicitement, ce qui l'intéresse c'est le découpage et les effets qu'il peut en tirer: oppositions, parallélismes, échos, reprises, gradations et dégradations. Il conçoit le récit comme une série de temps forts - de scènes à faire - dont l'importance sur le plan de l'action est toujours déterminante, reliés entre eux par des passages narratifs, souvent brefs, eux-mêmes souvent *dramatisés*, pour reprendre un de ses termes favoris. Il sait tirer, de ce découpage en tableaux, une grand force dramatique, celle même que souligne Pierre Larthomas dans son étude du langage dramatique:

Il y a entre la pièce en actes et la pièce en tableaux, outre les différences de structure, une différence de style qui tient principalement au fait que l'auteur du second genre de pièces peut, comme le fait remarquer Marcel Pagnol, 'attaquer dix ou vingt fois en pleine action' et, 'dix ou vingt fois, par un simple coup de rideau, laisser le spectateur au sommet de l'action dramatique'.[32]

Les canevas des scènes qu'il traite, il les choisit parmi ceux que lui offre la tradition. Dans *Thérèse Raquin*, *Germinal*, *L'Assommoir*, *La Bête humaine*, par exemple, il reprend les représentations habituelles de la violence ouvrière telles que les divulguent pièces, romans, tableaux, gravures: 'Procéder par grandes scènes typiques. Ainsi les bordées des ouvriers, une seule fois, mais en plein et dramatisé', 'Les premières râclées', 'Le drame banal chez le peuple, c'est quelque jalousie brutale qui finit par jouer du couteau'.[33]

Il les choisit pour leur charge émotionnelle et pour leur efficacité visuelle, son travail consistant à accroître ce poids de l'image et du geste. Deux notations du dossier préparatoire de *L'Assommoir* révèlent cette volonté. Il précise de Gervaise: 'Restée seule avec deux enfants, l'un de huit ans, l'autre de quatre ans (La scène de l'abandon, les enfants, etc ...)'. Quelques pages plus tard, il revient sur cette idée: 'Une première scène dans un lavoir. L'abandon de Gervaise dramatisé, mis en scène'.[34] On pourrait multiplier les exemples de scènes du même ordre visant au pathos ou au sentimentalisme par l'impact de la représentation, essentiellement. Ainsi, dans des genres très différents, la mort des petites Lalie Bijard ou Alzire Maheu, la descente du cheval Trompette, l'eau poursuivant Bataille ou les mineurs, autant de scènes auxquelles on pourrait trouver une source de l'ordre du 'vu' et qui fournissent, à leur tour, des sujets de choix aux illustrateurs.

Les premières pages de *L'Assommoir* relèvent de cette technique de dramaturge–metteur en scène. La narration devient une suite d'indications scéniques. C'est bien à travers le regard de Gervaise que Zola décrit le lieu - 'Et lentement, de ses yeux voilés de larmes, elle faisait le tour de la misérable chambre' - mais ce regard est, en réalité, celui, précis, efficace, sensible au détail frappant, symbolique, d'un metteur en scène, bien plus que celui d'une jeune femme inquiète attendant son amant. Le décor est constitué d'un certain nombre d'éléments directement signifiants pour un lecteur–spectateur, choisis selon les codes qu'il connaît: 'lambeaux de perse déteinte' tombant 'de la flèche attachée au plafond par une ficelle', commode à laquelle il manque un tiroir, malle grande ouverte dans un coin, etc. Gervaise est en scène: ses attitudes, ses gestes sont aussi choisis pour leur expressionnisme: crises de sanglots qu'elle essaie d'étouffer et qui redoublent quand elle regarde ses deux enfants dormant 'sur le même oreiller'; 'Claude, qui avait huit ans, ses petites mains rejetées hors de la couverture, respirait d'une haleine lente, tandis qu'Etienne, âgé de quatre ans seulement, souriait, un bras passé au cou de son frère'. Image conventionnelle de l'innocence enfantine, mais très fortement appuyée, visant au pathétique d'attendrissement et formant, avec le décor et l'attitude de la mère, un de ces tableaux à sujet émouvant que Zola critiquait dans *Salons*.

Cette attirance pour la scène forte est telle qu'on peut lire, à quelques pages d'intervalle, dans l'*Ebauche* de *L'Assommoir*: 'il faudra que le caractère du livre soit précisément la simplicité, une histoire d'une nudité magistrale, de la réalité au jour le jour [...]. Pas de complications, très peu de scènes, et des plus ordinaires', et 'Je la fais passer (Gervaise) par toutes les crises et toutes les hontes imaginables. Enfin, je la tue dans un drame'. Et l'on se rappelle l'étonnant dénouement, digne des mélodrames les plus 'mélodramatiques' auquel Zola avait d'abord pensé: Gervaise est enceinte; elle découvre, grâce à des voisins charitables, Lantier 'en flagrant délit' avec la grande Adèle:

> Elle [...] leur casse une bouteille de vitriol sur leurs corps, dans leur lit. Alors Lantier, rendu fou par la douleur, la prend et la traîne par les cheveux dans la cour, devant les Boche. C'est là que Goujet peut arriver et engager un duel formidable avec Lantier, dans la cour, les portes fermées, avec des armes différentes et terribles. [...] Un détail épouvantable: Lorilleux peut s'approcher de Gervaise étendue sur le sol et râlant, et lui donner un coup de pied sournois, 'Tiens! garce!'. C'est de ce coup de pied dont elle meurt. La scène à la tombée du jour'.[35]

Ces quelques lignes extraites de l'ébauche d'un roman sont véritablement la mise en place très précise, avec dialogue, éclairages, mouvement des acteurs, d'une scène de théâtre.

La fin apocalyptique de *Germinal*, celle du *Rêve*, la vision du train fou filant dans la neige, bondé de soldats hurlant des chants patriotiques, Denise se jetant en sanglotant et bégayant des mots d'amour, au cou du bel Octave, tombé assis sur son bureau, 'dans le million', sous le regard souriant de Mme Hédouin, relèvent de cette même fascination du spectaculaire. Il n'y a pas de roman qui n'ait son (ou ses) 'clou(s)', terrifiant(s) ou splendidement émouvant(s), provoquant à l'excès angoisse, pitié, attendrissement, effroi, capable(s) de rivaliser, par la liberté d'invention, l'efficacité, la puissance, avec ceux de mélodrames célèbres.

Cette volonté de faire certaines scènes commande même la construction des lieux du roman. Ainsi, la topographie de *Germinal* est-elle, en particulier, dictée par le désir d'insérer un épisode, prévu avant même tout travail sur le récit et relevant de l'imaginaire de la mine: l'inondation des galeries.

On pourrait faire le même type d'étude à propos des personnages. Zola part aussi des stéréotypes du mélodrame: le héros, l'héroïne pathétique: Catherine, chassée la nuit, piétinant dans la boue, Denise, l'orpheline, qui se dévoue sans faillir à ses deux frères; l'innocente victime bafouée: Lalie Bijard; le traître: Chaval, Virginie; le comique, qui vient détendre l'atmosphère: la Mouquette, Mes Bottes, Bec Salé. Au mélodrame, il reprend aussi la répartition manichéenne des personnages: 'Diviser mes personnages en bons et méchants, le plus de bons possible', note-t-il dans l'*Ebauche* de *L'Assommoir*.[36] On reconnaîtrait facilement la même tendance à constamment dramatiser, la même exagération, l'utilisation de mêmes figures hyperboliques.

Pourtant, les romans ne sont pas une simple succession d'images fortes, critique faite aux adaptations qu'on en a tirées pour la scène. Outre la complication infiniment plus grande, plus subtile des programmes des personnages, le poids du fantasme, des obsessions personnelles du créateur, l'animation de l'inanimé, le passage au mythe, font éclater, revivifient, transforment le conventionnel.

Je m'attacherai à ce second point en prenant comme exemple *Thérèse Raquin*. Exemple privilégié. Zola a voulu faire un roman scientifique, volonté fortement affirmée, non pas seulement dans la préface de la seconde édition, mais aussi dans le texte et par la formule de Taine mise en exergue à la première édition: 'Le vice et la vertu sont des produits comme le sucre et le vitriol'. Or, pour écrire cette œuvre, il prend ses modèles parmi ce qu'il y a de plus conventionnel et de moins scientifique: *La Vénus de Gordes* d'Adolphe Belot et Ernest Daudet, 'terrible histoire de passion et de souffrance', selon ses propres termes,[37] *Atar Gull* d'Eugène Sue, *L'Assassinat du Pont Rouge* de Charles Barbara,[38] etc.

A *La Vénus de Gordes*, il prend le canevas d'ensemble, tout à fait banal: une femme décide de se débarrasser de son mari gênant, avec l'aide de son amant. Mais d'un côté, il va le rendre beaucoup plus dramatique, de l'autre, il le renouvelle en lui insufflant ses propres fantasmes.

Il construit, d'abord, un récit d'une habileté et d'une efficacité étonnantes, montant vers l'horrible résolution de la crise, à travers une succession de scènes fortes, de plus en plus violentes, séparées par des périodes d'accalmie de plus en plus brèves. Mais cette volonté de maintenir tensions et suspense est telle qu'elle tombe dans l'artificiel, le désir de frapper conduit à l'exceptionnel - Sainte-Beuve l'a bien senti[39] - la chronologie est pliée au romanesque, le temps est un temps symbolique, non celui des horloges. Un certain nombre d'effets de retardement, en particulier dans le chapitre XI, dans lequel Zola fait attendre le crime, ne tiennent pas aux nécessités de la situation mais visent simplement à maintenir le suspense, à imposer un certain rythme au récit.

Si Zola choisit la figure du trio - une femme prise entre deux hommes, l'un faible et l'autre fort - figure banale, même s'il la renouvelle en faisant que l'homme faible admire, comme la femme, la force de son rival,[40] c'est d'abord parce que ce schéma engendre un maximum de violences et de tensions. Il est créateur de suspense. Il permet les rebondissements et un certain nombre de scènes que le lecteur attend. Zola ne le déçoit pas: il fait monter Mme Raquin dans la chambre où se trouvent Thérèse et Laurent, scène de suspense, variante de la scène attendue, dans ce genre de situation, de la découverte de l'adultère. Autre scène attendue, que Zola reprend: la lutte des deux hommes, en présence de la femme, le vainqueur emportant sa proie. Après avoir lutté avec Camille pour le jeter à l'eau, Laurent ramène Thérèse à Paris. Se déroule, alors, dans la voiture, une scène d'amour où se mêlent violence, sang, désir, mort, composantes de la scène primitive, moment de grande intensité.

Thérèse Raquin comporte d'autres scènes typiques du mélodrame: les visites de Laurent à la morgue, les hallucinations des meurtriers, moments de terreur et de fantastique (le portrait de Camille s'anime, le fantôme du noyé revient), le dénouement, que critique Gustave Vapereau.[41] Toutes ces scènes visent à provoquer une émotion forte. Zola y utilise des images et un vocabulaire stéréotypés. Un seul exemple: 'Chaque nuit le noyé les visitait, l'insomnie les couchait sur un lit de charbons-ardents et les retournait avec des pinces de feu' (*OC*, I, 593).

Outre ces modèles d'un type de littérature, Zola suit les codes de représentation dont j'ai déjà parlé, popularisés par des gravures, des tableaux, des pièces. Quand il décrit, par exemple, les scènes de terreur et d'hallucination, il peut revoir un tableau ou un dessin représentant un fantôme revenant narguer les vivants, la mort narguant des amoureux, ou encore ouvrant ses bras pour les accueillir. Ainsi, au chapitre XVII, Laurent rêve-t-il que Camille est caché sous son lit qu'il secoue 'pour le faire tomber et le mordre', voit-il 'le cadavre lui tendre les bras, avec un rire ignoble, en montrant un bout de langue noirâtre dans la blancheur des dents' (*OC*, I, 589–90). Références qui ne vont pas sans une certaine ironie, mais qui contaminent le projet scientifique, comme la blessure de Laurent qui, telle 'une viande empoisonnée [...] pourrissait ses propres muscles' (*OC*, I, 655).

Outre ces stéréotypes de situations ou de langage et ces références diverses, on repère, dans *Thérèse Raquin* des stéréotypes idéologiques, en particulier dans les scènes de brutalité entre Thérèse et Laurent:

> Laurent, ivre, rendu furieux par les tableaux atroces que Thérèse étalait devant ses yeux, se précipitait sur elle, la renversait par terre et la serrait sous son genou, le poing haut.
> [...] Et Laurent, fouetté par ces paroles, la secouait avec rage, la battait, meurtrissait son corps de son poing fermé (*OC*, I, 650).

Ce texte - dont la source est peut-être une gravure ayant pour sujet une scène d'alcoolisme et de misère - annonce certaines pages de *L'Assommoir*.

La scène dans laquelle Laurent prend Thérèse sur le carreau, image du rut, est pareillement surdéterminée: dans cet homme du peuple, la bête humaine se déchaîne, comme elle se déchaînera dans les mineurs qui prennent les filles sur les terris. Degas, inspiré, dit-on, par cette page, intitulera son tableau: 'Le Viol'.

Zola insère même, dans *Thérèse Raquin*, une phrase-cliché, une 'phrase-peuple', qu'il met au compte de Thérèse? ou du narrateur? on ne sait trop: 'elle dormait mieux la nuit, quand elle avait été bien battu le soir' (*OC*, I, 650). Dans le tempérament sanguin de Laurent se conjuguent deux causes de violence: c'est un homme du peuple *et* un paysan. L'imaginaire zolien peut rêver autour de ce sang trop riche.

Les caractéristiques du jeune homme sont bien celles du 'criminel-né', telles qu'elles seront définies, en 1887, par César Lombroso dans *L'Homme criminel*, telles aussi qu'elles sont transmises dans l'inconscient culturel.[42] Laurent en a les mains grosses, les doigts carrés, le cou de taureau. Il en a encore la chevelure abondante, la paresse, la poltronnerie, l'insensibilité, l'absence de remords.

Ainsi, la volonté de faire un roman scientifique est-elle fortement pervertie par l'héritage technique et rhétorique du romancier, en particulier par l'influence d'une certaine forme de théâtre, dont il n'a pu se défaire, ou, plutôt, dont il n'a pas cherché à se défaire, ainsi que par un système d'idées reçues, d'images, d'associations. Mais ces recettes ou cet héritage culturel, il les revivifie, les nourrit de ses propres obsessions. Ils ne constituent pas une fin en soi. Ils deviennent, en quelque sorte, un tremplin pour son imagination.

J'étudierai un seul exemple de ce travail sur un stéréotype. Le mélodrame a, comme le rappelle Jean-Marie Thomasseau, 'une prédilection pour les personnages muets dont le langage mimé convenait à son éthique simplifiée'.[43] Ces personnages, par suite de leur infirmité, sont, en effet, le lieu de conflits extrêmes, ils servent à provoquer des émotions particulièrement vives. Zola tire de l'aphasie et de la paralysie dont il frappe Mme Raquin, la première d'une série de paralytiques ou de vieillards figés dans l'immobilité qui parcourt son œuvre,[44] des scènes d'une grande intensité dramatique. Mais la manière dont il utilise le regard de la mercière et sa condition d'emmurée vivante dans sa prison de chair ne relèvent pas du modèle, mais de ses propres hantises.

Mme Raquin est le témoin lucide de ce qui se passe dans la salle à manger close, comme le sont les autres paralytiques. Mais ce n'est pas à travers son regard que nous connaissons les événements. Zola utilise encore peu le style indirect libre qui permet de faire intérioriser des faits par un personnage au lieu de les raconter - technique qu'il emploiera beaucoup ultérieurement.[45] Le regard de Mme Raquin a un rôle dramatique. Ses 'yeux fixes et aigus' fascinent et subjuguent les deux meurtriers. 'Regarder l'autre', écrit Barthes, 'c'est le désorganiser, puis le fixer dans le désordre, c'est-à-dire le maintenir dans l'être même de sa nullité.'[46] Ce que fait la mère de Camille. Comme l'araignée qui guette, immobile, sa proie, elle attend que la folie conduise les deux meurtriers au crime. Elle se contente de les regarder, 'ses yeux s'attachaient sur les meurtriers avec une fixité aiguë' (OC, I, 642). Zola insiste sur cette toute-puissance du regard, qu'il étudiera dans d'autres œuvres.[47] Thérèse éprouve 'une sorte de malaise' sous 'le regard droit, qui semblait pénétrer en elle' de Laurent. Le romancier va plus loin. Non seulement Mme Raquin rappelle aux deux meurtriers, par sa seule présence, leur faute, mais Thérèse a besoin qu'elle la regarde: les attitudes successives que la jeune femme invente, remords, regrets de Camille, n'ont d'existence que dans la mesure où elle les joue devant sa tante.

Zola amplifie l'effet en donnant au chat François le même rôle dramatique. Ses yeux, d''une fixité diabolique' (OC, I, 656), ont enregistré l'adultère et en conservent la mémoire. Ils en renvoient l'image aux amants, provoquant la terreur de Laurent. Le chat est, pour lui, véritablement, une incarnation du diable - cliché auquel Zola redonne vie - parce que ses yeux l'ont à jamais fixé, réifié en amant, en pécheur, comme Thérèse tente, dans leurs huis-clos tragiques, de le figer en meurtrier, ce qui le rend fou (OC, I, 642–4). La morsure que lui a faite Camille a le même pouvoir de matérialiser le crime, de le faire vivre dans sa chair, qu'elle contamine alentour. La chair de Thérèse est pareillement 'imprégnée' par le crime: enceinte, elle a peur d'accoucher d'un noyé, alors que l'enfant est de Laurent, mais il lui semble 'sentir dans ses entrailles le froid d'un cadavre dissous et amolli' (OC, I, 654).

Il ne s'agit pas de remords, au sens moral du terme. Mais, autour et à partir d'un personnage stéréotypé, se développe une double rêverie, par laquelle Zola explore les zones secrètes des êtres, les impossibles rapports avec l'Autre, laisse libre cours à ses propres obsessions: la certitude qu'un acte, une fois accompli, ne peut jamais être effacé, qu'il continue à vivre, comme la blessure de Laurent, bête monstrueuse, la fascination de la déchéance, la hantise de l'enlisement, l'interrogation angoissée devant la folie et la décomposition physique et morale, le travail de la mort.

Tout créateur puise dans la tradition. Son originalité tient, essentiellement, à la manière dont il la fait sienne. Celle du mélodrame est importante pour la création zolienne. Le romancier y a trouvé des points d'appui et un langage à travers lequel parviennent à s'exprimer des angoisses que, par ailleurs, il cherche à canaliser et maîtriser - les dossiers préparatoires en font foi - ainsi qu'une esthétique en accord avec son refus de l'éparpillement dans le détail, de la dissolution de l'œil dans la multiplicité de la sensation et de la nuance, en accord avec sa recherche de la construction, son sens des masses et des ensembles, son affirmation du tempérament et de la liberté du constructeur.

Notes

1. Voir, par exemple, *L'Echo de Paris*, 7 juin 1891; *L'Echo de la semaine*, 22 février 1891; etc.
2. 'Au théâtre [...] le gain est formidable. Comme pour le livre, on touche un tant pour cent sur les recettes, seulement, comme les recettes sont ici énormes, comme un nombre considérable de gens qui ne mettent jamais trois francs à un livre, en donnent sept ou huit pour un fauteuil d'orchestre, il arrive qu'un drame ou une comédie rapporte beaucoup plus qu'un roman. [...] Et je ne parle pas des représentations en province, des traités à l'étranger, des reprises de la pièce. Cela est donc d'une vérité banale, le théâtre rapporte beaucoup plus que le livre, un nombre considérable d'auteurs en vit, tandis qu'on aurait vite compté les quelques auteurs qui vivent du volume' (*Le Roman expérimental*, 'L'Argent dans la littérature', *OC*, X, 1271).
3. *Corr.*, I, 199.
4. Paul Cézanne, *Correspondance*, édit J. Rewald (Grasset, 1937), p. 33.
5. Paul Alexis, *Emile Zola: notes d'un ami* (Charpentier, 1882), p. 131.
6. *Ibid*.
7. Ces états sont publiés en annexe dans Colette Becker, 'Emile Zola: 1840–1867: genèse d'une œuvre, Essai de biographie intellectuelle et esthétique', thèse de doctorat d'Etat dactylographiée, Université de la Sorbonne Nouvelle, 1987.
8. *Corr.*, I, 250–1.
9. A Baille, 3 décembre 1859: 'j'irai au premier jour voir ce que c'est', écrit-il en parlant du *Père prodigue* d'Alexandre Dumas fils (*Corr.*, I, 113). A Valabrègue, fin février–mars 1865: 'Je vais beaucoup au théâtre, j'ai besoin d'un peu de bruit et je sors plus souvent que l'année dernière' (*Corr.*, I, 445); cette lettre date bien de 1865 et non de 1866, date sous laquelle elle a été publiée dans la *Correspondance*.
10. Voir leurs lettres, B.N., N.a.f., Ms, 24511, fol. 132–3; Ms. 24518, fol. 23; etc.
11. Lettres inédites, coll. Fr. Emile-Zola.
12. *Le Temps*, 6 mai 1889.
13. A Lacroix, *Corr.*, I, 523.
14. Voir, *passim*, *Europe*, no. 542 (1974), *Le Roman-feuilleton*.
15. Voir mon étude, Colette Becker, '*Germinal*, roman populaire?', *Europe*, no. 678 (1985), 34–41. Fabriquer une œuvre qui réponde aux attentes du public est une des motivations essentielles de Zola, qui, dans ce but - les dossiers préparatoires des romans en font foi - applique deux des principales 'recettes' du roman populaire: la volonté d'être immédiatement lisible et la recherche de l'effet.
16. Dans une interview donnée à *L'Echo de Paris*, le 7 juin 1891, intitulée 'Zola musicien', il rappelle qu'il était clarinette dans la fanfare du Collège d'Aix, et même qu'il fut 'deuxième clarinette au théâtre d'Aix. Oui, j'ai joué *Fra Diavolo* et le *Postillon* et *La Dame blanche*. Vous voyez que je connais le vieux répertoire'.
17. *Corr.*, III, 93–101. Busnach reculera devant l'audace de Zola.
18. Voir à ce propos les articles de J.B. Sanders, 'Busnach, Zola et le drame

L'Assommoir', *Les Cahiers naturalistes*, no. 52 (1978), 109–21; 'Germinal mis en pièce(s)', *Les Cahiers naturalistes*, no. 54 (1980), 68–86.

19. Jean-Marie Thomasseau, *Le Mélodrame* (P.U.F., 1984, coll. 'Que sais-je?').

20. Peter Brooks, *The Melodramatic Imagination: Balzac, Henry James, melodrama and the mode of excess* (Yale University Press, 1976).

21. Ed. Noël et Ed. Stoullig, *Annales du théâtre et de la musique*, 1892, pp. 314–15.

22. Cité par J.M. Thomasseau, *op. cit.*, p. 75.

23. Peter Brooks, 'Une esthétique de l'étonnement: le mélodrame', *Poétique*, no. 19 (1974), 340–56.

24. Le spectacle de la vertu opprimée puis triomphante a passionné et ému le siècle et passionne encore, comme en témoigne l'actuelle série à succès de la télévision française, *Sentiments*.

25. Cité par J.M. Thomasseau, *op. cit.*, p. 111.

26. B.N., N.a.f., Ms. 10274, fol. 338: 'Je voudrais, après *Le Rêve*, faire un roman tout autre; [...] et comme sujet, un drame violent à donner le cauchemar à tout Paris, quelque chose de pareil à *Thérèse Raquin*, avec un côté de mystère, d'au-delà, quelque chose qui ait l'air de sortir de la réalité (pas d'hypnotisme, mais une force inconnue, à arranger, à trouver)'; etc.

27. B.N., N.a.f., Ms. 10318, fol. 505: 'Tout le livre/drame doit se passer sans éclat, sous la chair, une furieuse lutte à l'intérieur et la surface calme, polie.'

28. B.N., N.a.f., Ms. 10345, fol. 10/13, cité dans *RM*, V, 1742–4).

29. B.N., N.a.f., Ms. 10271, fol. 158.

30. B.N., N.a.f., Ms. 10307, fol. 412/11–413/12, dossier publié par Colette Becker, *La Fabrique de 'Germinal'* (SEDES, 1986), p. 259.

31. Martin Kanes, '*Germinal*: drama and dramatic structure', *Modern Philology*, LXI (1963), 12–25 (p.13).

32. Pierre Larthomas, *Le Langage dramatique* (Armand Colin, 1972), p. 120. Janine Godenne a souligné, elle aussi, l'importance du tableau pour Zola, mais en l'étudiant différemment, comme un microcosme, 'un monde complet et achevé, et monde signifiant d'une réalité plus vaste' ('Le tableau chez Zola: une forme, un microcosme', *Les Cahiers naturalistes*, no. 40 (1970), 135–43).

33. Dossier préparatoire de *L'Assommoir*, B.N., N.a.f., Ms. 10271, fol. 171, 160, 167.

34. *Ibid.*, fol. 160 et 165

35. *Ibid.*, fol. 169.

36. *Ibid.*, fol. 170.

37. *Le Figaro*, 24 décembre 1866.

38. Voir la préface d'Henri Mitterand à l'édition du roman dans la collection Garnier Flammarion.

39. Lettre du 10 juin 1868: 'C'est fait de tête et non d'après nature. Et, en effet, les passions sont féroces. Une fois déchaînées, tant qu'elles ne sont pas assouvies, elles n'ont pas de cesse. Elles vont droit au fait et au but, fût-ce sur un cadavre: si Clytemnestre et Egisthe, s'aimant à la fureur, n'avaient pu se posséder complètement qu'à côté du cadavre tout chaud et saignant d'Agamemnon, le cadavre d'Agamemnon ne les aurait pas gênés, au moins pour les premières nuits. Aussi je ne comprends rien à vos amants, à leurs remords et à leur refroidissement subit, avant d'être arrivés à leurs fins. Ah! plus tard, je ne dis pas' (*OC*, I, 681).

40. Schéma que l'on retrouve dans d'autres romans - ainsi *L'Assommoir*, *Nana* - et qui paraît relever du Moi profond de l'écrivain.

41. 'Il eût été plus logique, plus réel d'amener ces deux complices, ahuris de leur crime, devant les tribunaux et de les y laisser, sauf à terminer toute leur histoire psychologique par trois ou quatre lignes de citation d'une chronique judiciaire' (*L'Année littéraire*, X (Hachette, 1868), p. 47).

42. Voir, par exemple, *Le Curé de village* de Balzac.
43. J.M. Thomasseau, *op. cit.*, p. 32.
44. Voir Auguste Dezalay, 'Le Moteur immobile: Zola et les paralytiques', *Travaux de linguistique et de littérature*, VIII (1970), 63–74.
45. Son utilisation dans *L'Assommoir* a été étudiée par Marcel Cressot, 'La Langue de *L'Assommoir*', *Le Français moderne* (1940), pp. 207–18; et Jacques Dubois, '*L'Assommoir*' de Zola: société, discours, idéologie (Larousse, 1973, coll. 'Thèmes et textes').
46. Roland Barthes, *Sur Racine* (Seuil, 1963).
47. *La Conquête de Plassans*, etc. Voir David Baguley, 'Les Paradis perdus: espace et regard dans *La Conquête de Plassans* de Zola', *Nineteenth-Century French Studies*, VII (1980), 80-92.

5

CONSCIOUS ARTISTRY AND THE PRESENTATION OF THE PERSISTENT IDEAL

Joy Newton

While the accomplishment and subsequent defeat of each modest aim Gervaise outlines to Coupeau is the backbone of *L'Assommoir*,[1] she imparts to her husband early in their marriage another more ambitious purpose, one that is never realized: 'Au bout de vingt ans, si le travail marchait, ils pourraient avoir une rente, qu'ils iraient manger quelque part, à la campagne' (p. 476). Although not elaborated upon further, this concept and the accompanying visual leitmotifs associated with her origins remain with Gervaise throughout her life. Zola had initially intended his protagonist to retain stronger links with the countryside. The *premier plan*, which had twenty-one chapters, included: 'XIV: une partie de campagne avec les Goujet, ce qui fait du bien à Gervaise. [...] XVI: [...] une promenade à la campagne. [...] XXI: à la fin la partie de campagne. La dernière dégradation de Gervaise. Sa mort' (p. 1552). As the novel developed, however, Zola eliminated all such contact from the later stages, the better to depict Gervaise as a prisoner of the slums of the capital, sustained only by her nostalgic dream of a paradise lost. Moreover, he continues to make us keenly aware of the haunting resonances of her ideal in two satellite novels of the Gervaise cycle, for while Nana and Claude undoubtedly obey various negative imperatives issuing from *la tare héréditaire*, they each inherit from their mother a legacy of more positive aims, which form variations on the theme under discussion.

In order to enhance deliberately the reader's perception of Gervaise's plight, the author integrates a systematic structure of signs into the parent novel on two levels. First, with deliberate artistry, Zola weaves into the fabric of his work a series of images connected with - and often antithetical to - her ideal, but exterior to the character's consciousness. These images suggest from very early on that her ambition for her later years will never be realized. Second, Zola makes it clear by the careful manipulation of viewpoint that although Gervaise's desire stays with her to the end, it undergoes transformations within her own sensibility as it becomes increasingly unattainable: as her horizons shrink, so do her dreams. Initially her goal is expressed with lucid simplicity to Coupeau, but later it is restricted only to her own musings, through which Zola makes us painfully aware of the processes of her befuddled mind striving to evoke progressively impoverished images of that for which she has always yearned.

As a newcomer Gervaise is gifted with a clear vision of the metropolis, and Zola uses her as an excellent point of focalization to offer us a graphic view of the poor quarters, presented with documentary clarity in the opening chapters; her only source of comparison is Plassans, and it is through her evocations of this area that Zola sets up the parameters of her provincial ideal. Gervaise's most persistent memories of the countryside of Provence focus upon the river (the strongest of the separate strands which bind together to form a kind of lifeline once she becomes submerged in the metropolis), while the others, by association, centre upon the fresh air, blue sky, sunlight and trees of the south. The river naturally dominates the other images (all of which have diminished equivalents in Paris), for it was there that Gervaise had spent most of her time, working from the age of 10 as a laundress: 'Ça sentait meilleur qu'ici [...] il y avait un coin sous les arbres [...] avec de l'eau claire qui courait [...] à Plassans' (p. 388). The river has not merely an intrinsic value as a pleasing remembered image, but carries also all the connotations of cleanliness proper to her job; its presence in Gervaise's mind is also suggested, by contrast, in her repugnance both to the Paris equivalent, the stifling wash-house, characterized by its 'jour blafard [...] buée chaude [...] humidité lourde [...] odeur fade' (p. 386), and to the mockery of the open gutters by the hôtel Boncœur, with its 'allée noire, étroite avec un ruisseau longeant le mur, pour les eaux sales' (p. 402). Zola retrieves this debased image when he indicates that all the plans Gervaise subsequently evolves with her husband will in some way be thwarted, beginning, ironically, with the wedding; this sets the pattern for the rest of her life, with a radiant start to this happy day which degenerates into squabbles in the violent thunderstorm that spoils the afternoon. The bride and groom had originally agreed upon *une partie de campagne* by way of celebration, before gathering for dinner: 'On irait gagner la faim dans la plaine Saint-Denis; on prendrait le chemin de fer et on retournerait à pattes, le long de la grande route' (p. 434). Instead, because of the storm, they are drawn into the very heart of the city, and forced to take shelter under the Pont Royal, where the women of the party sit on the paving stones, 'arrachant des deux mains les brins d'herbe poussés entre les pierres, regardant couler l'eau noire, comme si elles se trouvaient à la campagne' (p. 448). In Zola's dispassionate assessment the reality is very different: 'La Seine charriait des nappes grasses, de vieux bouchons et des épluchures de légumes, un tas d'ordures' (p. 448).

Although much of the early part of the book is filtered through the consciousness of the main character, Zola is clearly entering into collusion with his reader here, by punctuating his text with poignant symbols (to which Gervaise is oblivious) of the increasingly meagre and squalid approximations for which she will have to settle. Similarly, when describing the first apartment to which she moves with Coupeau, the author sets up a deliberate tension between the subjective and objective perspectives: 'la jeune femme, charmée [...] croyait retourner en province [...] les constructions, en devenant plus rares et plus basses, laissaient descendre l'air et le soleil' (pp. 464–6). Yet she shows no reaction to the extremities of the street, which the disengaged narrator depicts at some length: 'du côté de la rue de la Goutte d'Or, il y avait des boutiques sombres, aux carreaux sales [...] un marchand de vin en faillite', while at the other end, 'vers Paris, des maisons de quatre étages barraient le ciel, occupées à leur rez-de-chaussée par des blanchisseuses' (p. 466). These indications ('blanchisseuses', 'sales', 'en faillite') form a subliminal commentary signposting Gervaise's future prospects and stress that her view of the present situation is too sanguine; her willing suspension of disbelief is reinforced because of her city-bred husband's attitude, since for him this suburb *is* practically the countryside: 'Coupeau, amusé par les rares passants qui enjambaient le ruissellement continu des eaux savonneuses, disait se souvenir d'un pays où l'avait conduit un de ses oncles à l'âge de cinq ans' (p. 466). For Gervaise, this is a fresh and respectable start, to which she responds with her usual optimism, characterizing it with comparisons with what she had valued most in Provence: the site of their new dwelling is 'un coin de tranquillité qui lui rappelait une ruelle de Plassans, derrière les remparts' (p. 464). But it is clear that her perspective is now falsified, for the aspects she evokes in this urban 'equivalent' no longer have the immediacy and plenitude of those recalled in *le lavoir* from her still recent past (p. 388). The abundant greenery is reduced in this 're-creation' to 'un acacia allongeant une seule de ses branches', which now becomes 'la joie de Gervaise' (p. 466). Again, this simple notation carries a clear subtext: she is already unconsciously making compromises, so that, although we cannot doubt her sincerity, we must henceforth question her reliability in her interpretation of what she sees.

The new apartment brings new friends, in the form of Madame Goujet and her son. In the early years of their marriage the Coupeaus liked to spend their Sundays with the Goujets, escaping the stranglehold of the metropolis for a day out in the fresh air, either to Saint-Ouen,[2] where they used to go before their move (p. 463), or venturing further afield, often 'du côté de Vincennes' (pp. 474, 476). It is also at this point that Gervaise formulates specifically to Coupeau her plans for retirement to the countryside, which had hitherto been only a nebulous idea. It would be fair to say that the Sundays on the outskirts of Paris with the Goujets are the nearest that Gervaise ever comes to achieving her ideal. However, these shared outings come to an end after Coupeau's accident, and once they move to the laundry premises Gervaise has to work non-stop to support her family and no longer has time to spare while her business is a going concern. From the point where the ideal was clearly stated (p. 476), Zola has less need, for a time, to exploit his authorial freedom to supersede the natural limitations of his character's vision. By locating the narrative focus within the confines of the sensibility of the protagonist and manipulating her increasingly selective perception, the author makes the widening gap between her ultimate ambition and the realities of her situation quite explicit. We become painfully aware of the decline in her powers of discrimination when we witness her eager acceptance of what at best are distant mocking echoes of her fading dream. In the rue de la Goutte d'Or there is not even a tree to provide a source of *rêverie*, but Gervaise is able to continue deluding herself because of the proximity of the water, whose artificial colouring - 'd'un azur profond de ciel d'été' (p. 432) - can imitate the sky's reflection. An ironic distance is obtained by her assertion of contentment and the objective evidence which contradicts it: 'ses trois mètres de ruisseau, devant sa boutique, prenaient une importance énorme, un fleuve large, qu'elle voulait très propre, un fleuve étrange et vivant, dont la teinturerie de la maison colorait les eaux des caprices les plus tendres, au milieu de la boue noire' (p. 500). The exaggerated importance she attributes to what is essentially dirty water stained with effluent underlines for us the discrepancy between what she has currently and the almost forgotten source of the original image, the clear stream of Plassans.

The tones chosen for the paintwork of the shop (brilliant blue and white like the skies of her native Provence), and the design on the wallpaper, now begin to act as subconscious substitutes for the real thing: 'couleur du ciel [...] le papier [...] représentant une treille où couraient des liserons', while the work-surface is covered with 'un bout de cretonne à grande ramages bleuâtres' (p. 497). In winter, when it is warm and cosy inside, with the noise from the street muffled by heavy snow, 'Gervaise disait en riant qu'elle s'imaginait être à la campagne' (p. 543). She has been lulled into a false sense of security, thinking she has everything she ever wanted, when she is in fact increasingly devitalized by her obligations, with her horizons now virtually limited to the shop, the milieu which exactly mirrors her diminished ideal: 'Est-ce que tous ses rêves n'étaient pas réalisés, est-ce qu'il lui restait à ambitionner quelque chose dans l'existence? [...] Et maintenant son idéal était dépassé, elle avait tout, et en plus beau' (p. 502).

It might seem by this stage that she has almost lost sight of her desire to retire to the countryside. In fact her intangible ideal remains with her in essence, but, like the once-indomitable Gervaise, it has been subjected to the influence of the metropolis and undergone a transformation. It is significant that the platonic idyll with Gueule d'Or is characterized by images taken from within her sensibility which are coloured less by her dwindling memories of the early days in Plassans than by analogies drawn from the more recent Sunday excursions she and Coupeau had shared with the Goujets. The protagonist has now reached a further stage in her involuntary estrangement from her goal, a stage at one remove, when an impoverished approximation is permanently superimposed on the totality of the original. Her brief Friday visits to the forge in the rue Marcadet - a place which she reckoned on her first visit to be 'une rue où elle n'aurait pas demeuré pour tout l'or du monde' (p. 526) - are now her only regular outings and as such are presented through her distorting subjectivity as the ultimate pinnacle of happiness at this point in her life: 'Dès qu'elle tournait le coin de la rue, elle se sentait légère, gaie, comme si elle faisait une partie de campagne; [...] la chaussée noire de charbon, les panaches de vapeur sur les toits, l'amusaient autant qu'un sentier de mousse dans un bois de la *banlieue*, s'enfonçant entre de grands bouquets de verdure' (p. 554). The water image has dwindled into a mere 'flaque d'eau' (pp. 526, 554), and the green trees and fresh air have given way to the soot-begrimed industrial urban wasteland. After one such visit they go to a spot nearby, 'entre une scierie mécanique et une manufacture de boutons, une bande de prairie restée verte, avec des plaques jaunes d'herbe grillée; une chèvre, attachée à un piquet, tournait en bêlant; au fond, un arbre mort s'émiettait au grand soleil' (p. 614); the only others trees in sight are 'les bosquets verts des cabarets borgnes' (p. 616). Zola operates a kind of structural recessing here: these moments snatched from work spent on a patch of waste ground are indeed very far removed from their previous days out, with a leisurely meal under the trees, 'du côté de Vincennes' (p. 474), just as those Sundays in turn were only an echo of the aim Gervaise voiced to Coupeau, of spending years of well-earned rest somewhere in the countryside. Yet at the conscious level Gervaise is unaware of the ironic discrepancy when she tells Goujet: 'Vrai! [...] on se croirait à la campagne'. Subconsciously, though, she is ready at this point to cling to any vestige of that now-distant ideal which will enable her to get away, however briefly, from the fetid atmosphere of the laundry and the misery of her domestic situation.

By the time of the party for her fête (a deliberate pendant to the meal at the wedding), it is evident that no escape will be possible, for she is by then too deeply in debt, entrenched in habits of self-indulgence and too exhausted to clear the slate. On this occasion the only *partie de campagne* mentioned features in the air sung by Clémence, 'Faites un nid'. Gervaise's reaction to this song is not particularized but deliberately lumped together with that of the other Parisians: 'Ça causa [...] beaucoup de plaisir; car ça rappelait la campagne, les oiseaux légers, les danses sous la feuillée, les fleurs au calice de miel, enfin ce qu'on voyait au bois de Vincennes, les jours où l'on allait tordre le cou à un lapin' (p. 587). This string of clichés recalls the remote unfulfilled plans for the wedding-day celebration: 'un petit tour de balade l'après-midi, en attendant d'aller tordre le cou à un lapin, au premier gargot venu' (p. 432). Gervaise's contribution to the songs is indicative of her inability to struggle any more against the overwhelming odds which have deadened her ambitions: 'Ah! laissez-moi dormir' (p. 586). Zola does not set up any critical distance by making an intrusive commentary on Gervaise's real situation here, but effectively controls our sympathy by the artistic consistency with which he gently echoes these thematic parallels.

After this point, with the return of Lantier, Gervaise's fragile connecting link with the countryside - always hitherto a kind of lifeline - is virtually severed, and the privileged status accorded to her point of view much diminished as her capacity for discernment falters. Her Sunday 'outings' with Coupeau and Lantier become a mockery - 'histoire de crâner dans la rue' (p. 618) - and are then abandoned in view of the domestic realignment; while Gervaise toils in the laundry the two men treat themselves to meals at her expense, their walks now reduced to 'un petit tour sur le boulevard' between drinks (p. 625). Eventually Coupeau reaches the stage where he is too drunk to get home, and a mockery of the dream he had once shared with his wife is evoked when Zola states: 'Il couchait dans un terrain vague, en travers d'un ruisseau' (p. 628). The pattern of imagery connected with the river (p. 388) has by this stage undergone a drastic alteration: all references to water are now sullied, metaphorically or literally. When Gervaise takes to drinking in *L'Assommoir*, adapting easily to the stifling atmosphere from which she had once recoiled, she initially feels threatened by the presence of the infernal 'machine à saouler [...] avec son murmure de ruisseau souterrain' but is soon intoxicated with its product - 'le ruisseau maintenant coulait au travers de son corps' - and on the way home 'elle s'assit au ruisseau, elle se crut au lavoir' (p. 708). Gutter imagery henceforth taints all the water with which she is associated: when reduced to scrubbing floors for Virginie, she is depicted 'dans la mare d'eau sale [...] dont les éclaboussures la mouchetaient de boue,

jusque dans ses cheveux [...] mouillée et laide comme un chien qu'on tirerait
d'un égout' (pp. 734–6).

By the end of chapter IX Gervaise awakens briefly from the torpor into
which she had drifted; the quality of her renewed acute awareness is made
explicit with the death of Maman Coupeau, which precipitates her realization
of just how many illusions she has lost. The one haven which had remained -
the forge in the *rue Marcadet* - is henceforth inaccessible, for Goujet,
convinced of her renewed liaison with Lantier, tells her after the funeral that
'tout est fini' (p. 669). The site of her former happiness now has only sad
associations for her:

> elle n'avait bien sûr pas laissé que Maman Coupeau au fond du trou, dans le petit
> jardin de la rue Marcadet. Il lui manquait trop de choses, ça devait être un morceau
> de sa vie à elle, et sa boutique, et son orgueil de patronne, et d'autres choses encore
> qu'elle avait enterrés ce jour-là' (p. 671).

The image of the cemetery, 'le petit jardin de la rue Marcadet', remains firmly
rooted in her mind, even when its other painful associations have long since
been blotted out, for this patch of green represents the tattered remnant of her
dream of the countryside and recurs at the very nadir of her fortunes.

Her plight is at its worst when she experiences the ultimate humiliation of
soliciting under the leafless trees on the streets of Paris in her 'promenade
dernière' (p. 771), for it is at this point that her long-term impaired capacity
for self-awareness returns again, albeit briefly, with painful acuity. The gas-lit
shadow of her silhouette, a caricature of her former self,[3] reveals to her what
she has become: 'une ombre énorme, trapue, grotesque [...] elle louchait si fort
de la jambe que, sur le sol, l'ombre faisait la culbute à chaque pas; un vrai
guignol!' (p. 772). From the darkness to the snowstorm, everything conspires
to stress the bleakness of her future prospects: 'le soleil avait étouffé sa
chandelle, la nuit serait longue' (p. 767). Upon the miserable actuality
Gervaise superimposes for a moment a happier recollection from her past:
'Son lavoir, rue Neuve, l'avait nommée reine [...]. Alors, on s'était baladé sur
les boulevards, dans des chars ornés de verdure [...]. Et, alourdie, dans les
tortures de sa faim, elle regardait par terre, comme si elle eût cherché le
ruisseau où elle avait laissé choir sa majesté tombée' (p. 767). The reality is
totally antithetical to this flashback, the greenery only a memory, the sunlight
absent and the water, following the now familiar pattern, merely the open
drainage of the gutter. All hope is now lost, as she reflects when she hears a
train leaving Paris: 'De ce côté elle devinait la campagne, le ciel libre [...]. Oh!
si elle avait pu partir ainsi, s'en aller là-bas' (p. 768).

The humiliating final brief encounter with Goujet releases in Gervaise's
consciousness the meaning of the scattered images of the almost forgotten
plans for retirement, for in later years it was only with the happiness that he
inspired in her that these images were associated. As Gervaise recalls their
distant origin, they are bathed in the climate of her mood and suffused with
overtones of death: 'dans la cour elle se crut dans un vrai cimetière' (p. 778);
the sight of the black stream she crosses[4] - 'une eau couleur de ses pensées' -
recalls 'son bel espoir de se retirer à la campagne, après vingt ans de repassage.
Eh bien, elle y allait à la campagne. Elle voulait son coin de verdure au Père

Lachaise' (p. 779). There will be no place in the sun for Gervaise, for the only source of radiant light is the dirty face of the undertaker Bazouge, registered paradoxically as 'belle et resplendissante comme un soleil' (p. 780). With death virtually welcome as the only alternative left to her, the reduction of imagery is complete; the bright colours suggested subliminally by the mention of Gervaise's dream give way in Zola's evocation of her thoughts to a study in black and white, foreshadowed by the snow/shroud image which envelops her as she walks the dark streets (p. 774). In the event, however, Gervaise is not, to our knowledge, accorded the dignity of the last tributes in death which the colours of mourning suggest here, for Zola tells us, with great economy and bitter irony, given the significance the colour has held throughout her life: 'on la découvrit, déjà verte, dans sa niche' (p. 796).

Zola was involved with the adaptation of *L'Assommoir* for the stage while he was writing *Nana*,[5] so that inevitably the earlier novel would be fresh in his mind; it is surely no coincidence that we find here strong echoes of Gervaise and her dreams. Zola's adherence to Nana's consciousness as adopted vantage point is in no way as close as that between the narrator and Gervaise, since he specifically wishes to dramatize his first presentation of the actress (significantly playing Venus), and quantify the fatally attractive quality of her visual impact on others. Furthermore, Nana as a product of the theatre cannot offer us a *perspective inédite* of her surroundings, so that the naive-eye viewpoint, especially of scenes backstage, is attributed to comte Muffat. Nevertheless, Nana's consciousness is on occasion presented through internal perspective, as the multiplicity of verbs tethering the narration to her senses underlines. This is particularly noticeable in the sequence where she gets her first view of the countryside, late one afternoon, towards dusk: 'Nana flairait l'odeur des feuilles, regardait le vallon [...] elle ne voyait plus clair, elle touchait avec les doigts' (pp. 1232–5). This inside view, which encompasses sequences of *style indirect libre* (p. 1232–4), is an effective means of controlling the reader's sympathy towards the protagonist, whom Zola insists is 'bonne fille toujours' (p. 1470),[6] in spite of the destructive power her sexuality exerts over others.

Nana, a tall blue-eyed blonde, inherits not only her mother's looks and many of her preferences,[7] but also her pride. Remembering, no doubt, Gervaise's desire to 'écraser les Lorilleux' at her fête (p. 563), she in turn wishes to mark her first successful role in the theatre with 'un souper dont on parlerait' (p. 1165). It is early the next morning, after the break-up of this all-night party, that Nana, perhaps by unconscious nostalgic association, suddenly hankers after the same image which had sustained Gervaise through much of her life: 'Devant ce réveil navré de Paris, elle se trouvait prise d'un attendrissement de jeune fille, d'un besoin de campagne, d'idylle' (p. 1193). It is not without irony that this desire is translated into an early-morning drive to drink milk in the Bois de Boulogne with the man destined to become her next lover, the financier Steiner. It is through his riches that she is able to realize her mother's wistful dream - the acquisition of a place in the country, La Mignotte (though in a somewhat grander manner than anything to which Gervaise had aspired). Nana is obsessed with the *idea* of the countryside rather than with the actuality, since she has never spent any time there; 'on voit bien que madame n'est pas de la campagne', comments her maid, on seeing Nana ecstatic at the mere sight of grass and corn. We remember her as a child in *L'Assommoir* wanting to paddle in the dirty water flowing in the gutter 'où elle cherchait des petits poissons' (p. 481) and, slightly older, leading her friends from the tenement to play in the only other 'stream' she knows: 'la bande pataugeait dans les eaux de couleur de la teinturerie' (p. 519).

Nana's first view of her domain is a clear example of Zola's attribution of selective perception to his character. The gathering storm is hardly auspicious or fortuitous, since for us it seems to echo the portents on her mother's wedding day. The heedless Nana, however, is overcome with delight at her first sight of fruit and vegetables growing in the garden: 'son besoin était [...] de prendre une possession immédiate des choses, dont elle avait rêvé autrefois, quand elle traînait ses savates d'ouvrière sur le pavé de Paris' (p. 1235). Her reactions to the countryside are very fervent, perhaps because for as long as she can remember it was held up as *the* ideal; certainly, it makes her think of her childhood, when Gervaise's ambitions were uppermost and still within her reach: 'Nana s'attendrissait, se sentant devenir toute petite' (p. 1238).[8] The acquisition of La Mignotte is the peak of her achievement: 'Maintenant cette propriété, toute cette terre à elle, la gonflait d'une émotion débordante, tant ses ambitions se trouvaient dépassées' (p. 1244). This is a further ominous echo of *L'Assommoir* and her mother's statement: 'son idéal était dépassé; elle avait tout, et en plus beau'. As such, it forms an integral part of Zola's systematic structure of warning signs to the reader. Inevitably, Nana's bucolic idyll does not last, not even for a week, for on the sixth day of her stay, her cronies from the theatre arrive, bringing with them 'une bouffée d'air de Paris' (p. 1246), and she is lured back almost immediately to the capital, her elaborate toy apparently forgotten and soon passed on to Caroline Héquet, for whom Labordette purchases this second-hand dream. Yet the fact remains that this is one of the rare sequences when we see Nana truly happy, playing at being a country girl, joyfully picking strawberries in the rain or innocently revelling in the unaccustomed fresh air and sunlight with her son Louiset: 'Elle emportait son fils au soleil [...] elle se roulait avec lui sur l'herbe' (p. 1245).[9] All of this is very far removed from her twilight existence in Paris, where she works at night and sleeps by day.

Nana's horizons, after this extravagant expansion, are soon narrowed when she falls for the actor Fontan. When we first meet him he is playing Vulcan 'en forgeron du village' (p. 1106) to Nana's Venus: 'elle était là chez elle [...] asseyant Vénus dans le ruisseau, au bord du trottoir' (p. 1113). Fontan is at odds with the image of Goujet as *forgeron*, being closer in character to Lantier as an unreliable womanizer. The psychological coherence of Nana's character is sustained when she recreates a setting which the young Gervaise might have chosen in the tiny apartment she shares with the actor: 'elle rêvait une jolie chambre claire, retournant à son ancien idéal de fleuriste, lorsqu'elle ne voyait pas au-delà d'une armoire à glace en palissandre et d'un lit tendu de reps bleu' on the sunny side of the building (p. 1293).[10] This setting awakens other memories in Nana, for she swears at the beginning of this new relationship: 'Jamais on ne me battra' (p. 1293), but is in fact brutalized by Fontan (p. 1307), and has to resort to prostitution to keep him. Although, with the same resilience which characterized her mother, she does make a come-back after this emotional and social disaster, it is in a fury of destructiveness as she goes through the fortunes of her remaining admirers, notably that of La Faloise, whose land is used not for her enjoyment at first hand, but sold to pay for her caprices in the capital: 'des terres, des prairies, des bois [...]. A chaque bouffée, Nana dévorait un arpent. Les feuillages frissonnant sous le soleil, les grands blés mûrs, les vignes [...] les herbes hautes [...] même un cours d'eau tout y passait, dans un engloutissement d'abîme' (p. 1455). After this it is not long before she disappears, following her last stage appearance as Mélusine, the water-sprite.

Zola shapes the reader's response and sharpens the narrative focus by making us share Nana's consciousness for part of the text, notably her interlude in the country, though she is in the main liberated from the intermittent sequences of painful introspection and self-appraisal which are apportioned to her mother. She achieved Gervaise's dream for a time, but when she tossed it carelessly aside she lost sight of any real chance of happiness. At the end of the novel she is removed from us as Gervaise was, for although she returns to Paris just before she dies, her death - from smallpox, 'le virus pris par elle dans les ruisseaux' (p. 1485) - is not witnessed by the reader but reported; our final glimpse of her as 'une pelletée de chair corrompue ... déjà une moisissure de la terre' (p. 1485) recalls the last image of Gervaise.

Claude, like his mother, spent his formative years in Provence, for after coming to the capital with his parents at the age of eight, his welfare and education were taken over a year later by a benefactor in Plassans, an elderly 'amateur de tableaux' (p. 34); he returned to Paris when he was sixteen (thus forming a contrast to his half-sister Nana, who, like her father, is totally city-bred). In L'Œuvre Zola adheres most closely to the consciousness of Claude as adopted vantage point, thus presenting us with a highly selective artistic perception of the scenes registered. His feelings, like his mother's, for the landscape, river and trees of his place of origin are very strong: 'les anciens horizons, l'ardent ciel bleu sur la campagne [...] des langues de sable altérées et achevant de boire goutte à goutte la rivière [...] des sentiers de chèvre, des sommets dans l'azur' (p. 41) afford the inspiration for some of his best works. Claude looks back with particular nostalgia on 'les belles journées de plein air et de plein soleil [...]. L'été surtout, ils rêvaient de la Viorne, le torrent dont le mince filet arrose les prairies basses de Plassans [...] et c'était une rage de barboter au fond des trous [...] à vivre dans la rivière' (p. 38). With Sandoz and Dubuche he tries to recreate one aspect of their adolescence with lengthy walks once they all live in the metropolis, but in a curious echo of Gervaise's situation he finds his wanderings increasingly circumscribed: 'ils partaient à pied, certains dimanches, par la barrière de Fontainebleau [...]. Mais ils accusaient Paris de leur gâter les jambes, ils n'en quittaient plus guère le pavé' (p. 42).[11] The same negative/positive counterpoint between town and country established in L'Assommoir is thus perpetuated.

When Claude and Christine fall in love, they find an isolated spot on the Ile

de la Cité, 'une berge solitaire, plantée de grands arbres' and this corner of
Paris is transformed by their love into a 'coin de campagne, le pays de plein air
où ils profitaient des heures de soleil' (p. 102). After his humiliating defeat at
the Salon, it is in the nearby countryside by the river that he seeks solace, 'à la
campagne [...] sous le grand soleil [...] il aurait là-bas le vrai plein air, il
travaillerait dans l'herbe jusqu'au cou' (p. 145). Unlike Gervaise, Claude *is*
given a second chance, for he does escape from the capital and reaches his
artistic peak after his inspiration has been renewed by his spell in Bennecourt:
'en pleine campagne, en pleine lumière, il peignait avec une vision nouvelle.
Jamais encore il n'avait eu cette science des reflets, cette sensation si juste des
êtres et des choses, baignant dans la clarté diffuse' (p. 155). Yet his
achievement is meaningful to him only in the context of the metropolis:
'C'était le rêve, vivre à la campagne, y entasser des chefs-d'œuvre, puis un
beau jour écraser Paris en ouvrant ses malles' (p. 160). Accordingly, the days
on the river and the long walks are soon presented with negative
connotations: 'La rivière les ennuyait [...]. Même les promenades le long des
berges avaient perdu de leur charme [...] et, quant au plateau, à ces vastes terres
plantées de pommiers qui dominaient le village, elles devenaient comme un
pays lointain, quelque chose de trop reculé, pour qu'on eût la folie d'y risquer
ses jambes' (p. 167).

In the end Claude falls prey again to the thralldom of the big city: 'le pis
était que, en lui, le peintre se dégoûtait de la contrée, ne trouvant plus un seul
motif qui l'enflammât' (p. 167). Yet his finest paintings were produced by the
positive catalyst of the milieu in Provence and in Bennecourt; he needs the
uncluttered space and sunlight of the countryside for technical as well as
psychological reasons, since it is the *sine qua non* of his pioneer work as a
Pre-Impressionist. *Plein air*, the first canvas we witness him painting, has a
country setting: 'Dans un trou de forêt, aux murs épais de verdure, tombait
une ondée de soleil' (p. 33). Indeed, it is only in the countryside that Claude
feels any real satisfaction with his creation: 'Son long repos à la campagne lui
avait donné une fraîcheur de vision singulière, une joie ravie d'exécution [...]
comme il le disait à Bennecourt, il tenait son plein air, cette peinture d'une
gaieté de tons changeants chantante [...] où pour la première fois la nature
baignait dans de la vraie lumière, sous le jeu des reflets et la continuelle
décomposition des couleurs' (p. 204). All his major works produced
subsequently for the Salon are essentially studies of light and/or water, but
lack the rural setting which had hitherto proved to be his only successful
source of inspiration: after his return to Paris he tackles 'les neiges de
décembre' (p. 204), followed by 'un bout du square des Batignolles, en mai' (p.
205); his third subject is essentially 'le plein soleil [...]. Le sujet qu'il traita fut
un coin de la Place du Carrousel, à une heure, lorsque l'astre tape d'aplomb'
(p. 206), while his fatal last picture, 'c'est Paris lui-même, glorieux sous le
soleil' (p. 216). All are failures, for many complicated reasons considered
elsewhere,[12] but certainly a contributory factor must be that in the case of this
painter treatment and subject are mutually inimical: he is applying the right
technique to the wrong motif.

Although Claude manages to realize for a time Gervaise's ambition to live
in the country, he is unaware that this is the high point of his happiness until

later - when he is reluctant to go with Sandoz to visit Dubuche who lives near Bennecourt and 'la Seine, les îles, toute cette campagne où des années heureuses étaient défaites et ensevelies' (p. 312). The calculated lack of authorial comment on the remorseless, progressive reduction of his horizons makes his wife's plea infinitely more poignant, for their early dream is now cherished only by Christine, who tries to lure him back to reality, to the only milieu where they had known true happiness, away from his unattainable ideal on canvas: 'Rappelle-toi, à Bennecourt! Ecoute mon rêve. Moi, je voudrais t'emporter demain. Nous irions loin de ce Paris maudit, nous trouverions quelque part un coin de tranquillité' (p. 345). But such a step for Claude is now impossible: his last vision of the *pointe de la Cité* is the antithesis of all that he had tried to depict under a clear sky in warm sunshine:

> une nuit d'hiver, au ciel brouillé, d'un noir de suie [...]. Et là dans la Seine éclatait la splendeur nocturne de l'eau vivante des villes, chaque bec de gaz reflétait sa flamme, un noyau qui s'allongeait en une queue de comète [...] les grandes queues embrasées vivaient, remuantes à mesure qu'elles s'étalaient, noir et or, d'un continuel frissonnement d'écailles, où l'on sentait la coulée infinie de l'eau (p. 340).

He cannot reconstruct the radiant vision which had dominated his inner eye in face of this Whistlerian nocturne: 'Où avait donc sombré l'île triomphale? Etait-ce au fond de ces flots incendiés?' (p. 340). He therefore gives up the struggle. Claude's death, like his mother's, is tinged with bitter irony: he is buried in the new cimetière de Saint-Ouen, that area near the river where many years before the Coupeaus and the Goujets had enjoyed days out in the countryside, which the sprawling metropolis now incorporates. His grave is for 'un loyer de cinq ans' and is depicted as being 'dans ce terrain vide de *banlieue* [...] *sans soleil* [...] au milieu de la verdure pâlie des *arbres nains*' (p. 357).

I would not suggest here that the patterns of imagery considered are given equal importance in the three works cited. Indeed, it is clear that after being in the forefront of *L'Assommoir* they are relegated to a relatively minor role in the satellite novels, where other themes dominate, though in each case the patch of green is truly attainable only in death, which for each protagonist takes place in Paris. But the very existence of these artistically consistent echoes of Gervaise's dream proves to what extent Zola went beyond simple genetic transmission when he created the minds of Nana and Claude, for in systematically establishing his network of internal relationships between the novels as one aspect of the due process of literary fabrication he ensures that they inherit also part of Gervaise Macquart's soul.

Notes

1. 'De travailler tranquille, de manger toujours du pain, d'avoir un trou un peu propre pour dormir [...] ne pas être battue [...] mourir dans mon lit' (chapter II, p. 140). All interpolated references bearing only a page number in the first section of the chapter (and in related notes) are to *L'Assommoir* (*RM*, II); in the second section to *Nana* (*RM*, II); and in the third section to *L'Œuvre* (*RM*, IV).
2. Zola stresses the physical and psychological importance of the need for the

workers of Paris to get away from the capital in his *Causerie, La Tribune*, 18 October 1868: 'J'ai découvert Saint-Ouen [...] cet énorme bouquet de peupliers jeté au fil de la Seine [...]. Les ouvriers étouffent dans les quartiers étroits et fangeux où ils sont obligés de s'entasser [...]. Mais ouvrez l'horizon, appelez le peuple hors des murs, donnez-lui des fêtes en plein air, et vous le verrez quitter peu à peu les bancs des cabarets pour les tapis d'herbe verte' (*OC*, XIII, 193–7).

3. Physically our character has changed tremendously: her formerly open gaze has turned downwards, both because of her gain in weight and resultant increased severity of limp and because of her desire to avoid the judgemental appraisal of neighbours and the tradesmen to whom she owes money. Zola deliberately stresses this shift in her perspective when she moves to the sixth floor, 'où l'on ne recevait jamais la visite d'un rayon' (p. 673); in the sunlit shop (p. 503) she had looked outwards at the bustle of the street and upwards to the teeming life of the tenement block; on the sixth floor she has to look down to see what is going on in the courtyard, where only 'le coin humide de la fontaine' and 'la mare coulée de la teinturerie' (p. 673) suggest, distantly, the river in Provence. Although initially she misses the sunlight, later she recoils from it when the slums are being cleared: 'Gervaise [...] se montrait ennuyée de ces embellissements, qui lui dérangeaient le coin noir de faubourg auquel elle était accoutumée [...] on n'aime pas, quand on est dans la crotte, recevoir un rayon en plein sur la tête' (p. 737).

4. The obvious parallel with Hades is avoided since this would be foreign to Gervaise's sensibility and the narrative at this point is clearly circumscribed by her terms of reference.

5. Zola began his preliminary work on *Nana* in July 1878 and completed the novel in January 1880 (*Corr.*, III, 152); he was involved both in the scenario and in the rehearsals for *L'Assommoir*, which had its première at the Théâtre de l'Ambigu on 18 January 1879; he devoted three articles to the play (*Le Voltaire*, 28 January, 25 February and 2 September 1879), which appeared as preface in Charpentier's edition of 1881 (cf. *OC*, XV, 277).

6. Zola says of Gervaise: 'Elle reste bonne jusqu'au bout' in his letter of 10 February 1877 to Yves Guyot (published in *Le Bien public* three days later; cf. *Corr.*, II, 535).

7. Gervaise's favourite colour scheme of blue and white is transposed into Nana's outfit at the races (p. 1376), and her own décor (p. 1137), while her 'meubles de palissandre' (p. 1122) recall Gervaise's great symbol of achievement, the 'pendule de palissandre' (*RM*, II, 476); Nana also recreates the 'trous' dear to her mother, notably the kitchen, 'ce refuge tiède où l'on pouvait s'abandonner dans l'odeur du café' (p. 1136), where she lingered with, among others, Madame Lerat, her aunt, who had been an habituée of the rue de la Goutte d'Or circle.

8. Without labouring specific analogies, Zola evokes Gervaise's interlude with Goujet when he says of Nana: 'Etant petite, elle avait souhaité vivre dans un pré, parce que, un jour, sur le talus des fortifications, elle avait vu une chèvre qui bêlait, attachée à un pieu' (p. 1244). This reminds us of Gervaise's meeting with Goujet on the wasteland, where 'une chèvre, attachée à un piquet, tournait en bêlant' (*RM*, II, 614).

9. Both Nana and Claude's sons, who thrive in the countryside, die young, casualties of the big city; there is a clear cross-textual echo when Claude, looking at the canvas of his dead son, sees superimposed on it the image of him 'à la campagne, frais et rose, quand il se roulait dans l'herbe' (p. 294).

10. Cf. the first visit to the rue de la Goutte d'Or: 'Si Gervaise avait demeuré là, elle aurait voulu un logement [...] du côté du soleil' (*RM*, II, 416).

11. Sandoz also experiences withdrawal symptoms from his Provençal background:

'J'ai rêvé des repos à la campagne [...] dans mes jours de misère; et, aujourd'hui que je pourrais me contenter, l'œuvre commencée est là qui me cloître: pas une sortie au soleil matinal' (p. 262).

12. Cf. the Introduction to *Salons*, ed. F.W.J. Hemmings and R.J. Niess (Geneva, Droz and Paris, Minard, 1959); and P. Brady, *'L'Œuvre' d'Emile Zola: roman sur les arts, manifeste, autobiographie, roman à clé* (Geneva, Droz, 1967).

6

POUR UNE POÉTIQUE DE L'ESPACE ROMANESQUE: L'EXEMPLE DE ZOLA

Henri Mitterand

Synopsis

The spatial organization of Zola's fiction is an area of critical investigation both more fertile and more complex than the assimilation of habitat and inhabitant proposed by nineteenth-century determinism. Zola's highly developed proportional sense has often been remarked upon, and recent studies have underlined the thematic significance of the spatial oppositions characteristic of his novels.

The narrative implications of this aspect of Zola's work can be seen in the pages of Germinal *devoted to Etienne Lantier's first descent into the mine. For this description is elaborated in perceptual and sensorial terms which give a properly existential dimension to the relationship between protagonist and context.*

Throughout the Rougon-Macquart, *however, social and geographical coordinates are seldom positioned merely to authenticate the fictional representation. Indeed, they foreground the psychological or political dynamic dramatized in each novel. And this is equally true of individual and collective conflicts. In both* La Fortune des Rougon *and* La Conquête de Plassans, *for example, territorial imperatives function as the precise register of developments in the plot.*

It is thus not sufficient to repeat that Zola's craftsmanship is responsible for a fictional world notable for its internal symmetries and rigorous formal design. Its topography is as deliberately mapped as that of a cartographer, and yet it is controlled by an inner logic rather than serving to reinforce the referential illusion. The movements of Zola's characters are plotted as strategically as those of chess-pieces within the active constraints of segmented spheres of operation. The preparatory dossiers of the novels, not least in the drawings included in them, pay particular attention to the defining borders and boundaries of rooms, towns and landscapes. Much work remains to be done to chart and account for what is distinctive about Zola's handling of spatial setting, as compared to that of other nineteenth-century novelists. What is clear is that the narrative energy of Zola's writing is often to be located at the intersection of ordered spatial delineations and taxonomical frames, especially in the breakdown of categories and regulatory systems.

Zola est doublement un grand romancier de l'espace. D'abord par la maniére dont il gère, et régit, l'espace du texte, dans la matérialité du livre, dans la succession des parties, des chapitres et des pages. Chaque roman est composé selon une pensée du nombre, au sens arithmétique et au sens rythmique, qui apparente pour une part l'art de Zola à celui de l'architecte des temps classiques, où certaines expansions baroques n'excluaient pas la rigueur des proportions. D'où une certaine prédilection pour l'impair, peut-être parce que le nombre impair des parties ou des chapitres permet d'installer au cœur de l'ouvrage, ou plutôt à son sommet, une clé de voûte: c'est le cas, par exemple, pour les treize chapitres de *L'Assommoir* ou les sept parties de *Germinal*. Ceci, bien sûr, fait de l'espace du texte le serviteur de la logique et de la dynamique narratives.

Je n'ai pas l'intention de poursuivre sur ce thème, qui mériterait à lui seul une longue étude. Ce souci des proportions s'accompagne chez Zola d'une grande attention aux variantes de la distribution des composantes du récit le long du parcours textuel. Son roman pourrait souvent se réduire à une épure abstraite d'enchâssement, d'alternances, de parallélismes et de symétries. Je n'évoquerai ici, pour mémoire, que le parallélisme des chapitres d'ouverture des deux premières parties de *Germinal* (un chapitre chez les Maheu, un chapitre chez les Grégoire), ou, dans la même œuvre, la symétrie du tout premier chapitre et du chapitre final: un homme qui entre, un homme qui sort ... C'est toute une typologie à construire, qui montrerait en Zola un assez extraordinaire ingénieur et orchestrateur de la relation entre l'espace du livre et la matière narrative.

Espace du livre, dans le concret de son papier et de ses lignes, mais aussi espace de la représentation, dans l'immatérialité des situations qu'elle fait surgir à l'imaginaire du lecteur. Là aussi l'œuvre de Zola s'offre à toutes sortes d'observations, aussi diverses que les domaines de l'expérience humaine auxquels touche la notion même d'espace: espace géographique, celui qui distribue le sol, voire le sous-sol, en régions, en paysages, en quartiers; espace de la vie individuelle, celui qui fournit à chacun de nous ce que j'appellerai son horizon d'atteinte, l'espace où il vit et qu'il vit, celui de ses mouvements, de ses désirs ou de ses souffrances; espace social, enfin, qui répartit les foules, organise et règle leur travail et leurs conduites. C'est la substance même de la description et de l'action romanesques. On ne conçoit guère une narratologie romanesque qui resterait indifférente aux problématiques de la représentation de l'espace (lesquelles ne se confondent pas avec les problématiques de la description). A l'inverse, on ne saurait étudier et commenter pleinement l'originalité de l'inspiration et des techniques de Zola sans scruter son expérience et sa rêverie du lieu, ni son traitement narratif du local et du spatial.

Les pages-types vous viennent par dizaines à la mémoire, de la marche des insurgés de 1852 à travers les forêts du Var jusqu'à l'odyssée lamentable de l'armée de Châlons, en passant par les stations du chemin de croix immobile de Renée à la fenêtre du café Riche, l'effarement nauséeux de Florent projeté dans les tas de légumes du *Ventre de Paris*, la première descente de Lantier au fond de la mine de Montsou, la noce de Gervaise déambulant à travers les salles du Louvre, bien entendu les cinq vues du Paris d'*Une Page d'amour*, mais aussi la chemise d'Angélique s'échappant au fil de l'eau de la Chevrotte, dans *Le Rêve*, ou la locomotive blessée et immobilisée dans la neige, ou les tiédeurs musquées de la loge de Nana, ou la course de Claude le long du quai de l'Hôtel de Ville, par quoi s'ouvre *L'Œuvre*, ou quoi encore? Quel romancier du XIXe siècle pourrait faire surgir à nos mémoires un tel kaléidoscope de vues à la fois si typées dans leur facture, et si chargées de significations psychologiques, sociales et symboliques? C'est à soi seul le musée et le film imaginaires du siècle. Qui aura assez de souffle pour le visiter et le commenter de fond en comble? Ajoutons que cela devrait se faire de manière comparative, de manière à poser dans leur singularité, dans leurs éventuelles analogies, mais aussi dans leurs différences, un espace Zola, un espace Flaubert - ce ne sont évidemment pas les mêmes, ni dans les contenus ni dans l'arrangement des signes - un espace Proust, un espace Céline ...

Quelle stratégie pour une telle exploration? Je n'ai pas de réponse globale à cette question. Et cet essai ne peut ouvrir que deux ou trois pistes. Ajoutons que ce travail a été récemment entamé, avec l'excellent livre de Chantal Bertrand-Jennings, *Espaces romanesques: Zola.*[1] Je me situerai cependant sur un autre plan que Chantal Jennings, qui, tout en jouant avec grand talent sur tous les claviers de l'œuvre, a surtout étudié, d'un point de vue thématique, les figures dialectiquement opposées de la claustration enfouie ou écrasée et de la ruée des forces de vie et de conquête.

Je voudrais essentiellement, pour ma part, m'intéresser à la manière dont Zola construit, compose et transforme son espace romanesque comme condition *a priori* de l'invention d'un personnel et d'une action romanesque. C'est une démarche qui ne peut pas ne pas croiser la perspective thématique, mais qui voudrait prendre davantage en compte les apports de la syntaxe et de la sémiotique narratives.

Arrêtons-nous d'abord sur le processus par lequel Zola inscrit dans le roman la relation que j'appellerai sui-spatiale, celle qui unit le héros à son milieu de vie. Relation phénoménologique capitale, qui institue, en même temps qu'un *je*, sujet principal de l'action romanesque, un *ici*, lequel sera le lieu de son existence. Relation très forte dans *Les Rougon-Macquart*: en premier lieu parce que ce lieu de vie, comme Philippe Hamon l'a montré,[2] est une véritable assignation, une assignation à résidence, un territoire dont le personnage ne sortira pas, ou ne sortira guère, et qui détermine tout son vécu: rappelons-nous la boutique de Gervaise ou l'atelier de broderie d'Angélique. Ensuite, parce que ce lieu-milieu est en quelque sorte, chez Zola, énoncé par le personnage, qui le fait découvrir au lecteur en même temps qu'il le découvre lui-même. Il n'y a pas d'espace en-soi dans l'œuvre de Zola, mais seulement un espace pour-soi.

Un des exemples les plus significatifs est à cet égard la première descente d'Etienne Lantier au fond. Deux pages de *Germinal* qui font connaître au personnage et au lecteur, en même temps, l'espace du puits et le parcours qui conduit de la surface jusqu'aux galeries de mine. Deux pages à partir desquelles le puits de mine et Lantier ne formeront plus qu'un seul et même existant - et peut-être aussi la mine et le lecteur même, sur le mode imaginaire et par la grâce des mots de la fiction. Zola a travaillé ces deux pages en combinant trois registres, trois modalités de la présence du sujet à ce qui l'environne: les affects organiques et sensibles, le jugement et l'action.

Le premier de ces registres met en jeu la perception, les réactions des sens, les signaux qui émanent du corps. Visiblement, le corps de Lantier, dans cette chute vers le fond, apparaît comme rétracté, paralysé, déréglé par le froid, l'humidité, l'obscurité, le déséquilibre, en proie à un mode d'être non naturel, anormal, dysphorique. 'Une secousse l'ébranla, et tout sombra; les objets autour de lui s'envolèrent, tandis qu'il éprouvait un vertige anxieux de chute, qui lui tirait les entrailles' (*RM*, III, 1159). Lantier a perdu les routines anciennes et n'a pas encore trouvé les nouvelles. L'espace dans lequel il pénètre lui est à proprement parler un espace invivable.

Zola joue d'une seconde modalité, qui est celle de la connaissance. La question à poser est alors: que sait, que comprend, que croit le personnage de l'univers où il pénètre, et qui se construit lui-même de ce savoir ou de cette illusion de savoir? Le personnage se livre à une activité de déchiffrement, d'identification du milieu inconnu où il fait incursion, ce qui est d'ailleurs une manière de narrativiser et d'authentifier la spatialisation, d'énoncer ensemble le personnage, ses conduites, son espace, et sa durée. Or, dans le cas de Lantier descendant pour la première fois au fond, en profane, en non-initié, cette activité de pensée, cette tentative de penser, s'institue non sur le mode du savoir, mais sur celui du croire, non sur celui d'une découverte de l'être, mais seulement d'une conscience du paraître. L'espace du puits est pour lui un espace sans repères, sans coordonnées, fuyant dans sa verticalité descensionnelle, obscure, opaque dans sa minéralité souterraine. Tout ce que Lantier croit pouvoir induire ou déduire est faux. Même Catherine, qu'il prend pour un garçon. Tous les indices sont brouillés. Toute activité sémiologique est perturbée, désorientée, dans un espace de l'incertitude. Ce que Zola décrit ici, c'est en somme une impossibilité de décrire. Aporie qui ne lui est pas propre, qu'il partage avec Flaubert, et qui est née probablement de la découverte, par les peintres, les romanciers, et les photographes, de l'instantanéité et de la fugitivité de la vision.

Quant au registre du devoir-faire et du pouvoir-faire (après celui du sentir et celui du savoir, ou plutôt, en l'occurrence, du non-savoir), il s'ajuste exactement sur les deux autres. Si, naturellement, et logiquement, l'espace pour-soi est le lieu d'un faire, d'une appropriation pratique, d'une prise pragmatique des choses, dans les limites du possible et du permis, dans l'entre-deux du facultatif et de l'obligatoire, l'espace du puits, dans cette nuit du premier matin de *Germinal*, se situe au degré zéro du pragmatique. L'abondance des tournures indéfinies, passives, impersonnelles, atteste une totale passivation du personnage. Il ne peut ni bouger, ni agir.

Voilà comment se construit, sur ces deux pages du début de *Germinal*, un espace rigoureusement formalisé et fini dans sa forme (un puits), et rigoureusement sémantisé dans sa relation au sujet: un espace qui fait sens par le non-sens dans lequel le sujet se trouve jeté. Un lieu, un homme, un parcours, mais dans la redondance triplement insupportable d'un même effet de sens: la dysphorie organique, la cécité intellectuelle, l'impotence pragmatique. Certes, cela ne durera pas. Lantier acquerra à son tour les routines d'espace et de temps, il deviendra un parfait danseur du ballet quotidien des descentes, du travail et des remontées. Et pourtant il restera toujours en lui quelque chose du traumatisme de cette initiale descente aux Enfers.

On devrait chercher dans *Les Rougon-Macquart* d'autres structures équivalentes, même si aucune n'a l'expressivité et la poésie sombre de cette ouverture. Le même modèle de construction–énonciation d'un espace dysphorique, par le héros-sujet du roman, se laisse percevoir dans *Le Ventre de Paris*, et au début d'*Au Bonheur des dames*. Dans *La Conquête de Plassans*, Zola a mis en œuvre une variante, en retardant l'apparition du modèle: le personnage de Mouret, qui jusqu'à l'arrivée de Faujas était demeuré le possesseur-maître de son espace domestique, sur les trois plans de l'affect, du connaître et du faire, s'en voit dépossédé peu à peu, sur ces trois plans également: il finit par n'être plus maître de rien, il ne reconnaît plus rien, et il en deviendra fou. Ailleurs, dans le pavillon du Paradou, Albine se laisse mourir au milieu des fleurs. L'espace de *La Bête humaine* n'est pas plus rassurant, avec sa population de demi-aliénés. Les sentiers du Paradou se transforment en prison; la ligne Paris–le Havre devient un vecteur de la névrose et du meutre; Silvère mourra, dans *La Fortune des Rougon*, abattu sur la pierre même où il venait s'asseoir avec sa bien-aimée.

On n'en finirait pas d'énumérer les exemples de ces lieux de vie, de travail ou d'amour qui, dans *Les Rougon Macquart* s'affirment, d'emblée ou à retardement, comme ambivalents, et associent le double signe de la rationalité et de la névrose, ou du désir et de la mort. Le lecteur ne les connaît que dans cette exacerbation de point de vue subjectif, dans cette sorte d'imprégnation mutuelle des qualités du lieu et de l'état psychique de son occupant. Si l'on empruntait à la peinture, ou à la linguistique, la notion de valeur, on pourrait dire que les valeurs locales, au plan thématique, symbolique, poétique, sont modelées par cet échange entre un être malade et un horizon d'atteinte hostile, jamais totalement maîtrisé. C'est peut-être en ce sens qu'on peut voir dans le naturalisme de Zola un expressionnisme.

Espace pour le sujet psychique individualisé dans sa position de héros, l'espace romanesque de Zola est aussi un espace pour le sujet collectif. Il est toujours déjà un espace social, ou plutôt un espace socialement réglé. C'est une deuxième donnée également intéressante à explorer. On se souvient de la partie de crosse, dans *Germinal*, au chapitre 6 de la IVe partie, (*RM*, III, 1372–3), où l'on voit Zacharie et Mouquet, derrière leur cholette, parcourir tout le territoire avoisinant Montsou, 'deux lieues et demie en une heure', de la ferme Paillot au Pré-des-vaches, et puis encore des Herbes-Rousses à Chamblay: 'La terre sonnait sous la débandade de leurs pieds, galopant sans relâche à la suite de la cholette, qui rebondissait sur la glace'. Au terme de la course, ils débouchent sur le Plan-des-Dames, cette clairière vers laquelle convergent 'par les routes, par le sentier de la plaine rase, depuis le crépuscule', ce 'ruissellement d'ombres silencieuses', 'cette foule en marche' qui s'en va au rendez-vous des charbonniers. Deux courses simultanées et convergentes, celle du jeu de crosse et celle de la révolte, balisant le même terrain, les uns à travers champs, les autres sur les routes et les sentiers. Cette partie de crosse, métonymie de la liberté conquise, mais aussi peut-être de l'errance ludique des révolutionnaires, me paraît, de plus, une figure de la manière dont Zola, pour sa part, compose et balise les surfaces sur lesquelles vont se déployer ses personnages.

Il existe en effet une cartographie soigneusement délimitée des lieux de chaque roman. On le sait bien, les dossiers préparatoires de plusieurs des *Rougon-Macquart* contiennent de véritables plans dessinés: le plan de Plassans dans *La Fortune des Rougon*, celui de Montsou dans *Germinal*, celui du quartier de la Goutte d'Or dans *L'Assommoir*. C'est pour le romancier le moyen de repérer et de mémoriser les stations et les déplacements des personnages. C'est aussi une procédure au service de l'illusion réaliste. Mais c'est encore, contradictoirement, un moyen de déréaliser l'œuvre, en tirant son espace de représentation du côté d'une forme close, épurée, abstraite (elle est quasi-circulaire dans le cas de Plassans), coupée du monde, regardant vers son centre plus que vers l'extérieur: telle qu'un espace de jeu, ou bien un espace de manœuvre, au sens guerrier du terme. Philippe Hamon utilise la notion de *territoire*; elle est fondée, du point de vue d'une critique phénoménologique; mais du point de vue d'une critique qui s'attacherait, comme il le faut bien pour Zola, à la dynamique, ou 'cinétique' du roman, on devrait peut-être utiliser ici la notion de *terrain*.

Terrain de jeu, terrain de lutte, Zola circonscrit et segmente toujours, ou en tout cas souvent, un terrain pour l'action, pour le *drama*. Et c'est bien la raison pour laquelle on ne saurait analyser et interpréter la structure dramatique des *Rougon-Macquart* sans prendre en compte la relation du programme narratif et de sa topographie. Le paysage n'y est pas un icone réaliste, impressionniste, symbolique, etc., mais plutôt un cadre régulateur, consubstantiel au système des personnages et à la logique des actions, comme l'échiquier aux pièces du jeu. La rigueur de cette fonctionnalité me semble sans exemples équivalents en dehors de l'œuvre de Zola. Espace de jeu, espace d'enjeu. Espace, en allemand, du 'Kriegspiel'.

Revenons un instant à l'exemple du plan de Plassans, dans le dossier de *La Fortune des Rougon*. L'espace qu'il circonscrit y apparaît comme circulaire, et cloisonné, avec ses rayons et ses secteurs, où se rangent les trois quartiers, ses 'trois parties indépendantes et distinctes', dit le texte: le quartier des nobles, le quartier de la bourgeoisie, 'tout le petit monde aisé et ambitieux qui peuple la ville neuve', et 'le vieux quartier', où vivent 'le peuple, les ouvriers'. 'Une seule fois par semaine, dans la belle saison, les trois quartiers de Plassans se rencontrent face à face. Toute la ville se rend au cours Sauvaire le dimanche après les vêpres.' Ce qui ordonne cette cartographie urbaine, c'est une taxonomie sociale. On peut songer à la lointaine influence de Balzac, qui découpait de manière analogue Paris, dans *Ferragus*, ou à l'influence plus proche de Taine.

Mais Zola isole plus que son grand devancier le champ d'exercice de ses personnages. Autour de la ville, l'espace devient indéterminé, dessiné par le seul hasard des marches et des contre-marches des insurgés. Au contraire, dans l'enceinte de Plassans, la contiguïté des lieux marqués, tels que l'impasse Saint-Mittre ou le Jas-Meiffren, rend les rencontres inévitables, avec leurs conséquences heureuses ou malheureuses, et engendre la série des épisodes et des péripéties dramatiques. Ainsi se construit une sorte d'aire expérimentale, où la nécessité remplace le hasard, comme sur la scène tragique. Chaque secteur de cette aire devient une base d'opérations (qu'on pense au Salon jaune, dans *La Fortune des Rougon*), mais aussi un enjeu, un lieu stratégique à conquérir ou à garder (qu'on songe à l'Hôtel de Ville, dans le même roman). *La Fortune des Rougon* est ainsi l'histoire de la partie engagée pour la fortune et le pouvoir, par Pierre Rougon et Antoine Macquart, avec comme arrière-plan un affrontement plus collectivement tragique, mais plus lointaine, qui oppose les insurgés et le pouvoir bonapartiste. Cette partie se déploie dans les demeures, les rues, les quartiers, les points stratégiques de la ville, selon des parcours, des arrêts, des offensives et des retraites, qu'il vaudrait la peine de décrire en détail, car ils fournissent les schémas selon lesquels se profile la mise en mouvement de tout le roman. Curieusement tout revient au point de départ: Zola affectionne ces structures en boucle, telles que le lieu où se joue la fin de partie soit identique au lieu où elle a commencé. Voyez à cet égard *La Curée*, *La Conquête de Plassans* et *Germinal*.

Ce traitement de l'espace romanesque me paraît déborder de très loin la vision tainienne du déterminisme géographique et historique, aussi bien que la thématique du vécu subjectif, et ouvrir au roman français du XIXe siècle des perspectives tout à fait novatrices, dont il faudrait du reste sonder les sources épistémologiques et idéologiques. Pourquoi le roman, à ce moment-là, se construit-il de manière si précisément analogique aux jeux de stratégie? Je laisse cette question en blanc. Sur ce point, l'expérience personnelle de Zola, sa compétence en matière de zones d'influence et de réseaux d'intervention dans le microcosme parisien de la presse et de l'édition, n'est sûrement pas négligeable.

Pour nous en tenir à un objectif strictement descriptif, nous aurions donc à pratiquer deux séries d'observations: la première, sur le réglage des places occupées successivement par les personnages sur cet espace-échiquier, et la seconde sur la régulation de leurs parcours et de leurs manœuvres. On verrait d'ailleurs que de moment en moment le champ de forces se modifie et se recompose, pour des équilibres ou des déséquilibres nouveaux, jusqu'à l'issue finale, et que le temps joue ici sa partie, fort importante.

La Conquête de Plassans offre également un bel exemple pour cette interprétation polémologique du territoire romanesque. Quelle est en effet la stratégie de l'abbé Faujas? Réunir en terrain neutre monarchistes et bonapartistes, afin qu'ils acceptent de se saluer, de se parler, et de trouver un thème d'entente. La demeure du républicain Mouret, qui a vue sur les territoires opposés du légitimisme et du bonapartisme, offrira à l'abbé le lieu de sa manœuvre: installé là, il contrôlera la totalité du champ. Au surplus, grignoter l'espace domestique de Mouret, le rejeter dans les marges, le priver de ses points de repère, c'est le conduire à sa perte, et éliminer le principal adversaire après avoir investi sans combat ses positions.

Dans les romans de cette sorte, dont on retrouve le modèle dans *La Curée*, dans *Pot-Bouille*, peut-être aussi dans *Au Bonheur des dames*, l'histoire peut donc s'analyser comme une série de coups, dont les auteurs se déplacent au fur et à mesure sur un ou plusieurs secteurs donnés, et selon un type de vecteur déterminé. Dans *La Fortune des Rougon* et dans *La Conquête de Plassans*, il s'agit d'un modèle tabulaire, comme l'échiquier ou le jeu de go; dans *La Curée*, le parcours de Renée évoque plutôt le jeu de l'oie - ceci dit sans intention désobligeante à l'égard de cette jolie jeune femme - avec les cases où se prépare et s'infléchit son destin, les lieux pivots où tout bascule, la 'prison' où elle finit par tomber, sans parvenir à un terme heureux du voyage. De là l'importance, dans un modèle comme dans l'autre, des points de passage, des lieux de préparation, des points d'observation et des points de manipulation, des lieux de rencontre, des croisements, des issues, des bordures périphériques et des centres, de tous les points sensibles d'une topologie. Chaque roman a sa régie topologique et stratégique propre. Si l'objectif est dans *La Fortune des Rougon* de conduire un camp à la victoire sur l'autre, par embuscades et traîtrises, dans *La Conquête* il s'agit pour le maître du jeu d'amener deux factions adverses en un point où elles uniront leurs forces au lieu de se combattre, pour se tourner ensemble contre un ennemi commun, tout en s'inclinant devant l'ordonnateur de la manœuvre. Il y a quelque chose de Machiavel, sinon de Clausewitz, dans cet art zolien de l'espace narratif. Zola a peut-être pour modèle plus ou moins conscient la thermodynamique de Carnot.[3] Je me demande parfois si, non moins inconsciemment, il n'a pas en tête les modèles de la guerre moderne, tels que l'Europe du XIXe siècle les a mis au point. Espace de l'occupation réglée, de l'investissement calculé, donc. Mais aussi, nous l'avons vu, espace de la névrose, de la pathologie. Or l'un ne s'harmonise pas exactement avec l'autre. Et cette dysharmonie serait un troisième trait à examiner. Car elle crée le déséquilibre d'où naît, comme dans une chute d'eau, l'énergie, l'énergie narrative. Zola a très bien senti que l'essence du narratif tient à la perturbation des équilibres qui se sont constitués dans la mise en place initiale ou progressive des personnages et de leur lieu d'exercice. Ce que le lecteur attend, et sans quoi il n'y a pas de plaisir du roman, c'est, si je puis dire, le dérèglement du réglage. C'est la mise en question brutale, voire la transgression ou la destruction des frontières; c'est éventuellement la subversion de tout le système établi de positions et de parcours. Alors s'ouvre l'éventualité de la crise, du suspens, du pathétique. Le jeu tourne mal, parce que quelqu'un, quelque part, n'en admet plus les lois. Dans *La Conquête de Plassans*, la redistribution de l'espace politique entreprise par Faujas porte en elle le germe de son détraquement. Le finale du roman est exemplaire: c'est au moment où tout l'espace disponible a été conquis et astreint à un nouveau code de la cohabitation domestique et politique - la maison de Mouret tout entière à la tribu Faujas, le champ politique de Plassans tout entier à l'Empire - que l'exclu, le refoulé, qui est aussi le fou, reclus dans la folie du fait même de son exclusion, resurgit et détruit dans les flammes tout l'édifice du curé bonapartiste. Dans *L'Assommoir*, le retour de Lantier, revanche de la rue sur la maison, balaie et renvoie au néant tous les efforts obstinément amassés par Gervaise pour arranger, discipliner, décorer de signes rassurants, l'espace de son travail et de son repos. Pour elle, la marche inexorable du malheur se confond avec la réduction progressive de son lieu de vie.

Les romans de Zola résultent ainsi d'une triple attention de l'écrivain aux structures spatiales: celle qu'il porte à l'être-là, à l'habitus du sujet et en particulier aux situations de déracinement, de dépaysement, de déstabilisation, d'inadaptation, bref aux accidents et aux malaises d'espace qui peuvent frapper un sujet et le rendre étrange, ou étranger, à son milieu ou à lui-même: ainsi de Lantier, Florent, Renée, Marthe, Mouret ou Lazare Chanteau. Libre aux psychobiographes de s'interroger là aussi sur ce que cette curiosité peut puiser dans les souvenirs personnels.

En second lieu, l'intuition attentive des compartimentages de l'espace social, et notamment de l'espace urbain. Les acteurs du jeu social sont installés, malgré eux ou délibérément, dans un système d'espaces, avec deux possibilités: ou bien se laisser porter d'une halte à l'autre (selon un peu l'image de Renée, de Gervaise ou de Nana), ou bien, si j'ose dire, exploiter le terrain (c'est ce que fait Aristide Saccard, en tous les sens du terme), faire de l'espace assigné par le destin le champ clos d'une aventure qui prévoit et organise ses voies et ses points d'appui. Cette vision systématisée et dynamique de l'espace social contemporain s'accompagne bien entendu d'une intuition lucide du rôle qu'y jouent la propriété et le pouvoir, comme forces régulatrices mais aussi comme objets du désir de l'aventurier.

En troisième et dernier lieu, et non la moindre, une attention plus proprement poétique, et plus ironique, au désordre, à la négation ou à la dénégation subite de l'ordre institué, à la catastrophe, minime ou grandiose, qui anéantit le dispositif. Cela commence dès *La Fortune des Rougon*, avec l'exécution de Silvère par le gendarme Rengade, qui jette une lueur de sang et de malédiction sur le chemin ouvert par Pierre Rougon à toutes les ambitions et à toutes les cupidités de sa descendance. Et cela peut s'observer dans la plupart des grands romans du cycle. C'est en fin de compte l'image du train aveugle incontrôlable, qui, à la fin de *La Bête humaine*, sème la folie d'un bout à l'autre de la ligne: or, quel univers mieux ordonné et mieux réglé, dans l'espace et dans le temps, qu'une ligne de chemin de fer? Lorsque le monde selon Zola va jusqu'au bout de sa logique, il arrive un moment où celle-ci implose.

L'œuvre de Zola nous incite donc à ne pas réduire l'étude de la spatialité romanesque au repérage thématique et symbolique des substances ou des formes fondamentales d'un univers de fiction, à la manière bachelardienne, ni au relevé des affects sensibles et psychiques associés au séjour des sujets dans leur site ou dans leur gîte, ni à la répartition respective des milieux et des sociétés. Les problèmes d'analyse les plus importants commencent lorsqu'on s'avise d'explorer les modes d'engendrement, de constitution et de transformation de l'espace comme composante organique de la narration: comment, selon quelles procédures s'énonce-t-il? Comment se dispose-t-il, non lui-même en actant, mais pour le déploiement du système actanciel et pour la programmation des phases de l'histoire? Comment enfin s'y opèrent les ajustements, les bouleversements ou les liquidations du jeu des positions et des trajets?

A toutes ces questions, qui se posent à propos de toute œuvre romanesque, mais que l'observation de son métier nous aide à mieux cerner, Zola apporte des solutions complexes, à la fois toujours étroitement corrélées les unes aux autres dans une combinatoire savante, et toujours ouvertes à la variation, à l'inventivité. Sa mise en œuvre de la spatialité relève d'une technologie narrative plus élaborée, moins aléatoire que chez ses devanciers, tout en laissant place à d'heureuses dérives poétiques. On comprend mieux en ce sens l'admiration que lui portait Mallarmé. Celui-ci avait bien compris que sous l'enseigne d'Emile Zola, fabricant de romans en tous genres, on trouve un extraordinaire virtuose des formes.

NOTES

1. Sherbrooke, Naaman, 1987.
2. *Le Personnel du roman: le système des personnages dans les* Rougon-Macquart *d'Emile Zola* (Genève, Droz, 1983).
3. Voir Michel Serres, *Feux et signaux de brume: Zola* (Grasset, 1975).

7

ROMAN DE L'ART ET ART DU ROMAN: A PROPOS DES DESCRIPTIONS DE PARIS DANS *UNE PAGE D'AMOUR*

Jean-Pierre Leduc-Adine

Synopsis

It is important to situate Zola's descriptive practice in relation to the visual arts of the period. For there is an interdependence between his own procedures and those of contemporary iconography at a cultural moment notable for a shift in the traditional relationship between text and image. We should, however, privilege modes of representation rather than base such comparative analyses merely on the subjects represented by both writers and painters at this time.

   Zola's description of Paris in Une Page d'amour *(1878) provides us with an exemplary case. While the urban landscape is, of course, a new and fertile subject exploited by countless poets, artists and photographers, Zola's originality lies in his integration of narrative and pictorial imperatives. The novel's five panoramic descriptions of Paris may well find more than an analogy with series of paintings such as Monet's haystacks or Rouen Cathedral at different times of day. In the translation from preparatory notation to fictional arrangement, the descriptions of* Une Page d'amour *part company with possible sources and trans-generic pre-occupations. The pace and rhythms of the novel, as well as its overall design, are determined by these repeated and extensively fashioned views of the city from the heights of Passy. That vertical perspective is consistent with the pedagogic instrumentation of contemporary discourse. But the function of such textual interludes is both structural and emblematic. For Paris is less a background to the emotional vicissitudes of characters set in context than an articulating presence in its own right. The very terms of Zola's descriptions endow the capital with human qualities which are juxtaposed to, rather than simply reflecting, the psychological drama played out in the love affair of the novel's title. It is also necessary to explore the ways in which narrative threads are absorbed in descriptive texture. This includes the discursive import of colour-values and the properly theatrical modulation of the passages concerned. Zola's descriptions can thereby be aligned with Expressionist techniques and Classical principles. But it would be tendentious to postulate a synonymity of descriptive practice discernible on the one hand in Zola's writing and, on the other, in the painters he so notoriously championed as an art critic. Further research in this area must stress the related but contrastive visuality of such representations of the modern world, not least because Zola's technical resources in this respect militate against associating him with an aesthetic of indeterminacy.*

Si le rapport de Zola à la peinture, à l'art de son époque, s'est clairement concrétisé dans les textes de critique d'art qu'il a publiés pendant environ une quinzaine d'années, de 1866 à 1881, cette relation existe aussi, moins nettement peut-être, mais tout aussi massivement, dans les romans dans l'ensemble des *Rougon-Macquart*, comme dans les *Trois Villes* ou dans les *Evangiles*.

Il conviendrait de procéder à l'étude d'une genèse double et inversée témoignant des rapports dialectiques constants entre texte et image dans la seconde moitié du XIX⁰ siècle. 'Le roman réaliste et naturaliste, en particulier, ne se conçoit guère sans son alliance consubstantielle avec la photographie, et avec la peinture de paysage et de portrait, la gravure - qui ne sont d'ailleurs pas plus que lui une reproduction neutre et innocente du réel', recommande Henri Mitterand dans son Introduction à *Images d'enquêtes*, où il appelle de ses vœux une 'histoire iconographique de la littérature'.[1] En effet, la genèse de nombreuses descriptions, la recherche du motif, les 'choses vues' ne peuvent trouver leur principe d'explication qu'en référence à des visions et à des visées picturales, plastiques, à la transformation des fonctions de la peinture, à la transformation du regard porté sur le monde.

L'amorce de travail que je souhaite présenter ici voudrait mettre en rapport un ou des textes, des formes textuelles, ici essentiellement des 'descriptions littéraires', et des formes objectales, c'est-à-dire, des lieux, des espaces, des paysages d'une part, des représentations picturales de ces espaces d'autre part. Il s'agit donc dans cette perspective d'une démarche double: analyse et compréhension des objets représentés eux-mêmes d'abord, analyse sémiologique de la représentation picturale et littéraire de ces objets, et ceci dans une étude comparative et contrastive. Il s'agit ensuite de montrer comment s'effectue le travail d'un texte qui ne doit pas être envisagé et appréhendé au seul niveau du contenu supposé, mais au niveau de la constitution et de la construction même du discours, compte tenu de la spécificité du genre, le roman, qui impose des contraintes différentes de celles que nous pouvons trouver dans d'autres textes de la 'littérature d'art', que ce soit les comptes-rendus de Salons, les monographies, les textes polémiques, les manifestes, voire les poèmes.

Le problème premier qui se pose à nous vient de la difficulté pour accorder au plastique un statut dans la constitution même du texte. On pourrait certes envisager, naïvement, un mode de fonctionnement analogique où le texte constituerait une sorte de modèle. Deux étapes génétiques s'articulent ici. Les rapports du texte littéraire au pictural se font ou peuvent se faire chez Zola en deux étapes, d'abord dans le dossier préparatoire, véritable relais discursif entre la représentation iconique et la représentation linguistique, ensuite dans le texte définitif (ou considéré comme tel), à partir des ébauches, plans et notes du dossier, en particulier dans la constitution même de la description.

Il est essentiel de noter ici le renversement des rôles, ou plutôt le renversement des pôles entre peinture et littérature au cours du XIX⁰ siècle. Jusqu'alors, le texte générait le plus souvent les images, il en constituait même souvent l'autorité, la justification: ainsi dans les livrets de Salon de l'époque, la référence historique textuelle était érigée en légitimation du tableau d'histoire. Désormais, le texte change de statut, car c'est l'image qui génère très souvent du texte. Sous l'effet de certains genres picturaux, en particulier sous l'effet du paysage, la description envahit le domaine poétique et le domaine romanesque. Le texte en constitue souvent une adaptation, une sorte de transcription métaphorique de la peinture (la 'peinture' d'un paysage); mais il nous semble plus important et plus intéressant de montrer au delà de l'analogie du contenu dans les textes et dans les tableaux, comment le détour plastique permet des développements propres au système littéraire, de même que le traitement d'un thème littéraire par des peintres se caractérise surtout par une problématique spécifique. Le tableau comme le texte sont des miroirs dont les modes de vision et de présentation peuvent être quelquefois identiques, et dans des romans comme ceux de Zola, ils se fabriquent l'un par rapport à l'autre. Il est bien évident que la peinture dans *Une Page d'amour* sert de véritable pôle à la création littéraire, que l'image, la visualité, le tableau exercent sur l'écriture une fascination d'un autre ordre que celle de la parole et du texte.

Cette fascination, c'est d'abord celle d'un *nouvel espace de représentation*; le contenu, comme la fonction des paysages représentés dans la peinture et dans le roman à partir des années 1850 à 1860, vont fondamentalement changer; c'est ensuite celle d'une *nouvelle représentation de l'espace*. Les tableaux de paysages relèvent désormais de la visualité pure, de la matérialité pure même, et Flaubert, les concourt, comme Zola ou Huysmans ont associé à ces expériences des transformations de l'écriture.

L'étude des rapports entre l'image plastique et le texte impose d'envisager trois moments, trois actes chez l'écrivain: *le voir, le construire, l'écrire*; opérations qui souvent sont concomitantes, mais que l'analyse nous impose de séparer, car elles constituent les diverses médiations par lesquelles le romancier s'efforce de représenter, de 'traduire' l'espace.

Quels paysages les romanciers, comme les peintres regardent-ils, décrivent-ils, peignent-ils alors? Il s'agit dans *Une Page d'amour*, comme dans de nombreux autres romans du cycle des *Rougon-Macquart*, comme dans de nombreux autres romans contemporains, de marquer les paysages du signe de la contemporaneïté, de refuser le paysage historique, et de choisir en les esthétisant tous les espaces possibles de représentation, même les plus communs. Nous n'en donnerons ici qu'un exemple, emprunté à la description qui clôt la première partie du roman.

Quand, après la disparition du brouillard, l'image de Paris s'accentue et sert de rêve, ce ne sont pas d'abord les grands monuments parisiens que l'héroïne, Hélène Grandjean regarde, tels Notre-Dame, la Madeleine, la Tour Saint-Jacques; elle consacre plutôt son attention à la vie urbaine, à 'la foule active', à la 'caisse jaune d'un omnibus', 'aux camions et aux fiacres'; elle regarde un bâtiment industriel, 'les hautes cheminées de la Manutention', ou la construction représentant la nouvelle architecture du fer et du verre, 'les grandes verrières du Palais de l'Industrie' (*RM*, II, 851–2).

Partout, dans son œuvre, dans ses préfaces, dans ses lettres, Zola proclame son amour pour Paris et, comme les autres artistes, les artistes 'd'avant-garde', il éprouve un 'amour profond du Paris moderne'. S'il a critiqué avec une vigueur polémique d'une rare violence la construction du Paris hausmannien et qualifié le style Napoléon III de 'bâtard opulent de tous les styles', ce n'est pas sans une jubilation certaine qu'il a vu se créer une ville nouvelle; et la transformation de l'espace urbain devient même pour lui sujet artistique, littéraire ou plastique. Zola loue Jongkind d'avoir compris que Paris reste pittoresque jusque dans ses décombres. Hélèn Grandjean éprouve une émotion profonde, quasi trouble, devant le nouveau Paris; car, comme Zola, elle 'aime d'amour les horizons de la grande cité', car 'il y a là toute une mine féconde, tout un art moderne à créer'.[2]

L'inventaire, nécessaire, des lieux romanesques montre les éléments communs de représentation entre le Paris des peintres et celui des écrivains. Il marque un lieu restreint, et Paris revient constamment, dans son ensemble, ou métonymiquement dans le quartier de Passy; il conduit chacune des cinq parties: la charge naturaliste en est particulièrement forte; l'album parisien, exceptionnellement riche dans les *Rougon-Macquart*, prend ici valeur polaire tout à fait remarquable, véritable lieu monocentrique, lieu même d'accomplissement et d'élection de la modernité. Il constitue la rythmique même du roman.[3]

Mais il ne suffit pas de tenter de répondre à cette seule question: quels lieux les artistes peignent-ils? quels lieux les romanciers décrivent-ils? Il convient aussi de définir les modalités de leur représentation. Le système de la série de descriptions adopté ici par Zola (analogue aux systèmes des séries picturales comme les *Cathédrales* de Monet) dissocie, 'éparpille' l'ensemble peint ou l'ensemble décrit en une multitude d'éléments. Il tend ainsi à mieux rendre compte des sensations de l'artiste, à permettre à celui-ci d'exprimer mieux sa personnalité.

Fromentin, à peu près à cette date, établit dans un jugement sur le paysagiste Théodore Rousseau les fondements mêmes de cette transformation:

> Dans la Nature, il découvre mille choses inédites. Le répertoire de ses sensations est immense. Toutes les saisons, toutes les heures du jour, du soir et de l'aube, toutes les intempéries [...] il n'est rien qui ne l'ait tenté, arrêté, convaincu de son intérêt, persuadé de le peindre [...]. Il fallait une langue pour exprimer cette multitude de sensations nouvelles; et ce fut Rousseau qui, presque à lui tout seul, inventa le vocabulaire dont nous nous servons aujourd'hui. Dans ses esquisses, dans ses ébauches, dans ses œuvres terminées, vous apercevez les essais, les efforts, les inventions heureuses ou manquées, les néologismes excellents ou les mots risqués dont ce profond chercheur de formules travaillait à enrichir la langue ancienne et l'ancienne grammaire des peintres.[4]

Ce texte, précieux à bien des égards, démontre à merveille, comment l'originalité propre à l'art du paysage, à partir des années 1840 à 1850, c'est *d'abandonner toute situation discursive* (anecdotique, religieuse, mythique ou historique) et de *mettre le peintre en face du visible pur*.

L'image alors ne propose plus de sujet de réflexion au langage; elle en enseigne simplement l'efficacité sensorielle: le plaisir des yeux remplace celui de l'âme. L'espace n'est plus en rien traversé par l'éloquence: l'espace plastique suffit à l'art; il est muet, permettant toutefois à l'artiste, peintre ou écrivain, de s'affirmer comme le dispensateur du plaisir des sens éprouvé.

La révolution picturale, qui consiste à s'intéresser non plus tant à l'objet représenté, mais à la représentation de l'objet, a sans aucun doute modifié le statut de l'œuvre littéraire. Toute description rigoureuse est abstraction, puisque le peintre comme l'écrivain se font illusionnistes quand ils représentent l'espace, et que leur représentation ne concerne en rien la réalité perçue, mais la précision de leur système optique, ou de leur système linguistique, ce que Maupassant (dans *Le Roman*) avait parfaitement saisi quand il condamnait l'utopie naturaliste de Zola: 'le réaliste, s'il est un artiste, cherchera non pas à nous donner la photographie de la vie, mais à nous en donner la vision plus complète, plus saisissante, plus probante que la réalité même.' Et Valéry avait très finement ressenti ces liens quand il notait que 'l'invasion de la littérature par la description fut parallèle à celle de la peinture par le paysage'.[5] Il convient enfin de cerner les finalités de la spatialisation romanesque: je m'en tiendrai simplement aux quatre plus importantes d'entre elles.

La localisation est indispensable à toute narration, aussi a-t-elle une fonction narrative spécifique en situant de manière indispensable à la fois les personnages et le temps du récit. Malgré l'opposition constamment soutenue par les théoriciens de la narration, comme par les lecteurs mêmes du texte romanesque, entre description et narration, l'une et l'autre se trouvent presque toujours complémentaires: l'espace appartient à la logique même du récit, en tant qu'actant, en tant que sujet, en tant que destinateur et en tant qu'auxiliaire. Des relations obligées s'instaurent ainsi entre les personnages de la fiction et les lieux objets des valeurs. Dans *Une Page d'amour*, les indications précises de situation temporelle (et temps est à prendre et à comprendre dans plusieurs sens du terme: météorologique, narratif, historique) qui accompagnent l'espace parisien décrit n'ont évidemment pas d'autre finalité. Zola justifiait ainsi ces cinq descriptions, en avançant cet argument dans *De la description*: 'Dans ce qu'on nomme notre fureur de description, nous ne cédons jamais au seul besoin de décrire: cela se complique en nous d'intentions symphoniques et humaines' (*OC*, X, 1296).

La description des lieux marque aussi un travail du romancier et de l'artiste sur le monde, qui est la marque d'un savoir. Sa finalité est à la fois donc encyclopédique et didactique et les cinq descriptions de Paris vu des hauteurs du Trocadéro ont valeur emblématique. *Une Page d'amour* est un roman pour voyageurs: ce point de vue est particulièrement recommandé dans les Paris-Guides de l'époque, surtout en 1876, à l'occasion de l'Exposition Universelle, installée dans le Champ de Mars. Ce panorama appartenait au parcours obligé de tous les Brésiliens de *La Vie Parisienne*, des Monsieur Bénichou, débarquant à la Gare de Lyon; parcours obligé des peintres aussi: Manet expose en 1867 un tableau intitulé *Exposition Universelle de 1876*[6] et qui représente ce panorama, comme le fait le tableau de Berthe Morisot, intitulé *Vue de Paris des hauteurs du Trocadéro*.[7] Tout en provoquant l'effet de réel nécessaire, constitutif même, du roman réaliste, cette description analogue thématiquement aux panoramas des peintres prend ici une finalité très nettement didactique.

Ces descriptions ont aussi une fonction universalisante. En effet, chaque texte romanesque mobilise simultanément un objet particulier et un objet universel, et l'espace romanesque prend valeur quasi mythique, puisqu'il est re-production tout à fait conventionnelle d'un lieu, mais qu'il tend à devenir le lieu lui-même, et la tension dialectique qui s'instaure entre ces deux fonctions, ces deux valeurs, surdétermine la signification de la topologie romanesque, d'où l'importance du début et de la fin du texte. La fin d'*Une Page d'amour* reste ouverte; Hélène contemple toujours le même lieu mais son histoire n'est pas terminée; la fin dynamise ici l'ouverture; le roman n'est pas fini.

La description, enfin, a fonction esthétique. Les espaces décrits servent la cause de la description littéraire et du paysage pictural. Le paysage se suffit à lui-même sans avoir besoin de la justification d'une scène dont il ne serait que le décor, sans être une composition de l'imagination, ni une image de la mémoire; il est peint en plein air, hors de l'atelier et hors de toute convention: on quitte le temps pour l'espace, le texte pour l'image.

Il convient toutefois de quitter le stade de l'inventaire, de montrer comment, à partir d'un certain nombre d'éléments référés, la description se construit, est construite; les problèmes de stylistique génétique se posent à son propos, une fois vues les différences fondamentales entre le pictural et le scriptural, une fois bien montrée et démontrée l'hétérogénéité absolue qui sépare ces deux ordres, le voir et le dire; de dégager par quels procédures à la fois de structure et d'écriture, Zola essaie de rendre compte d'un paysage qui a été vu, ordonné déjà dans un autre système, celui du tableau. Quelles sont les procédures de transposition auxquelles Zola a recours et qu'il a menés jusqu'à ses extrêmes limites, avec à la fois une jubilation intense et une naïveté plus grande encore, malgré la rupture consommée entre le réel et le décrit? Une génétique de la structure se dégage avec vigueur dans les descriptions d'*Une Page d'amour*, à la fois une *macrostructure* qui envisage la distribution des descriptions de Paris dans le roman et une *microstructure* qui étudie la distribution des éléments décrits à l'intérieur même de chaque description.

La reprise des cinq descriptions dans le roman a valeur picturale à deux niveaux: tous les analystes ont remarqué qu'il s'agissait là d'un procédé emprunté aux peintres qui construisaient des séries, ainsi Monet et *Les Meules*, et ces séries renvoient surtout à la volonté d'étudier la lumière, et les variations de celle-ci, la 'décomposition' et la 'recomposition de la lumière',[8] procédé que Zola avait particulièrement apprécié chez les impressionnistes.

Il a par ailleurs dans ces reprises descriptives (re)constitué ce qui était un grand succès populaire de l'époque: le *panorama* ou le *diorama*, 'vaste tableau circulaire placé autour d'une rotonde de façon que le spectateur voit les objets représentés comme si, placé sur une hauteur, il découvrait tout l'horizon environnant'.[9] L'ensemble des traits démarcatifs des descriptions orientent vers le panorama, notamment la position du 'regardeur-voyeur', la position de la maison et du village de Passy ('en hauteur').

La structure de ces cinq descriptions terminales relève aussi du cahier des charges narratives permettant une intégration de la description dans la narration. Celle-ci ponctue le roman en donnant une explication qui se veut psychologique des états d'âme d'Hélène, qui est presque toujours le personnage descripteur. Des traits humains caractérisent souvent Paris, depuis 'sa gaité' et son innocence d'enfant, son mystère et sa tendresse, jusqu'à la 'sérénité de sa face géante, témoin muet des rires et des larmes' de la dernière description. Ils ont valeur de contrepoint par rapport à la narration dont il ne constitue plus seulement le décor, mais aussi le commentaire ou la paraphrase. Et on peut et on doit considérer aussi que Paris a un véritable statut actanciel, c'est un personnage du roman.[10] Notons aussi que la structure de ces descriptions a une valeur mythique. Il s'agit d'un drame en cinq actes, composé chacun de cinq scènes, cette dernière scène/chapitre/description étant toujours de longueur identique, environ une dizaine de pages. L'importance des structures numériques pourrait s'expliquer ici par l'arithmo-manie de Zola; et par la nécessité de la dynamique et de la dynamisation du roman. Mais la référence littéraire, textuelle, générique au théâtre classique est certainement plus riche d'interprétation et de conclusions. Nous retrouvons encore la structure de la tragédie, dans le temps: une année; dans le sujet: une passion; dans l'espace: un lieu, Paris/ Passy; et celle-ci enfin dans les structures elles-mêmes du roman, qui, selon une problématique très positive et très positiviste, renvoient aux exigences mêmes d'un scénario, défini dès le début par Zola, comme un 'drame', ajoutant ensuite: 'il faudrait organiser cela en quelques belles et larges scènes'.

Il y a donc théâtralisation de la description, au sens propre du terme. Paris est un actant de ce drame, au même titre que les autres personnages. Le texte descriptif prend là les modalisations nécessaires au texte théâtral. Les descriptions de Paris constituent également dans le roman une théâtralisation de l'espace parisien, du monde défini comme 'la toile de fond de cette rêverie' par Mallarmé. Enfin, parmi les nombreuses métaphores descriptives, relevons celle de l'eau, métaphore omniprésente pour caractériser Paris, défini comme océan, mer, ... qui prend ici valeur fantasmatique, dans ce roman sur la passion ('Passion, amour, calvaire').

A l'intérieur même de chacune de ces descriptions, Zola procède à un certain nombre de transformations structurelles qui renvoient aux problèmes picturaux. Dès 'l'affaire Manet', les critiques académiques reprochaient aux peintres modernes, aux 'réalistes' ou plus tard aux 'impressionnistes' de dissoudre les personnages dans les fonds de tableau, accordant ainsi la primauté au paysage, qui jusqu'alors constituait un motif décoratif. Or, dans les descriptions d'*Une Page d'amour*, les passants sont définis comme 'foule active de points noirs emportés dans un mouvement de fourmilière' (*RM*, II, 851), et plus tard, 'la foule s'émiette et se perd'.

A l'absorption du personnage dans le paysage, correspond structurellement l'absorption de la narration dans la description. La plupart des cinquièmes chapitres n'ont pas de véritable dynamique narrative. Un certain nombre de traits démarcatifs situent Hélène comme personnage descripteur, certes, mais en réalité, même si elle joue le rôle de focalisateur du système descriptif, très rapidement, elle s'efface pour céder la place à la dynamisation du paysage, les éléments décrits devenant tous sujets, voire à l'énonciation même du narrateur.

Les éléments descriptifs retenus sont les éléments essentiels des arts plastiques, lignes d'une part et couleurs d'autre part. Les notes du dossier préparatoire, 'Vue de Paris' (fols. 521 à 525), montrent que Zola, à la recherche du motif, retient ces seuls éléments, la géométrie est même essentiellement linéaire et il donne, assez rarement, l'impression de volume, sinon dans une reprise de fausse perspective indiquée par des notations du type 'au loin', 'plus loin'. La couleur est par contre omniprésente: c'est elle qui donne leur réalité, leur existence même aux choses, et leur prégnance est telle qu'elles existent en elles-mêmes, pour elles-mêmes: 'les couleurs gris bleuâtre, ardoise, jaune pâle, blanchâtre, brun rouge effacé' (fol. 523). La couleur s'autonomise presque totalement par rapport aux objets et, au début comme à la fin de chaque description, dans une visée panoramique récurrente, le regard du personnage ne voit quasi rien ou saisit un simple ensemble indistinct.

Il conviendrait enfin de montrer comment Zola, par l'écriture, construit ce nouvel espace littéraire. En raison de l'opposition entre la logique et les automatismes des éléments plastiques et ceux des éléments linguistiques, le narrateur dans une description n'a d'autre possibilité que de mettre en jeu une série de clefs et de mécanismes lexicologiques, syntaxiques, sémantiques et stylistiques. Certains indices langagiers sont des indices du genre descriptif, de la transposition d'une image en texte, de la description d'une image; le système descriptif s'actualise dans le texte par le jeu de ces différents procédés.

Le roman, et en particulier la description dans le roman, n'est pas une plate copie, une plate reproduction de la réalité, ce qu'en 1851, soulignait un critique d'art rappelant qu''un tableau n'est point l'image fidèle des objets qu'on voit en ouvrant au hasard sa fenêtre. C'est un ensemble de lignes et de couleurs, une combinaison de plans et d'effets, une chose voulue, raisonnée où intervient la puissance créatrice de l'homme.'[11] L'œuvre artistique, plastique, ou textuelle est la vérité de la réalité, parce qu'elle fait apparaître, par une observation juste les lois et les systèmes d'organisation. A cet égard, elle équivaut à une prise de conscience, à une prise de connaissance du monde. Le roman produit du savoir, en particulier il révèle l'organisation du vivant. C'est peut-être là la leçon, quelquefois mal perçue, du *Roman expérimental*. C'est peut-être ce que veut dire ce mot 'vie' qui revient constamment dans les romans comme dans les écrits théoriques de Zola.

Mais, au delà, Zola, malgré ses prises de position en faveur de la modernité, refuse l'obscurité, l'inintelligibilité, l'opacité de la description, telles qu'elles pourront être pratiquées par le nouveau roman. Même s'il a ressenti, pressenti la valeur heuristique du concept d'autonomie de l'art (la description comme le tableau n'ayant d'autre fin qu'eux-mêmes) Zola souhaite que la description soit intégrée dans le roman, qu'elle prenne donc sens narratologiquement, que la scène soit intelligible. Comme le récit romanesque est soumis au dialogue, à la scène, la description est soumise au modèle du réel, de l'immédiat. Ces contraintes sont celles de Zola, celles de la littérature de son époque, et peut-être aussi celles de la littérature.

NOTES

1. *Images d'enquêtes d'Emile Zola* (Plon, 1984), p. 11.
2. *Mon Salon, Manet, écrits sur l'art* (Garnier-Flammarion, 1970), p. 192.
3. Très vite, Zola a trouvé la distribution finale du roman: cinq parties contenant chacune cinq chapitres, dont le cinquième constitue une description de Paris: I - 'Hélène devant le paysage de Paris. 1ère Description. Avec sa fille qui la questionne sur Paris. Une matinée de clair soleil, toute blonde'; II - 'Hélène devant la fenêtre. 2ème Description. La petite à la fenêtre. Une après-midi de Mi-Carême, *rouge et or*, avec quelques nuages'; III - 'A la fenêtre, Hélène et l'abbé. Confession. Le vieil ami arrive. Paris la nuit'; IV - 'La petite malade à la fenêtre. Toute seule. Un crépuscule. Paris gris et boueux de la pluie. Navré'; V -

'Dernière description de Paris. L'hiver par un froid sec, avec quelques filets de neige. Temps clair. Pas de verdure. La Seine charriant' (B.N., N.a.f., Ms. 10318, fols. 418–19).

4. Eugène Fromentin, *Les Maîtres d'autrefois* (1876) (9ème ed., Plon, 1898) pp. 277–80.

5. *Œuvres*, (Gallimard, Bibliothèque de la Pléiade, 1960), II, 1219, cité par Philippe Hamon, *Introduction à l'analyse du descriptif* (Hachette, 1981), p. 15.

6. Ce tableau est actuellement à la Nasjonalgalleriet d'Oslo: cf. à son propos, le catalogue *Manet and Modern Paris*, Washington, National Gallery of Art, 1982–1983, et l'article de P. Mainardi, 'Edouard Manet's View of the Universal Exposition of 1876', *Arts Magazine*, LIV (1980), 108–15.

7. Ce tableau est actuellement aux Etats-Unis, Santa Barbara Museum of Art: cf. Catalogue *L'Impressionnisme et le paysage urbain*, R.M.N. (Musées nationaux), 1985, p. 186.

8. Zola, *Mon Salon*, p. 335.

9. Voir, l'article 'Panorama' dans le *Grand dictionnaire universel du XIXe siècle*.

10. Voir, Jean-Pierre Leduc-Adine, 'Paris et l'ordre spatial dans *L'Œuvre*', dans *Emile Zola and the Arts* (Washington, Georgetown University Press, 1988), pp. 165–75.

11. Paul Mantz, 'Salon de 1850–1851', *L'Artiste*, février 1851.

8

ZOLA'S ART AND DISCOURSE OF RÉSUMÉ

Geoff Woollen

A bewildering number of cognate words, notoriously difficult to translate from one language to the other, immediately confront attempts to define résumé: summary, blurb, synopsis, paraphrase, *précis*, *sommaire*, *compte rendu*, even *mise en abyme*, all implying the reduction of the discursive content of a piece of prose. Yet another word was used in a specific sense by Zola himself, as we shall see, in his tireless elaboration of the poetics of naturalism.

Stricto sensu,, anything shorter than the original would qualify as a résumé; but questions of length and terminology such as those that have so bedevilled French short-story theory are not our concern.[1] Indeed, word-count seems of minor importance; far more interesting are questions of thematic and emblematic mirroring or reduction, where the carefully selected part is metonymically representative of the very spirit of the whole, which have preoccupied critics such as Lucien Dällenbach and Philippe Hamon. Both have approached the main subject of this essay, the breathless, vertiginous encapsulation of the lives of the Rougon-Macquart dynasty in *Le Docteur Pascal*. For Hamon, it is an epic example of the 'parole finale', the explicative gloss. He gives the standard lapidary examples from Maupassant, but does not neglect to say that the six relevant pages of *Le Docteur Pascal* constitute a huge *explicit* in which 'le narrateur commente et paraphrase son propre texte':[2]

> Cela peut prendre des proportions importantes: Zola termine par exemple la série des 19 volumes de ses Rougon-Macquart par *le Docteur Pascal*, récit où le héros, un docteur qui 'connaît les dossiers de la famile', revient sur chacun des volumes précédents.

Dällenbach, while maintaining that in general the *mise en abyme* (such as the celebtrated *La Mouche d'or* article on Nana) is 'une espèce de *citation de contenu* ou de *résumé intratextuel*',[3] allows a special status to 'la super-mise en abyme du *Docteur Pascal*', which 'dramatise la "table des matières" des *Rougon* et fait en quelque sorte que l'œuvre monumentale soit un *cycle*'.[4] Hence, from 'intratextuel' we would be moving towards 'intracyclique'. In Gérard Genette, the term 'sommaire' is used for an analeptic résumé along the lines of the biography of César Birotteau, to emphasize its paucity in Proust;[5] this would no doubt make the relevant section of *le Docteur Pascal* a 'super-sommaire'. We should also be aware of the potential usefulness of his interpretation of the prefix *meta*; admitting his idiosyncrasy *vis-à-vis*, say, Dällenbach and Hamon, for whom it connotes beyond or *extra*, he chooses to read it as an indicator of *intra*, in particular, internal narrative subordination.[6] Within the framework of the *Rougon-Macquart* globally summarized by Pascal Rougon, protagonists such as Gervaise and Etienne could therefore be held to tell their life story in metarésumé. Then, too, there are interesting hybrid examples of the intratextual and extratextual; for Jacques Lantier, 'la famile n'était guère d'aplomb, beaucoup avaient une fêlure. Lui, à certaines heures, la sentait bien, cette fêlure héréditaire' (*RM*, IV, 1043). It has been claimed of Tante Dide's cry 'Le gendarme!' that 'this minimalist text is an Ur-text, a model of narrative generation in the *Rougon-Macquart*'.[7] In my argument, it represents *le degré zéro du résumé*.

Writers may be more reliable when it comes to summarizing themselves than in their reception-conditioning prefaces, and it can confidently be predicted that a fully-fledged theory of *le discours résumiel* will in due course take its place alongside the *préfaciel*; both discourses, after all, are *ex-post facto*. In *le résumiel*, too, there exists a desire to rattle the ideological handcuffs: the key feature of exercising control over literary reception is that a need is felt for a 'discours d'assistance',[8] or the roughly similar 'discours d'escorte'.[9] However, to reap fully the harvest of this narratological fruit is beyond the scope of the present study. It is to be situated between F.W.J. Hemmings's 'Intention et réalisation dans *Les Rougon-Macquart*',[10] and Halina Suwala's invitation to subject 'les particularités stylistiques' of Zola's critical discourse to further investigation.[11]

Henri Mitterand makes the point that Zola came to literature via paraliterature, that is, accompanying *prières d'insérer* and even what we would now call publishers' 'junk mail'.[12] It is worth stressing that Zola's literary output, from his early days as 'publiciste' with Hachette, was résumé-led, summary-driven; indeed, he was very much a pioneer of a style that was later to be used against him. Colette Becker and Halina Suwala have related in great detail the early days of the reporter on prestigious public lectures,[13] tireless producer of in-house publicity 'fliers' (neatly termed by Becker 'tracts-annonces')[14] and contributor to the *Bulletin de l'amateur du livre*. Mitterand gives examples of the *prière d'insérer* Zola composed for the *Contes à Ninon*, the kind of manna that normally conditioned critical responses, and publishes an appreciation suspected to be his very own![15] Zola's early work as book reviewer and art critic developed in him the procedures of a résumé that attempted to capture the spirit and the substance of the works under consideration. Henri Marel points to Eli Berthet's *Les Houilleurs de Polignies* as a likely inspirational source for *Germinal*, underlining that, geographically *inter alia*, Zola's résumé 'n'est pas complet':[16]

M. Eli Berthet sait admirablement dramatiser ses récits et leur donner un intérêt poignant et familier à la fois. Il a le don de la terreur, des larmes et du sourire.

Jadis, il introduisait ses lecteurs dans les catacombes de Paris, et il obtenait un succès qui dure encore. Aujourd'hui, il nous fait descendre dans une mine de houille, et il traite avec un égal talent ces scènes de désespoir et d'angoisse qui se passent dans les entrailles du sol. Les houilleurs de Polignies, les ouvriers de M. Van

Best, se sont révoltés et demandent une augmentation de salaire; le maître refuse,
mais la fille du maître, Amélie, descend dans la mine pour apaiser les ouvriers, et elle
y trouverait la mort, sans le dévouement d'un jeune houilleur que son père a engagé
depuis, et qui, au dénouement, se trouve être un jeune ingénieur déguisé, M.
Léonard de Beaucourt. Il y a mariage, et l'ingénieur, qui a relevé la fortune de M.
Van Best par la découverte d'une mine très riche, devient son associé et son gendre.

Le livre est plein de très curieux détails sur la vie et les mœurs des houilleurs.
C'est là un monde particulier et étrange dont le romancier a tiré parti en conteur
pittoresque et intéressant. La partie de description est excellente; elle fait faire au
lecteur un voyage très émouvant dans ces couloirs étroits et troubles que visitent le
feu grisou et les inondations. La partie dramatique est habilement mêlée aux détails
techniques, et rien n'est plus attachant que les amours d'Amélie et de Léonard, se
déroulant au milieu des péripéties de la révolte des houilleurs, conduits par un
coquin qui finit par expier ses crimes. Depuis *Les Catacombes de Paris*, M. Elie
Berthet n'a pas conté une histoire plus touchante et d'intérêt plus vif.

An entire novel, *Thérèse Raquin*, was synopsis-generated before being
preface-clad, evolving from the barest outline of 'Un Mariage d'amour'. It was
as a critical résumist that Zola wrote the *Rougon-Macquart*, themselves pre-
and post-summarized and completing an aesthetic cycle represented by his
favourite metaphor of Ouroboros, the snake biting its own tail.[17]

We know that Zola's enthusiam for Berthet's work, even in 1866, was not
great; but as it was published by Hachette, his job was to write copy that
would sell it, and he could reserve his private views on Berthet and
feuilletonistes of his ilk for 'Les Romanciers contemporains'.[18] What will
become a familiar pattern can already be seen: plot synopsis plus a few more
appropriate remarks - in contemporary terminology, an *analyse*. If Zola
summarized others' works, as a prelude of alimentary necessity prior to
original writing, in mid-course he returned by choice to the exercise before, in
Le Docteur Pascal, applying it to himself. Vapereau had indulgently said of
Zola's *Contes à Ninon*: 'On imite toujours quelqu'un, même avec du talent,
avant d'être soi-même.'[19] For the verbs 'imiter' and 'être', one can easily
substitute 'résumer' and 'se résumer'.

In his article mentioned above, Hemmings deals with the majority of the
Documents et plans préparatoires, a veritable goldmine for the student of the
Zola novel, which includes notes on the scientific works of Letourneau and
Lucas, résumés of these notes, general declarations of intent for the cycle,
proposals for the first ten volumes, and consecutive versions of the family
tree. The preliminary synopses, or pre-résumés of intent to deliver that
follow, were submitted to the publisher Lacroix in 1868. What should be
stressed is a certain myopia, compared to the expansive later vision. Zola may,
unlike Balzac, have seen his plan mapped out in advance, but there is a
considerable gap between his twenty-novel cycle and this first résumé: folio
23 of Zola's *Notes générales* (*RM*, V, 1735) is a sheet listing the following
novels (numbered for convenience).

Un roman sur les prêtres (Province) [1]
Un roman militaire (Italie) [2]
Un roman sur l'art (Paris) [3]
Un roman sur les grandes démolitions de Paris [4]

Un roman judiciaire (Province) [5]
Un roman ouvrier (Paris) [6]
Un roman dans le grand monde (Paris) [7]
Un roman sur la femme d'intrigue dans le commerce (Degon) Paris. [8]
Un roman sur la famille d'un parvenu (effet de l'influence de la brusque fortune
    d'un père sur ses filles et garçons) Paris. [9]
Roman initial, province. [10]

The plan is fairly reductive, and to arrive at the total of ten novels actually composed one has to suppose that 'le roman sur les prêtres is applicable both to *La Faute de l'abbé Mouret* and *La Conquête de Plassans*; and that 'le roman sur la femme d'intrigue dans le commerce', eventually Sidonie Rougon the procuress, can have its repercussions on *Le Rêve* and *Une Page d'amour*. It clearly does on *La Curée*, which is touched by the ramifications of four of the projects: 4, 7, 8 and 9.

The preliminary résumés themselves are so conditioned by the common theme of decadence that again the grand total of ten as conceived will be less in its realization. Precursory to *La Curée* are:

> Un roman qui aura pour cadre la vie sotte et élégamment crapuleuse de notre jeunesse dorée, et pour héros les fils d'Auguste Goiraud, Philippe, un de ces avortons, que l'on a nommés avec énergie 'des petits crevés'. Ces misérables pantins sont bien la caractéristique de l'époque. Education de Philippe, sa tête et son cœur vides. Il est un produit des appétits de son père et de cette fortune rapide et volée qui le met à même, dès quinze ans, de se vautrer dans toutes les jouissances. Il y a là un monde à peindre et à marquer d'un fer rouge. Dans l'œuvre entière, Philippe représente le produit chétif et malsain d'une famille qui a vécu trop vite et trop gorgée d'argent. Le père est puni par le fils. (Ms. 10303, fol. 53, *RM*, V, 1772)
>
> Un roman qui aura pour cadre les spéculations véreuses et effrénées du Second Empire, et pour héros Aristide Rougon, l'homme de Plassans, qui flairait la fortune et qui a laissé assassiner Silvère afin de débarrasser la famille d'un garçon compromettant. Venu à Paris après la proclamation de l'empire, il se mêle au grand mouvement d'achat et de vente de terrains, déterminé par les démolitions et les constructions de M. Haussmann. L'œuvre sera le poème, ou plutôt la terrible comédie des vols contemporains. Aristide réalise en quelques années une immense fortune. Remarié à une poupée parisienne, il souffre par sa femme. Peinture d'un ménage parisien, dans la haute sphère des parvenus. (Ms. 10303, fol. 54, *RM*, V, 1772)
>
> Un roman qui aura pour cadre le monde officiel et pour héros Alfred Goiraud. [...] Il épousera la fille d'un comte quelconque, rallié à l'empire, *ce qui introduira dans l'œuvre des types affaiblis de notre noblesse agonisante.* (Ms. 10303, fol. 55, *RM*, V, 1773; my emphasis)
>
> Un roman qui aura pour cadre le monde artistique et pour héros Claude Dulac. [...] Tableau de la fièvre d'art de l'époque, *de ce qu'on nomme la décadence et qui n'est qu'un produit de l'activité folle des esprits.* (Ms. 10303, fol. 62, *RM*, V, 1775; my emphasis)

The remainder are *La Fortune de Rougon*, of course, summarized prior to publication in great detail, and the stereotypically introduced 'roman qui aura pour cadre les fièvres religieuses du moment', 'roman qui aura pour cadre le monde militaire', 'roman qui aura pour cadre le monde ouvrier', 'roman qui aura pour cadre le monde galant', and 'roman qui aura pour cadre le monde judiciaire'.

We can see in the way that *La Curée* encroaches on *Son Excellence Eugène Rougon* and *L'Œuvre* the desire to arm what Michel Euvrard has called a 'machine de guerre contre l'Empire, contre les idées et l'ordre établis'.[20] Beyond these three, it is possible to discern only *La Fortune des Rougon*, *La Faute de l'abbé Mouret* (plus, *à la rigueur*, *La Conquête de Plassans*), *La Débâcle*, *L'Assommoir*, *Nana*, and the judicial dimension of *La Bête humaine*. Again, this hardly constitutes ten novels, and we must note the narrow political indignation of these preliminary sketches, and marvel at the flux of life that is monumentally summarized in *Le Docteur Pascal*. Realization is so far beyond intention, the rhetoric of the résumés is finally so captivating, that one marvels that 'ceci n'a pas tué cela'.

Huysmans might never be forgiven, said Zola, his 'pisses de chat',[21] nor did the latter avoid mockery for what was considered to be his flagrant abuse of a universal 'solvent', the word *analyse*. And yet a contemporary dictionary, the *Littré*, gives as one of its meanings: 'En littérature, extrait, précis, examen d'un ouvrage'. One may well wonder why Zola's remarks such as 'J'ai été fou d'analyse exacte'[22] were held up to scorn.

Perhaps *Littré's* qualification, 'en littérature', should be underlined; less rigorous standards pertained here than in the scientific domain, whose systematic thoroughness, exactness and objectivity Zola so enthusiastically assimilated in *Le Roman expérimental*. The Larousse encyclopedic dictionary voiced the standard objections: 'Heureusement les œuvres de M. Zola valent mieux que les théories inventées après coup pour les expliquer', and if Brunetière is not cited it is because the (much longer) résumé of *Le Roman naturaliste* follows immediately after, with particular reference to his disadvantageous comparison of Zola with Restif de la Bretonne.[23] Brunetière's fastidious semi-retraction - 'Il serait déloyal pourtant d'accabler M. Zola sous cette comparaison' - is ignored, and perhaps rightly so, but more interesting is the way in which a direct quotation is rendered more polemically offensive.[24]

In the name of science, Zola had erected an unforgiving (and unforgivable) critical position. What Zola meant by *analyse* is actually a conflation of a standard, workmanlike task and areas of literary and scientific prestige. If his use of it (before it became a stylistic tic) is examined, then it will be seen that he attached to *analyse* the senses of intuitive psychological penetration, scientific dissection and plot synopsis, and hoped that the favourable connotations of the former would rub off on the latter. Thus Zola could write of *Le Rouge et le Noir* (referring to the scene in which Julien takes Madame de Rênal's hand), 'Stendhal y a analysé merveilleusement les états d'âme de ses deux personnages'.[25] The subordination of Fabrice del Dongo to the picaresque events of *La Chartreuse de Parme* does not appeal to the critic who, rehearsing some of the points later to be made in Maupassant's 'Le Roman', calls it 'autant un roman d'aventures qu'une œuvre d'analyse'.[26]

Flaubert's art is said to combine 'l'analyse exacte de Balzac et l'éclat de style de Victor Hugo', in other words psychological penetration. *Madame Bovary* is concisely summarized: 'Le sujet du livre pourtant, l'intrigue, était des moins romanesques. Il tient aisément en trente lignes.' A few critical paragraphs then follow, though Zola bemoans the parsimonious word limit he has been set by the *Vestnik Evropy*. But when he turns to *L'Education sentimentale*, *analyse* clearly refers to plot résumé alone: 'L'analyse de *L'Education sentimentale* est impossible. Il faudrait suivre l'action page à page; il n'y a là que des faits et des figures. Pourtant, je puis expliquer en quelques lignes ce qui a donné à l'auteur l'idée du titre, fâcheux du reste.' For *La Tentation de Saint Antoine*, 'je vais tâcher, dans une brève analyse, de donner une idée de cette œuvre.' This turns out to be, largely, running paraphrase of a superior kind. Nevertheless, because he wrote two studies of Flaubert, before the latter's death in 1875 and after it in 1880, grouped in *Les Romanciers naturalistes* under the headings 'L'Ecrivain' and 'L'Homme', two studies of each novel are thereby provided, enabling him to come closer to the bipolarity of systematic analysis here than elsewhere.

To turn to the scientific, the Goncourt brothers' avowedly scientific pretensions are quite appropriately termed 'la nudité de l'analyse' and 'l'analyse du tempérament de cette fille [Germinie]', and one remembers the excitement with which, at the beginning of one of his first review articles, Zola talked of 'l'œuvre excessive et fiévreuse que je vais analyser'.[27] There analysis, then, would inspire his, and the work of physiologico- or chirurgico-analytical protonaturalists such as Claretie and Malot is described in similar terms, the latter article being entitled 'Un Roman d'analyse'.

But where Zola is more damning with faint praise, he tends to use the word in a throwaway manner; hence of a lengthy summary of Daudet's *Fromont jeune et Risler aîné*, he writes: 'J'ai analysé cette œuvre tout au long, pour bien en montrer le côté vivant';[28] of *Jack*: 'Il m'est bien difficile, dans cette analyse rapide, de donner une idée complète de ce long roman'; of *L'Arlésienne*: 'voici une analyse exacte', a full and faithful synopsis; and of *Le Nabab*; 'D'abord, il me faut analyser *Le Nabab* d'une façon précise et détaillée. On ne me comprendra bien que lorsqu'on aura sous les yeux un résumé exact du roman' neglecting the sub-plots and secondary characters 'pour tout de suite terminer l'analyse du drame'.

The word 'drame' is an invitation to cull from *Le Naturalisme au théâtre* and *Nos Auteurs dramatiques* further examples from the mid-seventies period; a sample only will be given, because the use becomes mechanical. Of a complicated plot: 'Je vais tenter d'analyser son (M. Talray) *Spartacus* en quelques mots; et je demande à l'avance pardon si je me trompe, car ce ne serait pas ma faute.' Of Poupart-Davyl's *Coq-Hardy*: 'Je ne chercherai pas à analyser la pièce dans son intrigue puérile et compliquée.' Of Dumas *fils*'s *Le Demi-Monde*: 'Mais avant de me prononcer sur la façon désastreuse dont l'auteur a gagné la partie, il me faut donner une analyse de la pièce, la plus claire possible, de façon à pouvoir ensuite me faire nettement comprendre', ending: 'J'ai analysé l'œuvre avec impartialité, en évitant d'indiquer un seul de mes jugements, de façon à exposer d'abord purement et simplement les faits. Je commencerai maintenant par louer les quelques scènes qui ne me déplaisent pas.'

Hence what historically was a term of hallowed critical deference eventually has the status of, on the one hand, a pseudo-objective synopsis prior to a critical massacre; or, on the other, any straight synopsis of a play. It gives a gloss of authority to what he deals with perfunctorily. More candidly, on *Tartarin de Tarascon*, he ends 'telle est cette œuvre dont je n'ai pu donner malheureusement que la carcasse'; his playsmiths such as Busnach were indeed content to be known as 'carcassiers' rather than 'analystes'.

Zola's normal critical *tour d'horizon* as a reviewer evolved into a plot résumé, followed by abbreviated attempts to define a work's particular flavour, spirit or genius. The less sympathetic he was, the less well it worked; he was perceived to become more and more ill-tempered, and it was very much on the corpus of his increasingly offhand and formulaic reviews, his 'modèle de réception', that his 'modèle de production', *Le Roman expérimental*, was judged.[29] In a sense he was his own worst enemy, disinclined as he was to lard his reviews with long quotations from the works themselves or from other critics. Hence his pioneering work in the critical résumé, which, though interesting, fell short of the high and difficult standards he set for the modern novelist. It would have implications for his reception.

There were reasons for Zola, in late career, to feel that his literary fortune might have been better. The most reliable barometer to it could not, to his mind, have been a faithful résumé of his substance and spirit. Entries relating to Zola in the *Grand Dictionnaire universel du XIXe siècle*, published in fifteen volumes (1866–76) and two supplements (1878 and 1890), are characteristic. There might well have been alphabetical reasons for none but *La Fortune des Rougon* (the F volume appearing in 1872) and *Le Ventre de Paris*, in the final volume (1876), being summarized, though they were in fact omitted. However, honourable amends were made with entries for 'Zola' in the final volume and the two supplements, and detailed and generally positive synopses of *Madeleine Férat* (1873) and *Thérèse Raquin* (1876). The second of these quoted freely from Gustave Vapereau's *L'Année littéraire*; this seems less to afford evidence that one of Hachette's leading encyclopedic contributors protected him than to indicate that this was an invaluable source of plunder for contributors working up against a deadline. Later, the unsympathetic Francisque Sarcey and Anatole France were also to be used.

The controversial and successful *L'Assommoir* was the first to have, in résumé form, a dictionary entry in its own right, in the first supplement of 1878; some others followed in 1890. The ending of this long and serious study, including a thousand-word plot synopsis - '[le] roman que nous venons d'*analyser*' - was on the whole well disposed towards him: 'beaucoup de détails ont été pris dans *le Sublime*, mais M. Zola en a formé un livre tout nouveau, plus mauvais peut-être au point de vue moral, mais plus vivant, et cette vie qu'il lui a donnée est bien l'œuvre propre de M. Zola.' The conclusion is not without its restrictions, but is so reminiscent of the letter written to Auguste Dumont of *Le Télégraphe* (18 March 1877), justifying the borrowings from Poulot in these terms and glossed by the editor of the newspaper, that it seems likely to have been written by somebody familiar with the controversy.[30] Certainly it is symptomatic of the tendency of the encyclopedia contributors to cannibalize the best available articles for their purposes.

So what cause, if any, had Zola for complaint? He might have accepted the plagiarism of existing critical discourse; extensive quoting - see the résumés of *Madame Férat*, *Nana* (the *Mouche d'Or*, of course) and *L'Œuvre* - had not been unknown to him in his early days; nor was a degree of flippancy (see that of *Le Ventre de Paris*). A poor knowledge of novels claimed to have been read - for instance the statement that Claude Lantier is 'fils de Gervaise, de l'*Assommoir*, et d'un alcoolique quelconque' - were more irritating. It was not so much that Zola was not perceived to rise above overall mediocrity as that he was held to be a very uneven talent, with as many faults as virtues. This type of *discours résumiel* was essentially bland and neutral to unexceptionable novelists, but even his later works were not received with unmitigated favour. Any publicity may be good publicity, and Zola had a fairly good spread in the pages of the *Grand Dictionnaire*, but most synopses referred to his brutality, vulgarity or crudity, or else, somewhat treacherously, applauded their absence in the novel under consideration. For instance, 'malgré ses défauts, *Au Bonheur des dames* semble marquer une étape nouvelle dans la carrière de M. Zola; on n'y retrouve plus les malades, les imbéciles et les coquins qui composaient le personnel ordinaire de ses précédents ouvrages'.[31] As for *Le Rêve*, 'ce n'est pas la première fois que le grand maître du naturalisme essaye d'appliquer à de chastes et idéales peintures la puissance descriptive qu'il sait si bien mettre en œuvre pour nous présenter des êtres abjects et dégradés, mais très réels'.[32] The closest to admitting the legitimacy of low-life naturalism comes in the entry on *Germinal*; again, the difficulty of synopsis is referred to - 'Impossible de donner autre chose que cette maigre charpente du livre de M. Zola: le drame est tellement touffu qu'il échappe à l'analyse' - but a certain appropriateness is conceded:

> Le sujet était dans son tempérament. Les rudesses, les grossièretés, qui rentrent dans sa manière et semblent parfois cherchées par lui comme un appât au lecteur blasé, naissent ici, pour ainsi dire, du fond même du roman et lui donnent une partie de sa force et son homogénéité.[33]

Hence it is no surprise to find that the best reception should be reserved for arguably his worst novel, *Au Bonheur des dames*, in which the conflicting ideologies do not exist in vital, dialectical tension but in awkward, uncomfortable juxtaposition. A *donnée* productive of the former - 'la lutte du capital et du travail'[34] - will be dismissed as '[les] théories socialistes les moins limpides'. Clearly there were still many outstanding scores to settle with the iconoclast of 'Les Romanciers contemporains' and 'Documents littéraires', in which 'l'auteur se montre la plupart du temps d'une sévérité à outrance ou d'un dédain mal justifié'.[35] Or else there was the recourse to silence: sixteen, or perhaps seventeen novels could have had fully-fledged alphabetical listings in the *Grand Larousse*: of these, *La Fortune des Rougon*, *La Curée*, *La Conquête de Plassans*, *La Faute de l'abbé Mouret*, *Son Excellence Eugène Rougon* and *Une Page d'amour* were but briefly mentioned, in the 'Zola' biographical sections. *La Joie de vivre* was cited only as a title.

The 'companion of literature' has not evolved much since the nineteenth century. The Laffot-Bompiani *Dictionnaire des œuvres* is full of careful but often carping résumés. It devotes more pages to the synopsis of Goethe's *Faust* than to the whole of Zola's output, omitting *Son Excellence Eugène*

Rougon, Au Bonheur des dames (curiously), *La Joie de vivre* (predictably) and *L'Argent*, though they are briefly summarized under *Les Rougon-Macquart*. Politics-occulting, moralizing judgements are also a direct inheritance: the early Third Republic, in either 'ordre moral' or later manifestations, was not disposed to stress the political dimension of the *Rougon-Macquart* that was so important in the pre-résumés. Since Zola's satirical blast became less strident, perhaps it was of little import. Yet it was unsatisfactory to have let it fade by default; temperamentally unable to postpone being understood to 1880 or 1935, like Stendhal, and unwilling to take Gide's calculated risk - 'Mais, tout considéré, mieux vaut laisser le lecteur penser ce qu'il veut - fût-ce contre moi'[36] - Zola had to 'faire contre mauvaise fortune bon cœur', and do the summarizing task himself.

In any case, Zola was far from being universally misunderstood; there were those who could point in the direction he appeared to have strayed from. The biographer of Zola in the 1878 first supplement to the *Grand Larousse* proclaimed himself unimpressed by the theories of heredity, but continued:

> M. Zola trahissait beaucoup mieux ses propres aspirations lorsqu'il s'écriait, dans la préface des *Contes à Ninon*: 'Je n'ai rien fait encore; j'ai des besoins cuisants de réalité. Je pleure sur cette montagne de papier noirci. Je me désole à penser que je n'ai pu étancher ma soif du vrai, que la grande nature échappe à mes bras trop courts. C'est l'âpre désir: prendre la terre, la posséder dans une étreinte, tout voir, tout savoir, tout dire. Je voudrais coucher l'humanité sur une page blanche, tous les êtres, toutes les choses, une œuvre qui serait l'arche immense.

The work is, of course, the *Nouveaux Contes à Ninon*, but more interesting is the painstaking incorporation of 'Je me sentais des besoins cuisants de réalité' from the previous collection of short stories.[37] Whether this is conscientious scholarship or an approximately remembered citation is irrelevant to the fact that it constitutes genuine reception of the kind an author might think he deserves. Indeed, predating Sandoz's passionate credo in *L'Œuvre* (*RM*, IV, 161–3) and *Le Docteur Pascal* itself, it is a valuable reminder of a strain of lyrical pantheism evident in Zola before 1878, *La Faute de l'abbé Mouret* notwithstanding - a strain clearly subordinate to the 'machine de guerre' of *Les Rougon-Macquart* in their original form.

These so appositely quoted prefaces point to the narrative technique and rhetoric ultimately deployed by Zola to deliver 'toute l'âme résumée' of his cycle. If *mises en abyme* could explicitly condition the understanding of individual works, its epic, panoramic sweep - occasionally glimpsed in the *Grand Larousse* résumés - needed more dynamic, intracyclical projection. Critics were too fixated on the 'partial evil' of the constituent volumes to sense the 'universal good' that the whole could be said to represent. If he could not gain the scientific seal of approval for his ideal poetics of the novel, the 'modèle de production', then why not for his series just completed? His *Défense et illustration*, a true 'affirmation et explication',[38] was *Le Docteur Pascal*, dedicated privately and touchingly to Jeanne Rozerot, but publicly to his late mother and his wife as 'le résumé et la conclusion de toute mon œuvre' (*RM*, V, 915).

Hamon speaks of the two main resources of *métalangage*, or commentative discourse, as follows:

> Nous aurions alors deux usages du métalangage: celui de l'écrivain qui, dans la circularité infinie et invérifiable de la parodie (Apollinaire), des rewritings et des mises en équivalence généralisées, dissout l'autorité du véritable et de l'énonciation unique; celui qui mime le discours de l'Autre (le savant, le technicien, le 'classique') que l'on cite pour lui prendre son sérieux, son autorité, sa compétence linguistique et s'instituer, à travers un transcodage systématique de tous les lieux illisibles, à travers un contrôle de la polysémie, comme sujet et comme source du Vrai et du Savoir.[39]

Clearly it is this second variety with which we are concerned in *Le Docteur Pascal*. The power of explaining the overall significance was invested in the figure of Pascal Rougon, established as the figurative author in the opening novel. Though he may have weaknesses, as scientific persona he is complementary to Zola, that is, his *alter ego* figure, and in his moral superiority seems to function as 'implied auther'.[40] So too Clotilde, it has been suggested, is the ideal narratee.[41] It seems more reasonable to posit that Pascal is received by her 'loud and clear' in his oral exposé, so that Clotilde is the first *hearer*, performing a model *reading* of the charred sheets that remain.[42]

'Ideal' does not mean unproblematical, for the experience of hearing Pascal read from the dossiers is traumatic for Clotilde; but she does emerge from the searing experience equipped to be proxy author of *Les Rougon-Macquart* after Pascal's death and Félicité's burning of all the papers but the family tree. In the reconstruction of her bewilderment, nineteen novels and over six thousand pages are summarized in less than six. At the time, Clotilde is far from making total sense of it; her head spins as the giddy pageant of her flawed family unfolds before her eyes. Her résumés are tightrope performances, as the thread always threatens to break, but never snaps. Zola's great skill is apparent; the detail that Pascal would provide, whether imparted in direct or reported speech, would be paraphrase to an intolerable degree, whereas Clotilde's emotionally disoriented recollections are credible. The rhetorical effect created is extremely powerful: in single sentences always, even if of one hundred and fifty words, straining syntax to the maximum, the young woman somehow holds on to the detail of each of the stories of Rougons, Mourets and Macquarts that then unfolds. The language is unpretentious and immediate; the simple declarative 'c'était' and/or the 'et' of great 'mouvement' can serve to introduce a character and résumé: 'Et c'était Saccard encore...'; 'Enfin, c'était Jean...'; 'Et c'était Jean encore...'; 'Et Octave Mouret...'; 'Et Gervaise Macquart...' (*RM*, V, 1010–12, 1014). Massive use is made of present and past participles, without which sentences of this length could not be constructed. The other feature, a key to the psychological coloration, is that the narrative tense is the imperfect, which can stand in place of the past historic but would not be expected in standard biographical résumé - and the shocking but salutary story of Clotilde's family is hardly that.

It is because of this precise narrative focalization that Janet Beizer, playing on the ambiguity of the Anglo-Saxon genitive, justifiably contends that we are listening to 'Clotilde's Story', told *of* the unwanted-on-journey child of *La*

Curée, then told *by* her (and censored from her summary of it). The paraphrases are uneven; *Nana* becomes a cast, or casualty-list, of names noted by Clotilde for future research, although the prestigious *mise en abyme* of the *Mouche d'Or* of course structures the discourse:

> Nana, dès lors, devenait la revanche, la fille poussée sur l'ordure sociale des faubourgs, la mouche d'or envolée des pourritures d'en bas, qu'on tolère et qu'on cache, emportant dans la vibration de ses ailes le ferment de destruction, remontant et pourrissant l'aristocratie, empoisonnant les hommes rien qu'à se poser sur eux, au fond des palais où elle entrait par les fenêtres, toute une œuvre inconsciente de ruine et de mort, la flambée stoïque de Vandeuvres, la mélancolie de Foucarmont courant les mers de la Chine, le désastre de Steiner, réduit à vivre en honnête homme, l'imbécillité satisfaite de La Faloise, et le tragique effondrement des Muffat et le blanc cadavre de Georges, veillé par Philippe, sorti la veille de prison, une telle contagion dans l'air empesté de l'époque, qu'elle-même se décomposait et crevait de la petite vérole noire, prise au lit de mort de son fils Louiset, tandis que, sous ses fenêtres, Paris passait, ivre, frappé de la folie de la guerre, se ruant à l'écroulement de tout (*RM*, V, 1013–14).

Elsewhere, epic sweep and pathos can be more instantly apprehended:

> Etienne, à son tour, chassé, perdu, arrivait au pays noir par une nuit glacée de mars, descendait dans le puits vorace, aimait la triste Catherine qu'un brutal lui volait, vivait avec les mineurs leur vie morne de misère et de basse promiscuité, jusqu'au jour où la faim, soufflant la révolte, promenait au travers de la plaine rase le peuple hurlant des misérables qui voulait du pain, dans les écroulements et les incendies, sous la menace de la troupe dont les fusils partaient tout seuls, terrible convulsion annonçant la fin d'un monde, sang vengeur des Maheu qui se lèverait plus tard, Alzire morte de faim, Maheu tué d'une balle, Zacharie tué d'un coup de grisou, Catherine resté sous la terre, la Maheude survivant seule, pleurant ses morts, redescendant au fond de la mine pour gagner ses trente sous, pendant qu'Etienne, le chef battu de la bande, hanté des revendications futures, s'en allait par un tiède matin d'avril, en écoutant la sourde poussée du monde nouveau, dont la germination allait bientôt faire éclater la terre (*RM*, V, 1013).

We see how the *dossiers* come to life. Authorial prompting, i.e. Pascal's, is kept to a reasonable minimum; the evolutionary glosses stressing a surging current of life in which good and evil are biologically irrelevant - 'Il y a de tout, de l'excellent et du pire, du vulgaire et du sublime, les fleurs, la boue, les sanglots, les rires, le torrent même de la vie charriant l'humanité!' (*RM*, V, 1018 *et passim*) - his updates, and his proleptic résumé of his own dossier lose much of their potential didacticism in order to remain subservient to Clotilde's feelings. Nevertheless, they add spirit or 'âme' to the substance, so that, as Beizer points out, 'Pascal gets her with text well before he gets her with child'. After the impregnation, a period of incubation immediately follows - 'Ah! [...] que devenir?' (*RM*, V, 1022–4). For, at first, it makes no sense at all. Given Dällenbach's *rapprochements* with the *nouveau roman*, we may see, in a contemporary analysis of retrospective narration, analogues to her initial panic:

> Tenter de rapporter, de reconstituer ce qui s'est passé, c'est un peu comme si on

essayait de recoller les débris dispersés, incomplets, d'un miroir, s'efforçant maladroitement de les réajuster, n'obtenant qu'un résultat incohérent, dérisoire, idiot, où peut-être seul notre esprit, ou plutôt notre orgueil, nous enjoint sous peine de folie et en dépit de toute évidence de trouver à tout prix une suite logique de causes et d'effets là où tout ce que la raison parvient à voir, c'est cette errance, nous-mêmes ballottés de droite et de gauche, comme un bouchon à la dérive, sans direction, sans vue, essayant seulement de surnager et souffrant.[43]

But Clotilde becomes *matrice-narratrice*; the obligation to process his words is thrust upon her by the death of her initiator and lover, and competence develops. If *La Fortune des Rougon* and *La Curée* are an unshapely, unwieldy mix of contemporaneous and flashback narrative, at least Clotilde soon improves, and the awkwardness could be considered a symptom of the initial confusion. On the bare résumés of proper names and family relationships, her poetic fantasy embroiders, animating stills, buildings and machines in a way that her positivist master would never do (not having Zola's temperament). Such figurative authorship, envisaged from the beginning, is an ideal self-defensive posture. Ultimately Clotilde will be able to write the biography of her father, and think as kindly of the imprisoned visionary of *L'Argent* as of the altruistic Sigismond Busch. First, however, there are scores of moral abandonment to settle:

Aristide Rougon s'abattit sur Paris, au lendemain du 2 Décembre, avec ce flair des oiseaux de proie qui sentent de loin les champs de bataille. Il arrivait de Plassans, une sous-préfecture du Midi, où son père venait enfin de pêcher dans l'eau trouble des événements une recette particulière longtemps convoitée. Lui, jeune encore, après s'être compromis comme un sot, sans gloire ni profit, avait dû s'estimer heureux de se tirer sain et sauf de la bagarre. Il accourait, enrageant d'avoir fait fausse route, maudissant la province, parlant de Paris avec des appétits de loup, jurant 'qu'il ne serait plus si bête'; et le sourire aigu dont il accompagnait ces mots prenait une terrible signification sur ses lèvres minces (*RM*, I, 359).

Only later could Zola explain and affirm his pantheistic credo. Panoptic vision, colour and life were breathed into the dry and minimalizing summaries of *Les Rougon-Macquart*. A narrow and embittered *parti pris*, resulting in the vision-blocking ubiquity of *La Curée*, was then amplified into the lyrical recapitulation of *Le Docteur Pascal*. A long apprenticeship bore fruit in aesthetically compelling self-summary, the only kind he could rely on; and it may be critically appropriate that it is the unwanted encumbrance - 'une femme et un enfant lui [Aristide] semblaient déjà un poids écrasant pour un homme décidé à franchir tous les fossés, quitte à se casser les reins ou à rouler dans la boue' (*RM*, I, 359) - of the initially encumbering *La Curée* who recuperates the whole cycle.

NOTES

1. See R. Godenne, *La Nouvelle française* (PUF, 1974), pp. 11–12, *et passim*.
2. 'Texte littéraire et métalangage', *Poétique*, 8 (1977), 261–84 (p. 269).
3. 'L'Œuvre dans l'œuvre chez Zola', in *Le Naturalisme*, Colloque de Cérisy (UGE, coll. 10/18, 1978), pp. 125–39 (p. 129; Dällenbach's emphasis).

4. *Ibid.*, pp. 133 and 139, n. 9. This citation incorporates a reference to E. Ledrain (*L'Eclair*, 2 August 1893), on *Le Docteur Pascal*.

5. *Figures III* (Seuil, 1972), pp. 130–3.

6. *Ibid.*, pp. 238–9 and n. 1.

7. Janet L. Beizer, 'Remembering and Repeating the *Rougon-Macquart*: Clotilde's Story', *L'Esprit créateur*, XXV (1985), 51–8 (p. 57).

8. Jacques Derrida, 'Hors livre: préfaces', in *La Dissémination* (Seuil, 1972), pp. 9–67 (p. 35).

9. J.-F. Deljurie, 'René à travers les manuels ou le discours d'escorte', *Littérature*, 7 (1972), 27–47.

10. *Les Cahiers naturalistes*, 42 (1971), 93–108.

11. Halina Suwala, 'Première campagne critique de Zola', *Revue de l'Université d'Ottawa*, 48, 4 (1978), 310–22.

12. 'Les Titres des romans de Guy des Cars', in *Sociocritique* (Nathan, 1979), pp. 89–97 (p. 97).

13. H. Suwala, 'Zola et les conférences de la rue de la Paix', *Les Cahiers naturalistes*, 37 (1969), 1-19, and 38 (1969), 128–45.

14. 'Zola à la librairie Hachette', *Revue de l'Université d'Ottawa*, 48 (1978), 287–309 (p. 293).

15. See the 'Notice' following the *Contes à Ninon*, (*OC*, XI, 189–91). It was claimed that 'l'analyse de chaque conte' had been briefly given.

16. Henri Marel, '*Germinal* et *Les Houilleurs de Polignies*', *Cahiers de l'UER Froissart*, 5 (1980), 113–26 (p. 114).

17. Edmond de Goncourt's diary entry for 13 April 1893 has Zola speaking of his diligent background research for *Le Docteur Pascal* 'pour que l'œuvre eût quelque chose de *l'anneau du serpent qui se mord la queue*' - *Journal: mémoires de la vie littéraire*, ed. R. Ricatte (Monaco, Editions de l'Imprimerie Nationale, 1956–8), XIX, 96; Goncourt's emphasis.

18. Already in the more independent medium of *Le Salut public* of 26 November 1866 he is referring to a work, *La Peine de mort*, 'qui semble dater de cinquante ans', and implying that Berthet is a mediocre *feuilletoniste*, before the later harshness of 'Les Romanciers contemporains'; see *OC*, X, 690–1 and XI, 237–8, 255 (n.)

19. Gustave Vapereau, *L'Année littéraire* (Hachette, 1865), VII, 82–3.

20. *Zola* (Editions Universitaires, 1967), p. 21.

21. 'Céard et Huysmans', in *Une Campagne*, (*OC*, XIV, 580–5) (p. 581). The exact quotation, from Chapter One of *Les Sœurs Vatard*, is 'l'âcre pissat du chat'.

22. 'A Ninon', *Nouveaux Contes à Ninon* (*OC*, IX, 349–50).

23. For both of these entries, see the *Grand Dictionnaire Universel du XIXe Siècle*, supplément II (1890), p. 1792.

24. F. Brunetière, 'Le *Roman expérimental*', in *Le Roman naturaliste* (Calmann-Lévy, 1882), p. 127, has: 'Restif, sous le manteau couleur de muraille dont il s'enveloppait, était vraiment l'aventurier du naturalisme, j'ai grand peur que M. Zola n'en soit que le maître de cérémonies', the last part of which becomes: 'j'ai bien peur que M. Zola n'en soit que le Prudhomme.'

25. *Les Romanciers naturalistes* (*OC*, XI, 75–6)

26. *OC*, IX, 105–15.

27. *OC*, X, 62.

28. *OC*, XI, 192–204.

29. Henri Mitterand, 'Le Naturalisme théorique de Zola', *Cahiers de l'UER Froissart*, 5 (1980), 181–93 (p. 181).

30. See *Corr.*, II, 548–9 and 550–1, n. 7.

31. *Grand Dictionnaire Universel du XIXe Siècle*, supplément II (1890) p. 396.

32. *Ibid.*, p. 1778.

33. *Ibid.*, p. 1313–14.

34. *Ebauche* of *Germinal*, B.N., N.a.fr., Ms. 10307, fol. 402/1.

35. *Grand Dictionnaire Universel du XIXe Siècle*, supplément II (1890) p. 2018.

36. *Journal des 'Faux-Monnayeurs'* (NRF, Gallimard, 1927), p. 87. Dällenbach (p. 128) points out that Zola's *mises en abyme* are purposely obvious. To say nothing of *La Mouche d'Or*, the one in *Pot-Bouille* was immediately picked up by its reviewer: 'Au second [...] un homme qui fait des livres, peuh! un romancier naturaliste!' (*Grand Dictionnaire*, supplément II (1890) p. 1732).

37. See 'A Ninon', *Nouveaux Contes à Ninon* (OC, XI, 351), and 'A Ninon', *Contes à Ninon* (*ibid.*, p. 30).

38. For C. Becker, *loc. cit.*, p. 293, his earliest polemical open letters, as well as being publicity-seeking, are 'toujours l'affirmation et l'explication de ses conceptions et de ses principes littéraires'. At the time under consideration, he wrote to J. Van Santen Kolff: 'Ce qui m'amuse, c'est que j'y mets l'explication et la défense de toute la série des dix-neufs romans qui ont précédé le vingtième'; letter of 22 February 1893 (OC, XIV, 1485).

39. Hamon, p. 278; see also his 'Un Discours contraint', *Poétique*, 16 (1973), 411–45 (pp. 428–9).

40. Or author's 'second self'; see, Wayne C. Booth, *The Rhetoric of Fiction* (Chicago University Press, 1973 [1961]), p. 67.

41. For a summary of the relevant theory, see Jaap Lintvelt, *Essai de typologie narrative: le point de vue* (Corti, 1981), pp. 17–18; in particular, 'le lecteur abstrait fonctionne d'une part comme image du destinataire présupposé et postulé par l'œuvre littéraire et d'autre part comme image du récepteur idéal, capable d'en concrétiser le sens total dans une lecture active'.

42. Naomi Schor, *Zola's Crowds* (Baltimore, Johns Hopkins University Press, 1978), p. 69.

43. Claude Simon, *Le Vent* (Editions de Minuit, 1975), p. 10.

9

ZOLA'S PARTING SHOTS

Colin Boswell

When one considers the craft of fiction from the point of view of the writer rather than from the point of view of its reader and critic, there are three textual segments which might possibly test that craft to a disproportionate extent: the title, the *incipit* (the opening words of the text) and the *explicit*[1] (the words of the sentence with which the text ends). This study will be particularly concerned with the *explicit* which Zola wrote as the conclusion of 28 of his novels. The main emphasis will be on the *explicit* of the 20 novels of the *Rougon-Macquart* series, but the final sentences of *Thérèse Raquin*, *Madeleine Férat*, of the three novels of the *Trois Villes* and of the three novels which remain of the projected *Quatre Evangiles* will also be examined. The title, the *incipit* and the *explicit* seem to me to be amongst those elements which Philippe Hamon has called the 'lieux stratégiques, des articulations ou stases privilégiées'[2] of any narrative and, on account of the close functional relationship between them, the *explicit* will on occasions be compared to the other two.

The title will usually be reader's first point of contact with the novel and will also normally be one of the shortest syntagma to be encountered in the narrative discourse. And yet this tiny fragment of language frequently acts as a signpost to the multiplicity of interpretations which are possible. The brevity of Zola's titles is demonstrated by the fact that in the 28 novels I am examining he only once created a title of more than four words (the six-word title *La Faute de l'abbé Mouret*). On two occasions Zola selected a three-word title (*La Bête humaine* and *Le Docteur Pascal*) but his preference was normally for titles of one, two or four words. One-word titles became standard from *Lourdes* onwards but had already been used three times in the *Rougon-Macquart* series (*Nana*, *Germinal*, *Pot-Bouille*[3]) and they account for nine of the 28 titles, close to one third of the total. Exactly the same number of times Zola chose two-word titles, initially merely citing the name of the eponymous heroine (*Thérèse Raquin* and *Madeleine Férat*) but then in later works stating the theme(s) of the novel in a two-word noun-phrase consisting of an article followed by a noun (e.g. *La Curée*, *L'Assommoir*, *La Débâcle* etc.). Only slightly less frequently[4] he used a four-word phrase with a structure in most cases consisting of Article + Noun + *de* + Noun/Proper Name.

We have evidence that, despite the apparent banality of many of these titles,

Zola sometimes did not choose them without a considerable amount of hesitation. Henri Mitterand cites no fewer than 134 possible titles for *La Bête humaine* to be found in folios 297–304 of the *Ebauche*.[5] The list of alternatives titles for *Germinal* is only slightly less impressive: *L'Assiette au beurre, Le Cahier des pauvres, Le Quatrième ordre, Table rase, Liquidation, Les Affamés, Légion, Le Feu souterrain, Le Feu qui couve, Château branlant, Coup de pioche, Moisson rouge, La Maison qui craque, La Lézarde, Sous terre, Le Grain qui germe, Le sang qui germe.* In Zola's own words:

> Et c'est un jour, par hasard, que le mot: *Germinal* m'est venu aux lèvres. Je n'en voulais pas d'abord, le trouvant trop mystique, trop symbolique; mais il représentait ce que je cherchais, un avril révolutionnaire, un envolée de la société caduque dans le printemps. Et peu à peu je m'y suis habitué, si bien que je n'ai jamais pu en trouver un autre.[6]

And so, if we take Zola at his word, it is almost by chance that we have what Henri Mitterand has called 'la plus belle invention verbale de Zola' (*RM*, III, 1884). In the case of the novel *L'Œuvre* we have evidence from one of Zola's letters that he was not particularly happy with the title: 'Autre malheur, je n'ai pas encore trouvé un titre dont je fusse content. Le seul possible jusqu'à présent est: L'Œuvre, et je le juge bien gris.'[7] The title of the novel would therefore seem to be for Zola a linguistic unit of more than usual significance and one to which he paid particular attention. Later in this study the *explicit* will be examined in relation to the titles.

The final sentences will also frequently be compared with the initial sentences. This is because there are clear similarities of function between them. In the words of Alexander Welsh: 'Beginnings and endings of narrative have much in common since both are arbitary designations in a sequence of events that is presumed continuous, extending before and after the events which are narrated.'[8]

Because we do not possess the manuscripts which would allow us to see to what extent Zola changed his mind over the particular phrases he chose for his novels we have no evidence that he suffered from the sort of 'writer's block' exemplified by the fictitious character of Joseph Grand in *La Peste*, who is unable to progress beyond a continual reworking of the first sentence of his novel. A comparison of the variants cited in the notes to the Pléiade edition shows that Zola made only very minor alterations to the *incipit* between different editions of the novels.[9]

A short but stimulating and provocative survey of the *incipit* of the *Rougon-Macquart* was undertaken by Jacques Dubois, who concluded: 'Dans la plupart des cas [des *incipit*] pourtant, le dispositif du texte vise à laisser l'impression d'une histoire en cours, d'un moment prélevé sur une durée et faisant suite à un moment antérieur.'[10]

Dubois then described the technique with which Zola opened no fewer than 10 of the 20 novels as follows: 'Le plus opérant et le plus repérable consiste à désigner, dès la première phrase, un personnage-sujet par son nom de famille ou, mieux, par un prénom ou un surnom, comme si ce personnage était déjà connu de toujours et ne demandait pas à être présenté.'[11]

According to Dubois the *incipit* of a realist work has two primary functions: first, the obvious one of setting the narrative in motion; second, that of giving the reader some guarantee of the authenticity of what is being recounted. In the words of Dubois: 'Pour donner figure à la contiguïté qu'il prétend entretenir avec le réel, le récit réaliste s'évertue à se présenter comme une simple intervention dans le continu des "choses" et des "faits", intervention qui en prolonge le mouvement, sans en briser le cours.'[12]

By implication therefore the function of the *explicit* of the realist novel might also seem to be a dual one: first, to bring the narrative to its conclusion and, second, to set it against 'le continu des "choses" et des "faits"'. If one views the literary text, like language itself, as an essentially linear phenomenon, as what Hamon called 'un espace sémiologique linéairement matérialisé',[13] then the way it conveys its multiplicity of possible interpretations is through the constant interplay of paradigmatic oppositions and syntagmatic combinations. The *explicit*, occupying as it does the last slot in the syntagmatic structure of the text, finds itself in a particularly privileged position. Talking of the interpretation of poetry Barbara H. Smith wrote:

> As we read the poem, it is a hypothesis whose probability is tested as we move from line to line and adjusted in response to what we find there. And [...] the conclusion of a poem has special status in the process, for it is only at that point that the total pattern - the structural principles which we have been testing - is revealed.[14]

But not all critics agree with this accumulative theory of how the meaning of a literary text is evaluated by the reader, a theory which is based upon the assumption that the last meaning is the 'true' one, for, as Hamon writes: 'le sens d'un texte est sans doute autre chose que la somme ordonnancée, l'addition des différents sens de ses différentes parties constitutives, et l'acte de la lecture - d'un texte écrit - ne s'arrête sans doute pas à la fin du texte.'[15]

The accumulative theory is, of course, based upon the presupposition that the *explicit* contains the last words of the narrative discourse encountered by the reader. This could be questionable on two accounts. Firstly some readers might, out of idle curiosity or for some other motive, skip to the end of the text and capture the *explicit* out of its syntagmatic sequence. Secondly there is always a possibility that the *explicit* is not really read at all in any true sense, the reason for this being that in any linear linguistic sequence, the later elements usually become more and more predictable and therefore carry less information. In other words they become increasingly redundant. We have all experienced that moment in the cinema when the audience senses that the film is drawing to its close and prepares to leave, often obscuring the last words and images in the process. The reader of the text not only has narrative clues (for example the death or marriage of the protagonists) which signal the imminent end but also the turning of the last page and the eye's downward rush towards the final blank space. Culler has described the different speeds at which we read a novel:

> When reading a nineteenth century novel we speed up and slow down, and the rhythm of our reading is a recognition of structure: we can pass quickly through those descriptions and conversations whose functions identify; we wait for something more important, at which point we slow down. If we reversed this rhythm no doubt we would become bored.[16]

Although it is quite possible that some readers slow down over the last page in order to postpone the disappointment caused by the fact that their pleasure in the text is soon to end, it is also likely that many, having perceived the end, speed up and do not in any true sense 'read' the *explicit*. For these readers the story is already over, even if a few words of the narrative discourse still remain. If my assumption is correct the *explicit* may differ in a very important respect from the title and the *incipit*, neither of which is likely to be skipped by the reader. It would also be doubly ironical if it could be demonstrated that the writer took particular trouble over a fragment which many readers tended to ignore.

If there is anything at all of Zola in his character Claude Lantier then we may have evidence that Zola found that endings could be troublesome. Claude does not often have difficulties in starting paintings, his problem is knowing how to finish them:

> Et Claude, en effet, comme si cette ironie d'un habile homme [de Fagerolles] lui eût porté malheur, ne fit ensuite que gâter son ébauche. C'était sa continuelle histoire, il se dépensait d'un coup, en un élan magnifique; puis, il n'arrivait pas à faire sortir le reste, il ne savait pas finir (*RM*, IV, 234).

There is slender evidence from a comparison of the *explicit* of the different published versions of the same novel that Zola ever felt it necessary to make significant alterations. There is, however, evidence that Zola did not wait until the end of the final chapter before drafting the *explicit* but that instead he had often planned it well in advance. Richards claimed that the poet might even begin with the *explicit*: 'The order of parts within a poem may change greatly during composition. Quite often, I believe, the first phrase to occur - the phrase to which the rest of the poem is a response - becomes, in the final version, the close.'[17]

It seems highly unlikely that Zola would always have worked in this manner but we do have evidence of how some of his *explicit* were planned in advance and of some of the problems by which Zola found himself confronted. At the end of a short debate over a possible political end for *La Conquête de Plassans* he noted: 'Cette fin est à arranger' (*RM*, I, 1674). 'Et finir par *Germinal*', Zola had written in folio 391 of the *ébauche* of that novel (*RM*, III, 1940). The *Premier plan détaillé* of *La Terre* contains a long debate about the ending of the novel at the end of which Zola warned himself: 'Se méfier du dénouement de *Germinal* et de *L'Œuvre*' (*RM*, IV, 1607–8).

The preparatory *dossier* of *Le Docteur Pascal* contains a long meditation on the end of that novel which concludes as follows:

> Enfin Clotilde faisant toujours téter [Description du dehors], avec les sept étoiles. Finir, en tout cas, par la bravoure qu'il y a à créer un Rougon encore, après la terrible ascendance. Une musique lointaine, celle de la cérémonie. Et l'enfant tête toujours, sa petite main en l'air, comme un drapeau d'appel à la vie (*RM*, V, 1665–6).

In this extract we see that Zola had not only planned the final scene of the novel but had even sketched out a rudimentary form of the *explicit* which is similar in many ways to the final version. It would therefore seem that for Zola the *explicit* could be a narrative segment of greater-than-average significance and in what follows is a detailed analysis of a corpus consisting of the *explicit* of 28 of this novels. The corpus will first be examined from a linguistic point of view, including a survey of such features as sentence length, word length, choise of vocabulary, type of discourse used. It will then be examined in relation to the wider topic of narrative closure.

Here first of all is the corpus:

Et pendant près de douze heures, jusqu'au lendemain vers midi, madame Raquin, roide et muette, les contempla à ses pieds, ne pouvant se rassasier les yeux, les écrasant de regards lourds. *Thérèse Raquin* [TR][18]

Quand elle eut distingué le cadavre aplati à terre, comme piétiné par ce fou qui riait et dansait diaboliquement dans l'ombre vague, elle redressa sa haute taille, elle dit de sa voix sèche. 'Dieu le Père n'a pas pardonné.' *Madeleine Férat* [MF]

Et, au loin, au fond de l'aire Saint-Mittre, sur la pierre tombale, une mare de sang se caillait. *La Fortune des Rougon* [FR]

La note de Worms se montait à deux cent cinquante-sept francs. *La Curée* [Cu]

Et Claude, qui avait certainement oublié de dîner la veille, pris de colère à les voir si bien portantes, si comme il faut, avec leurs grosses gorges, serra sa ceinture, en grondant d'une voix fâchée: 'Quels gredins que les honnêtes gens!' *Le Ventre de Paris* [VP]

Puis elle joignit les mains avec une épouvante indicible, elle expira, en apercevant, dans la clarté rouge, la soutane de Serge. *La Conquête de Plassans* [CP]

'Serge! Serge!' cria-t-elle plus fort, en tapant des mains, 'la vache a fait un veau!' *La Faute de l'abbé Mouret* [FM]

Lorsqu'il parut, rajeuni, comme allégé, ayant démenti en une heure toute sa vie politique, prêt à satisfaire, sous la fiction du parlementarisme, son furieux appétit d'autorité, elle céda à un entraînement, elle alla vers lui, la main tendue, les yeux attendris et humides d'une caresse, en disant: 'Vous êtes tout de même une jolie force, vous.' *Son Excellence Eugène Rougon* [ER]

'Fais dodo, ma belle!' *L'Assommoir* [As]

Jeanne, morte, restait seule en face de Paris, à jamais. *Une Page d'amour* [PA]

'A Berlin! à Berlin! à Berlin!' *Nana* [Na]

'C'est cochon et compagnie.' *Pot-Bouille* [PB]

Il ne lâchait pas Denise, il la serrait éperdument sur sa poitrine en lui disant qu'elle pouvait partir maintenant, qu'elle passerait un mois à Valognes, ce qui fermerait la bouche du monde, et qu'il irait ensuite l'y chercher lui-même, pour l'en ramener à son bras, toute-puissante. *Au Bonheur des dames* [BD]

Et ce misérable sans pieds ni mains, qu'il fallait coucher et faire manger comme un enfant, ce lamentable reste d'homme dont le peu de vie n'était plus qu'un hurlement de douleur, cria dans une indignation furieuse: 'Faut-il être bête pour se tuer!' *La Joie de vivre* [JV]

Des hommes poussaient, une armée noire, vengeresse, qui germait lentement dans les sillons, grandissant pour les récoltes du siècle futur, et dont la germination allait faire bientôt éclater la terre. *Germinal* [Ge]

Puis il ajouta: 'Allons travailler.' *L'Oeuvre* [OE]

Des morts, des semences, et le pain poussait de la terre. *La Terre* [Te]

Et au sommet du bonheur, Angélique avait disparu, dans le petit souffle d'un baiser. *Le Rêve* [Rê]

Sans conducteur, au milieu des ténèbres, en bête aveugle et sourde qu'on aurait lâchée parmi la mort, elle roulait, elle roulait, chargée de cette chair à canon, de ces soldats déjà hébétés de fatigue, et ivres, qui chantaient. *La Bête humaine* [BH]

L'amour est-il moins souillé, lui qui crée la vie? *L'Argent* [Ar]

Le champ ravagé était en friche, la maison brûlée était par terre; et Jean, le plus humble et le plus douloureux, s'en alla, marchant à l'avenir, à la grande et rude besogne de toute une France à refaire. *La Débâcle* [Dé]

Et dans le tiède silence, dans la paix solitaire de la salle de travail, Clotilde souriait à l'enfant, qui tétait toujours, son petit bras en l'air, tout droit, dressé comme un drapeau d'appel à la vie. *Le Docteur Pascal* [DP]

Là-bas, Bernadette, le nouveau Messie de la souffrance, si touchante dans sa réalité humaine, est la leçon terrible, l'holocauste retranché du monde, la victime condamnée à l'abandon, à la solitude et à amort, frappée de la déchéance de n'avoir pas été femme, ni épouse ni mère, parce qu'elle avait vu la Sainte Vierge. *Lourdes* [Lo]

Le surlendemain, au lever du jour, il serait à Paris. *Rome* [Ro]

Paris flambait, ensemencé de lumière par le divin soleil, roulant dans sa gloire la moisson future de vérité et de justice. *Paris* [Pa]

Et c'était l'exode, l'expansion humaine par le monde, l'humanité en marche, à l'infini. *Fécondité* [Fé]

Table 1   Mean length of *explicit*

Novel	Number of words in *explicit*	Novel	Number of words in *explicit*
TR	32	Ge	30
MF	41	Œ	5
FR	19	Te	11
Cu	12	Rê	15
VP	42	BH	39
CP	21	Ar	11
FM	17	Dé	40
ER	60	DP	39
As	4	Lo	58
PA	10	Ro	10
Na	6	Pa	21
PB	5	Fé	18
BD	51	Tl	13
JV	47	Vé	33
Sub-total	367	Sub-total	343

	TOTAL	710
	MEAN x̄	25.36
	STANDARD DEVIATION σ *	16.7

* The standard deviation (σ) is a means of calculating the degree of dispersal around the mean of the scores of elements in a given population. A low standard deviation indicates that all the scores are close to the mean; a high standard deviation implies that the scores are very scattered. In normal distribution one would expect 66% of the population to be located within a range of plus or minus one standard deviation from the mean, in this case within a range from 42.06 to 8.66. In this table, 71% are within this range.

Et Luc expira, entra dans le torrent d'universel amour, d'éternelle vie. *Travail* [Tl]

Et, après la Famille enfantée, après la Cité fondée, la Nation se trouvait constituée, du jour où, par instruction totale de tous les citoyens, elle était devenue capable de vérité et de justice. *Vérité* [Vé]

The length of a sentence should be in a reasonable degree of correlation to its syntactical complexity, and an examination of the length of the *explicit* and its comparison with the average sentence-length of individual novels and of Zola's work in general may prove illuminating about one particular aspect of style.[19] The average sentence-length[20] expressed as a mean of the *explicit* in the corpus is as shown in Table 1.

In order to see how this figure compared with the average sentence-length of Zola's prose writing in general, I took 100 sentences at random from each of the 20 *Rougon-Macquart* novels, thus constituting a random sample of 2,000 sentences. The mean ($\bar{x}$) of these sentences was 20.14 with a standard deviation (σ) of 15.09. It seems therefore that, on average, Zola preferred a final sentence which was marginally longer than his normal style. Table 2 illustrates how the *explicit* compares with the *incipit* of each novel.

Table 2   Mean length of *incipit* (figures for *explicit* in brackets)

Novel	Number of words in *incipit*	Novel	Number of words in *incipit*
TR	35 (32)	Ge	42 (30)
MF	11 (41)	Œ	20 (5)
FR	46 (19)	Te	45 (11)
Cu	20 (12)	Rê	37 (15)
VP	44 (42)	BH	23 (39)
CP	4 (21)	Ar	27 (11)
FM	13 (17)	Dé	17 (40)
ER	16 (60)	DP	21 (39)
As	10 (4)	Lo	56 (58)
PA	23 (10)	Ro	38 (10)
Na	12 (6)	Pa	32 (21)
PB	21 (5)	Fé	37 (18)
BD	35 (51)	Tl	35 (13)
JV	15 (47)	Vé	62 (33)
Sub-total	305(367)	Sub-total	492(343)

	TOTAL	797	(710)
	MEAN $\bar{x}$	28.46	(25.36)
	STANDARD DEVIATION σ	14.4	(16.7)

The figures clearly show that the *incipit* is on average even longer than the *explicit* and that both are longer than the statistical norm. It can also be seen that there was a tendency for the *incipit* to get longer as Zola matured; the mean length of the first 14 novels being 21.79 against 35.14 for the last 14. No such tendency is observable in the *explicit*, except that between *L'Assommoir* and *Pot-Bouille* Zola did seem to prefer very short final sentences.

In order to make meaningful comparisons between the *incipit*, the *explicit* and the mean we need to examine the z-scores, or what French statisticians call the 'écart réduit'.[21] Table 3 examines a random sample of 2,000 sentences taken from the 20 novels of the *Rougon-Macquart* series. The z-scores

Table 3   z-scores for *incipit* and *explicit* of the *Rougon-Macquart* novels

Novel	Mean sentence length	Standard deviation	INCIPIT Length	Variance from mean	z-score	EXPLICIT Length	Variance from mean	z-score
FR	17.43	11.97	46	28.57	2.38	19	1.57	0.13
Cu	23.67	15.25	20	−3.67	−0.24	12	−11.67	−0.77
VP	18.33	10.4	44	25.67	2.46	42	23.67	2.27
CP	17.99	10.63	4	−13.99	−1.31	21	3.01	0.28
FM	18.37	11.92	13	−5.37	−0.45	17	−1.37	−0.11
ER	18.75	13.96	16	−2.75	−0.19	60	41.25	2.95
As	20.43	16.67	10	−10.43	−0.62	4	−16.43	−0.98
PA	16.42	11.99	23	6.58	0.54	10	−6.42	−0.53
Na	17.84	11.13	12	−5.84	−0.52	6	−11.84	−1.06
PB	18.66	11.24	21	2.34	0.20	5	−13.66	−1.21
BD	22.72	15.66	35	12.28	0.78	51	28.28	1.80
JV	18.64	13.28	15	−3.64	−0.27	47	28.36	2.10
Ge	18.49	13.75	42	23.51	1.70	30	11.51	0.83
Œ	22.79	16.63	20	−2.79	−0.16	5	−17.79	−1.06
Te	20.48	13.30	45	24.52	1.50	11	−9.48	−0.58
Rê	20.26	13.48	37	16.74	1.24	15	−5.26	−0.39
BH	20.62	13.22	23	2.38	0.18	39	18.38	1.39
Ar	24.13	19.85	27	2.87	0.14	11	−13.13	−0.66
Dé	23.25	21.88	17	−6.25	−0.29	40	16.75	0.76
DP	23.41	23.34	21	−2.41	−0.10	39	15.59	0.66

			INCIPIT			EXPLICIT		
		AVERAGE Z-SCORES	0.35			0.29		

confirm the overall view that Zola's *incipit* tended to be longer than his *explicit* and that both were longer than was the average for his *Rougon-Macquart* novels. From the figures in Table 3 we see that the *incipit* tended to be 0.35 of a standard deviation longer than average and that the *explicit* tended to be 0.29 of a standard deviation longer. On the other hand we note that in 15 of the 20 novels either the *incipit*, or the *explicit*, or both are shorter than average. For

Zola started and ended *La Curée*, *La Faute de l'abbé Mouret*, *Nana* and *L'Œuvre* with sentences which were shorter than the average for those novels. Novels which start with shorter-than-average sentences but where the *explicit* is longer than average are: *La Conquête de Plassans*, *Son Excellence Eugène Rougon*, *La Joie de vivre*, *La Débâcle* and *Le Docteur Pascal*. In five novels the *explicit* is relatively short whereas the *incipit* is longer than average: *Une Page d'amour*, *Pot-Bouille*, *La Terre*, *Le Rêve* and *L'Argent*.

The z-scores also show how the mean sentence-lengths of the *incipit* and *explicit* can be larger than average despite the fact that so many of them are relatively short. There are five positive z-scores higher than 2.0: the *incipit* of *La Fortune de Rougon*, *Le Ventre de Paris* and the *explicit* of *Le Ventre de Paris*, *Son Excellence Eugène Rougon* and *La Joie de vivre*. It would be impossible to have negative z-scores in that range because that would imply a sentence of, let us say, minus eight words long. The largest minus z-score is the −1.31 of the *incipit* of *La Conquête de Plassans* which is four words long.[22] Therefore the overall mean is skewed upwards on account of a small number of exceptionally long sentences. And so before we decide definitively that sentence-length is a significant stylistic feature of Zola's craft of fiction, we should quickly look at two other possible ways of measuring central tendency.

The median of a population is the score which divides that population into two equal halves. The median sentence-length for the population of 2,000 randomly chosen sentences is 16: in other words 50% of the sample consists of sentences of 16 words or fewer and 50% consists of sentences of 16 words or more. The mean sentence-length for the population was 20.14, but no single sentence can be of that length since a sentence-length clearly has to be a whole number. Medians are whole numbers whereas this is not necessarily the case with means. The median sentence-length for the *explicit* of the 28 novels is 20, because 14 of the novels have sentences of 19 words or shorter and 14 of the novels have *explicit* of 21 words or longer. Therefore the use of the median seems to confirm the original view that the *explicit* tends to be slightly longer than the norm: 20 compared with 16.

The other measure of central tendency is the mode, best seen in a histogram or bar-chart. The mode of a population is the score which occurs most frequently in that population. Like the median, but unlike the mean, the mode will always be a whole number. In Table 4 we see the histogram of sentence-lengths of the sample population of 2,000 sentences, with the alphabetical codes of the *explicit* of the 28 novels which concern us sited in the relevant bar, thus providing a second histogram to compare with the more general one. However the percentages given at the side of the table refer only to the histogram of sentence-lengths of the larger sample. The smaller histogram, which is conveyed by the vertical listings of the codes which designate the novels, is only provided so that general shape can be compared with that of the larger one.

From Table 4 we can see that, as far as the larger sample is concerned, the mode is situated in the bands of sentences of 6 to 10 and 11 to 15 words long, with over 40% of the population coming in these two bands. As far as the smaller sample is concerned, the *explicit* of eight novels come in these two bands but this only represents 28.6% of the total. In fact the smaller histogram is close to being bi-modal, with the major mode situated in the band 11 to 15 and a smaller one situated in the band 36 to 40.

We have measured central tendency in three different ways and in each case it appears that Zola had a preference for a more expansive *explicit* than the average sentence-length for the novels as a whole. We have seen too

Table 4   Histograms showing sentence-lengths in a sample taken from the *Rougon-Macquart* novels and those of the *explicit* of the 28 novels being examined

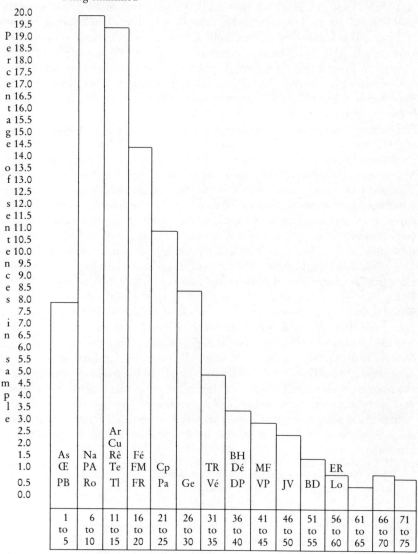

Sentence lengths (in groups of 5)

that he also usually preferred an even longer-than-average sentence for the *incipit*. Clearly the difficulties of opening and closing a narrative were not in most cases satisfactorily solved without recourse to a certain wordiness and when Zola did choose a curt *incipit* or *explicit* it therefore strikes the reader with even greater force. Using different statistical methods and with the aid of the computerized corpus at Nancy, Etienne Brunet also noted the tendency I have just described. Asking whether one might talk of 'une loi' or 'une habitude' on the part of Zola, Brunet concluded: 'Il y a donc l'indication d'une tendance. Zola raccourcirait sa phrase à l'intérieur d'un même texte.'[23]

The preponderance of monosyllabic words was confirmed by a straightforward count which showed that nearly two-thirds (65.6%) of the words used are in fact monosyllabic with a further 23.6% being of two syllables. This is not a significant stylistic feature of the *explicit*, however, for very nearly the same figures emerged from a random sample of other sentences. From Brunet's figures,[24] which show the average number of letter per word, it appears that Zola was absolutely typical of other novelists of his period in using words of 4.3 letters on average and one could assume that the majority of these would be monosyllabic.

There are occasions when Zola seemed to aim for an obvious musical effect, playing on the sonorities of certain sounds. One of the best examples is the final sentence of Part 1, Chapter 7 of La Débâcle: 'Le 7e corps entra dans Sedan, ivre de fatigue, de faim et de froid (*RM*, V, 534). Although this is not a standard feature of the *explicit* there are some effects which seem to be quite concious. For example the *explicit* of *La Bête humaine*, describing the driverless train racing through the night, contains nine sibilants; there are five examples of the phoneme /s/ ('sans', 'sourde', 'cette', 'ces', 'soldats') and four examples of the phoneme /ʃ/ ('lâchée', 'chargée', 'chair', 'chantaient'). The anger conveyed by the *explicit* of *Le Ventre de Paris* seems to be increased by the associations of the phonemes /g/ and /r/ in four of the last 17 words ('grosses', 'gorges', 'grondant', 'gredins'). Nearly one-third (five) of the 16 vowels contained in the *explicit* of *La Fortune des Rougon* are nasal vowels and create the effect of a bell, which not only reminds us of the tocsin which has sounded earlier but which is now perhaps the funeral bell tolling for the dead Silvère and the demise of republican idealism. In the final sentences of *Germinal* and *La Débâcle* Zola uses an internal rhyme based on repetitions of the phonic sequence /ɛR/: 'germait', 'germination', 'faire', 'terre' in *Germinal* and 'terre' coupled with 'refaire' in *La Débâcle*.[25]

In other *explicit* Zola creates some interesting rhythmic effects of which the most notable is that three of the final sentences could be regarded as alexandrines:

> 'L'a/mour est-il moins soui/llé, lui qui crée la vie?'
> 'Jeann(e), mort(e), re/stait seul(e) en fac(e) d(e) Pa/ris à ja/mais.'
> 'Des morts, des s(e)menc(e)s et le pain pou/ssait de la terr(e).'

At the lexical level one phenomenon which strikes the reader immediately is the fact that nine of the 28 *explicit* start with the banal conjunction *et*: three of the first five, four of the last seven, including each of the final three novels. In general Zola's choice of vocabulary for the *explicit* is an interesting blend of words which are amongst the most frequent in the *Rougon-Macquart* and words which he otherwise rarely used. Useful data on the 20 novels of the *Rougon-Macquart* and on *Thérèse Raquin* and *Madeleine Férat* are provided by Brunet. Each of the 22 novels is given a list of nine words (three nouns, three verbs and three adjectives) which are, from a statistical point of view, particularly characteristic of the novel in question. For *L'Assommoir* these are: 'zingeur', 'chapelier', 'blanchisseuse'; 'rigoler', 'pincer', 'croquer'; 'interne', 'établi', 'extérieur', and for *Germinal*: 'coron', 'fosse', 'mineur', 'crever', 'hurler', 'gifler'; 'gréviste', 'international', 'délégué'.[26] Not one of the 198 words listed by Brunet as characterstic of the 22 novels appears in any of the *explicit*.

Brunet's figures show that 84 nouns appear in the 22 novels with a frequency greater than 1,000. The ten most frequent nouns are, in decreasing order of frequency, 'femme', 'homme', 'heure', 'jour', 'main', 'yeux', 'fait', 'tête', 'coup', 'air' and six of these are to be found in the *explicit*: 'femme', 'homme', 'jour' (×2), 'main' (×3) 'yeux', 'air'. A further 21 of the most frequents nouns are found in the *explicit*: 'voix' (×2), 'enfant', 'maison', 'milieu', 'bras' (×2), 'fond', 'monde', 'père', 'vie' (×5), 'terre' (×3), 'cœur', 'pied' (×2), 'regard', 'dieu', 'bête', 'abbé', 'mois', 'sang', 'travail', 'ombre', 'salle'. This means that 27 of the 84 nouns (32.14%) which appear more frequently than 1,000 times in the novels also occur in the *explicit*. It is also surely not without interest that the noun which occurs most frequently in the *explicit* is 'vie'. A slightly smaller proportion of the most frequent adjectives appear in the final sentence for, of the 28 adjectives with a frequency greater than 1,000, we find eight (28.6%) in the *explicit*: 'grand', 'petit' (×2), 'nouveau', 'noir', 'mort', 'fort', 'gros', 'rouge'.

In all, slightly more than 21% of words used in the *explicit* are taken from the vocabulary which Brunet has demonstrated to be most typical of the *Rougon-Macquart*, but the final sentences also contain many words which were relatively rare in Zola's writing. The adverb 'diaboliquement' occurs only once in the 22 novels analysed by Brunet and that is in the *explicit* of *Madeleine Férat*. The noun 'parlementarisme' occurs only twice, and one of these occurrences is in the final sentence of *Son Excellence Eugène Rougon*. The noun 'germination' occurs only three times in all and its appearance in the *explicit* of *Germinal* is its only occurrence in that novel. The expression 'en friche' which occurs in the *explicit* of *La Débâcle* only occurs three times in all and only one of these three appearances is in *La Terre*. The verb 'se caillait', with which Zola ended *La Fortune des Rougon*, is its only appearance in that novel and only occurred four times in all. The *explicit* of *Rome* contains the noun 'holocauste' and yet despite Zola's often apocalyptic vision, this noun only occurs five times in the *Rougon-Macquart*. In terms of word-frequency the vocabulary of the *explicit* is thus an interesting blend of the characteristic and the uncommon.

Let us now examine the *explicit* in terms of the narrative voice employed, comparing this with the *incipit* and, where appropriate, with the figures obtained from our random sample of 2,000 sentences (see Table 5). I have divided sentences into four broad types: (a) those which consist entirely of the voice of the omniscient third-person narrator [N], (b) those which consist wholly or partly of the voice of one of the characters speaking directly [DS], (c) those which consist partly of the voice of one of the characters speaking indirectly [IS], and (d) those where the words of a character are conveyed in free indirect speech ('style indirect libre') [SIL]. The figures given are based on a very small sample and should therefore be treated with some caution, but the heavy use of free indirect speech in *L'Assommoir*, which seems curiously out of line with all the other figures, does correspond to some extent with the survey which Dubois reported in his monograph.[27] Using the statistical test to find the standard error of the samples and from this the confidence-limits of the averagees given in the Table, we clearly see that we must be wary of the figures given for the individual novels. Given that the standard error for the 32% of the sentences in *L'Assommoir* containing free indirect speech is 0.5, this means that we can only be 68% confident that the true figure lies between 37% and 27%, 95% certain that it lies between 42% and 22%, and 99% certain that it lies between 47% and 17%. The confidence-limits for the averages at the bottom of Table 5 are much stricter: we can for example be 99% certain that the true average of sentences which consist uniquely of the voice of the narrator lies between 60% and 54% since the standard error of this sample is 0.01.

Table 5   Proportions of different narrative voices used in the *Rougon-Macquart* novels

Novel	N	DS	IS	SIL	TOTAL
FR	61	25	10	4	100
Cu	60	24	13	3	100
VP	57	32	5	6	100
CP	49	45	4	2	100
FM	65	30	1	4	100
ER	56	35	4	5	100
As	40	25	3	32	100
PA	62	29	5	6	100
Na	50	34	5	11	100
PB	51	38	6	5	100
BD	54	28	6	12	100
JV	57	32	7	4	100
Ge	53	22	5	20	100
Œ	54	30	6	10	100
Te	60	25	2	13	100
Rê	76	19	3	2	100
BH	60	29	2	9	100
Ar	56	30	6	8	100
Dé	57	23	6	14	100
DP	63	21	5	11	100

Averages

	57.0%	28.8%	5.2%	9.0%	100%

For some nineteenth-century French novelists, the Goncourt brothers for example, it was an almost standard practice to begin the narrative by plunging *in medias res* with an initial dialogue. Zola clearly did not favour this device for he consistently employed the voice of the omniscient narrator for the *incipit* of every one of the 28 novels under discussion. But this uniform technique was not carried over into the *explicit* as we can see in Table 6. We

Table 6   Narrative voice employed in *explicit*

Novel	Narrative voice	Novel	Narrative voice
TR	N	Ge	SIL
MF	DS	Œ	DS
FR	N	Te	N
Cu	N	Rê	N
VP	DS	BH	N
CP	N	Ar	SIL
FM	DS	Dé	N
ER	DS	DP	N
As	DS	Lo	N
PA	N	Ro	N
Na	DS	Pa	N
PB	DS	Fé	N
BD	IS	Tl	N
JV	DS	Vé	N

note that in 16 of the 28 novels (57%) Zola used the voice of the narrator as the final voice we hear, and, as we saw in Table 5, this is probably very close to the percentage of sentences in the *Rougon-Macquart* series in which this voice is used. But we also observe a very distinct evolution, for in the early part of his career Zola seemed more content to leave us with the voice of one of the characters: Geneviève in *Madeleine Férat*, Claude in *Le Ventre de Paris*, Bazouge in *L'Assommoir*, the street crowd in *Nana*, Julie in *Pot-Bouille*, Chanteau in *La Joie de vivre*. The very last time that Zola used a character's voice to end a novel was in *L'Œuvre*, where it is Sandoz, a character who bears a close similarity to Zola himself, who concludes. From then on, with the exception of *L'Argent*, which ends with a reflexion in free indirect speed on the part of Madame Caroline, who is another character thought to be strongly based on Zola himself, he ended his novels exactly as he began them with the voice of the narrator. I will return to this question later when examining the types of discourse being employed.

Rarely is it the voice of the protagonist which is heard, although in many cases this would not be possible since the protagonist is dead before the *explicit*. But even where this is not the case Zola normally allowed another character to say the last word. In *Germinal*, however, the only novel apart from *L'Argent* to end in free indirect speech, it is, one assumes, Etienne's reflexions which are being reported to us. And in *Au Bonheur des dames*, a rarity in the *Rougon-Macquart* in that it is a novel with a comparatively happy end, it is the voice of Octave Mouret which is reported to us indirectly.

The type of statement which is being made is nearly always an affirmative sentence. But in three cases, *L'Assommoir*, *Nana* and *L'Œuvre*, Zola ends with some sort of imperative statement. In *L'Assommoir* Bazouge's injunction to the dead Gervaise is deliberately couched in the language that would be employed to lull a child to sleep, and this device increases the poignancy of the ending. The jingoistic tone of the generalized imperative with which *Nana* ends jars with the reader's privileged knowledge about the outcome of the Franco-Prussian war. At the end of the novel Nana has metamorphosed into a symbol standing for the soon to-be-destroyed Second Empire rather than being one of the elements which has provoked its downfall. At the end of *L'Œuvre* Sandoz enjoins himself and Bongrand to return to work, and on the surface this imperative underlines the importance of continuing the struggle.

To end a novel with a question would seem to be the equivalent of ending a piece of music with an imperfect cadence, and yet Zola did end one novel, *L'Argent*, with an interrogative. We note however that the question is in fact a rhetorical one which Madame Caroline silently poses herself; it scarcely requires an answer and is, in any case, a recollection of a question which Saccard had posed her earlier in the novel. The repetition of the same question in the final sentence implies that Madame Caroline has now come to terms with the positive as well as the negative aspects of the capitalist system. Despite the fact that *La Joie de vivre* ends with the verb–subject inversion which characterizes the interrogative, Chanteau's 'Faut-il être bête pour se tuer' is an exclamation rather than a question.

The question of narrative closure is not confined to the *explicit*, but clearly the last sentence of a work of fiction plays an important role in closure and I now wish to examine the *explicit* in relation to that question. As a work reaches its conclusion or peroration the author will frequently look for a sentence which, to some extent, encapsulates what has gone before. It might therefore be interesting to see how frequently Zola used part or all of the title of a novel in its *explicit*, since the title is also an attempt to encapsulate as much of the meaning of the novel into a short syntagm. The most obvious example is *La Terre*, where the last two words of the *explicit* happen to be the title of the novel. The *explicit* of *La Bête humaine* contains the phrase 'en bête aveugle' and the words 'Paris' and 'vérité' occur in the last sentences of the novels which bear those titles. But there are also more oblique references to the title in other novels. For example, although the word 'ventre' does not occur in the *explicit* of *Le Ventre de Paris*, we do find 'dîner', 'gorge' and 'ceinture'. The last word of the *explicit* of *La Joie de vivre* is 'tuer' and other words used in the final sentence which contrast stongly with the title are 'misérable', 'lamentable', 'douleur' and 'hurler'. The *explicit* of *Germinal*, although containing no occurrence of that word, has 'germait' and 'germination'. Finally there is a clear semantic relationship between the title *L'Œuvre* and the novel's final word 'travailler'.

Many critics have commented on Zola's frequent use of cyclical imagery and it is interesting to see to what extent the *explicit* has linguistic reminiscences of the *incipit*. The first novel of the *Rougon-Macquart* cycle provides us with an excellent example. *La Fortune des Rougon* opens with a long description of 'l'aire Saint-Mittre' and it is with a brief but chilling cut away from the Rougons' celebration dinner party to a one-sentence description of congealing blood on a tombstone in the former graveyard that the novel concludes. *La Conquête de Plassans* opens with the terse 'Désirée battit des mains' and the image of hands is picked up in the *explicit* with 'Puis elle [Marthe] joignit les mains'. It is odd to notice that this became something of a leitmotif, for in the *explicit* of the following novel, *La Faute de l'abbé Mouret*, we have Désirée 'tapant des mains'.

The *explicit* of *L'Assommoir* forms an antithesis to the *incipit*, for Gervaise has now gone to her final 'sleep', whereas in the *incipit* she had fought sleep until 2 a.m. In the *incipit* of *Germinal* Etienne enters Montsou through 'les champs' at night; in the *explicit*, as he leaves Montsou, he muses about what is happening in 'les sillons'. In the first sentence of *La Terre* we see Jean using a 'semoir'; the *explicit* contains the words 'semences'. The phrase 'plaine fertile' occurs in the *incipit* of *La Débâcle* but the *explicit* refers to 'le champ ravagé'. *Le Docteur Pascal* opens in Pascal's 'salle' and there are references to 'chaleur' and to 'calme'; in the *explicit* we find ourselves in the same room which is 'tiède' and where the prevailing atmosphere is of 'paix solitaire'.

At the beginning of *Lourdes* the train full of pilgrims is leaving Paris and at the end of the novel it returns with the disappointed pilgrims uncured, although the *explicit* has changed into a different rhetorical key. In *Rome* we again begin and end with a long all-night train journey, whereas in *Paris* we look down on Paris from above in both the *incipit* and the *explicit*.

For a major part of his creative life Zola was engaged in writing novels which were part of three organized series and it is interesting to see whether he ever uses the *explicit* as a link or 'trailer' to another work. For example the *explicit* of *La Conquête de Plassans* contains a reference to Serge the protagonist of the next novel, *La Faute de l'abbé Mouret*. The *explicit* of *Paris* contains the words 'vérité' and 'justice' and the same words recur in *Vérité*, by which time *Justice* was the projected title for the following novel. In the *explicit* of *Fécondité* we have the phrase 'l'humanité en marche' reminding us of the title *La Vérité en marche*.

In a recent survey of the question of narrative closure, Armine Mortimer claimed that:

> La conception de la clôture narrative dépend souvent d'un sentiment satisfaisant que toutes les données du récit ont abouti à leur fin plus ou moins nécessaire, que les problèmes posés par la narration sont résolus, qu'aucun bout du fil narratif ne reste flottant, que les signes composant l'univers narratif sont épuisés, en somme, que ce qui a été ouvert est clos.[28]

She went on to suggest that Zola's closures were particularly 'closed' and left no further scope for the reader's imagination:

> C'est ainsi que Zola répondit au désir de *savoir* que Balzac décrivit si nettement. Il y a dans ses clôtures quelque chose de issi totalement épuisant, de si pleinement complet, de si définitivement clos, qu'on n'imagine rien au-delà.[29]

One assumes that Mortimer is principally concerned with the closure of the 'story' rather than of the 'narrative discourse' but nevertheless her view seems to me at times questionable and at some variance not only with the evidence provided by a close reading of Zola but also with the classification system which Mortimer herself used. For example one of her categories is called 'les fins-fils', a category defined as 'les dénouements caractérisés par la naissance d'un enfant couronnant l'œuvre'.[30] One cannot imagine a more 'open' closure than this and it is the one with which Zola chose to conclude the *Rougon-Macquart* series. Another of Mortimer's categories is 'la fin–commencement' and *Germinal* is cited as an example of this type of closure: 'Ainsi *Le Père Goriot* se termine sur un acte plein d'avenir, et *Germinal* incorpore une velléité de commencement, de redémarrage, dans ce qui semble se terminer sur un échec.'[31]

This is not to say that there are no examples of particularly 'closed' endings. In the *explicit* of *Thérèse Raquin* for example the narrator describes the all-but-dead Madame Raquin feasting her eyes on the corpses of the murderers of her son. The *explicit* of *L'Assommoir* consists of Bazouge's short phrase as he cradles the dead body of Gervaise. The finality and infinity of death is underlined by the last two words ('à jamais') of the *explicit* of *Une Page d'amour* and nothing seems left to be said after the final sentence of *Le Rêve* where the narrator recounts, without sadness but with a note of sentimentality, the death of Angélique.

The genuinely happy end is something of a rarity and the only clear example seems to be *Au Bonheur des dames*, which ends with Octave Mouret deciding to marry Denise. Interestingly it is the only *explicit* amongst those I am examining which contains a substantial amount of indirect speech. It is of course open to the reader's imagination to wonder whether this story really does have a happy ending, for Octave Mouret's past record as a womanizer and adulterer might not necessarily make the reader particularly confident about the future of the relationship.

Very occasionally Zola would choose a cold, factual statement as his *explicit*. The best example of this technique is *La Curée* in which we are given the figure of Renée's debt to the couturier Worms. A similar example, although this time with clear emotive connotations, is the final sentence of *La Fortune des Rougon*.

A very frequent technique which Zola used in the earlier novels, particularly in those where the *explicit* is wholly or partly a direct account of the words of a character, is the epigrammatic final statement or what Mortimer called 'le "tag line" ou la clôture épigrammatique' and which she described as follows: 'Nous appelons "tag line" une seule phrase faisant paragraphe à la fin du text et où se concentre toute la force clôturale.'[32] In the case of *Le Ventre de Paris* and *Pot-Bouille* a character reveals, in one short and angry phrase, a hostile attitude to the bourgeoisie. In *L'Assommoir*, Bazouge's soothing words remind us of the title and suggest a form of oblivion from the sheer drudgery and meanness of working-class life different from that induced by drink. The anguished cry at the end of *La Joie de vivre* contrasts in an almost blackly comic way with the optimism of the title and allows for a range of possible interpretations by the reader. Clorinde Balbi's succinct statement of her admiration for Eugène Rougon's energy despite her opposition to his political position gives us the *explicit* to *Son Excellence Eugène Rougon*. The only epigram which is conveyed to us in free indirect speech is Madame Caroline's reflexion on the similarity between the workings of capitalism and the sexual act, a reflexion which poses as much of a paradox for her as it seemed to pose for Zola, tugged as he was between his naturalist's approval of the act of procreation and his socialistic leanings on the one hand, and his puritanical distaste for the sexual act and fascination with social-Darwinism on the other.

Towards the end of his career Zola seemed to develop a taste for endings where the narrative voice became markedly oratorical and the language used was of a particularly abstract type. The *explicit* of *Paris*, *Fécondité*, *Travail* and *Vérité* are all to some degree characterized by the vague clichés which are not uncommon in a political discourse and this style has already been seen in the final sentence of *La Débâcle*. In these closures Zola foresaw the apotheosis that awaited society in the twentieth century when science and rationalism would have pushed back the frontiers of ignorance and superstition.

The apotheosis however must frequently be preceded by the apocalypse and in a number of Zola's novels the ending is clearly apocalyptic. One of the earliest examples is in *La Conquête de Plassans* but they become more common later in the *Rougon-Macquart* series in novels such as *Nana*, *Germinal*, *La Terre*, *La Bête humaine*, *L'Argent*, *La Débâcle* and *Lourdes*. For Frank Kermode the narrative version of the apocalyptic myth is merely part of man's way of making sense of the world: 'The apocalyptic types - empire, decadence and renovation, progress and catastrophe - are fed by history and underlie our ways of making sense of the world from where we stand, in the middest.'[33] It is interesting to note that Zola used a degree of poetic licence to create the ending of *La Bête humaine*, for our imagination is left to create the final catastrophe of the driverless train despite the fact that Zola had been informed that the locomotive would probably have lost power as the fire under its boiler subsided and so would gradually come to a rather anti-climactic rest.

But one of the most characteristic endings that Zola used mainly but not entirely in the novels from the second half of the *Rougon-Macquart* series onwards is the closure in which the discourse ends on a note of hope although the story has ended with sad or even tragic events and in which humanity has been overwhelmed by events rather than been able to control them. Perhaps the first time that Zola used this device was in *La Faute de l'abbé Mouret* where the last sentence recounts the excited arrival of Serve's mentally retarded sister Désirée to tell him that the cow has calved. This clear contrast between the scene, the burial of Albine, and the diction, the words of Désirée, becomes almost a commonplace in many of Zola's *explicit* and it is interesting to note that many of his novels actually have a cemetery as the final setting of the novel but that, in most but not all cases, Zola found some final word of comfort. Novels which end with such a positive statement include *La Faute de l'abbé Mouret*, *La Joie de vivre*, *Germinal*, *L'Œuvre*, *La Terre*, *L'Argent*, *La Débâcle*, *Le Docteur Pascal*, *Rome* and the three novels of the *Quatre Evangiles*.

There is nothing particularly original in this technique. In the words of Kermode: 'the pairing of decadence and renovation, the apocalyptic end as beginning, are old subjects. Wastes can blossom.'[34] And Lewis Kamm saw these 'open' endings as evidence that Zola's view of time was not, as some critics argue, essentially circular, but rather that it was clearly linear:

> Such works as *Germinal*, *La Terre*, and *La Débâcle* end on optimistic notes, not because they present the beginning of a new cycle, inevitably condemned to repeat the previous one, but because they present a beginning, or, if one prefers, a transition to something else. The novel's endings are open because the linear time which is at the very heart of their form is itself infinitely open.[35]

They may also call into question an optimistic reading of the texts. The note of hope in *La Faute de l'abbé Mouret* is pronounced by a sub-normal child. The optimistic endings of *La Terre* and *La Débâcle* depend on the reader accepting the inevitability of war as a social counterpart to the survival of the fittest in Darwin's theory of evolution. The end of *Germinal* could be interpreted, on account of Zola's use of free indirect speech, as Etienne's attempt to justify to himself his leaving Montsou for Paris, since he is walking away from a situation which he has helped to create, leaving the miners who remain alive in a measurably worse position than they were when he arrived.

But one of the most problematical endings is created by the *explicit* of *L'Œuvre*. The setting is once again a cemetery, contrasting starkly with the final diction, the 'Allons travailler' of Sandoz. Life goes on or, perhaps more importantly, work goes on and here we seem to have Zola's version of the quantitative ethic which we later find in Camus's *Le Mythe de Sisyphe*. But only a few paragraphs previously Bongrand and Sandoz have been telling each other that they are both failures, constantly striving for but never achieving the unattainable goal of artistic perfection, and that Claude Lantier at least had the courage to admit this failure and to commit suicide. Sandoz concludes this earlier dialogue with the following words: 'Ma foi, oui. Puisque nous ne pouvons rien créer, puisque nous ne sommes que des reproducteurs débiles, autant vaudrait-il nous casser la tête tout de suite' (*RM*, IV, 363). Are we to believe then that, with his final 'Allons travailler', Sandoz is telling Bongrand and himself that they must return to their second-rate creations because, in the final balance, life is preferable to death, or are we to suspect that the statements about Claude's integrity and the praise of his suicide are in fact an understandable but insincere attempt to use language in order to soften the blow caused by a friend's untimely death?

In this study I have examined the *explicit* of Zola's novels in a number of ways in order to see whether a detailed analysis would shed any light upon one particular aspect of his craft of fiction, namely his technique of concluding a narrative. A detailed discussion of some of the characteristic linguistic features opened out on to the larger general question of how the *explicit* contributes to the narrative closure. But before we find ourselves tempted to use this evidence to decide such questions as whether the novelist presents us with a fundamentally optimistic or pessimistic world view, we would do well to remind ourselves that Zola's 'parting shots' are but part of the story.

NOTES

1. The term *explicit* has been chosen because it is an essentially neutral label for the final words of the narrative and leaves open for further discussion the status of this segment in terms of its rhetorical and narrative function. It also has the advantage of being in a neat structural relationship with the term *incipit* which is traditionally used to refer to the opening words of a text. I have chosen to define the *incipit* and the *explicit* more narrowly as the opening and closing sentences of a novel. In talking of the difficulties which the *incipit* and the *explicit* pose for the writer, I am clearly referring to forms of fiction which do not make use of the set formulae such as: 'Once upon a time'; 'And so they both lived happily ever after'; 'Il était une fois'; 'Il vécurent heureux et eurent beaucoup d'enfants'.

2. Philippe Hamon, 'Clausules', in *Poétique*, 24 (1975), 496.

3. I am treating *Pot-Bouille* as a compound lexeme, partly on the grounds that it is a hyphenated form, and partly on account of its nominal use in expressions such as *avoir pot-bouille chez quelqu'un*.

4. In seven novels (*La Fortune des Rougon, Le Ventre de Paris, La Conquête de Plassans, Son Excellence Eugène Rougon, Une Page d'amour, Au Bonheur des dames, La Joie de vivre*), which represent one quarter of the novels being examined.

5. *RM*, IV, 1758–9.

6. Letter to Van Santen Kolff (6 October 1889) quoted in *RM*, III, 1884.

7. Letter to Charles Chincolle (6 June 1885) quoted in *RM*, IV, 1379.

8. A. Welsh, 'Opening and closing *Les Misérables*', in *Nineteenth Century Fiction*, 33, (1978), 10.

9. For only two of the *incipit* of the *Rougon-Macquart* novels does Henri Mitterand provide us with alternatives: the replacement of 'trouble' by 'tumulte' in the first sentence of *Son Excellence Eugène Rougon* and two minor alterations to the first sentence of *La Débâcle*.

10. Jacques Dubois, 'Surcodage et protocole de lecture dans le roman naturaliste', in *Poétique*, 16 (1973), 491–8 (p. 492).

11. *Ibid.*, p. 493.

12. *Ibid.*, p. 491.

13. Philippe Hamon, 'Clausules', in *Poétique*, 24 (1975), 494.

14. Barbara H. Smith, *Poetic closure: a study of how poems end* (London, University of Chicago Press, 1968), p. 13.

15. P. Hamon, 'Clausules', in *Poétique*, 24 (1975), 506.

16. J. Culler, *Structuralist poetics* (London, Routledge & Kegan Paul, 1975), p. 263.

17. I.A. Richards, 'How does a poem know when it is finished?', in *Parts and wholes*, ed. D. Lerner (London, Macmillan, 1963), p. 172.

18. Each novel has been assigned a two-letter identification code which will be use in the statistical tables.

19. I am indebted to a number of works which have assisted me in the statistical analysis of style. These include Anthony Kenny's *The Computation of Style* (Oxford, Pergamon Press, 1982); Charles Muller's two works *Initiation aux méthodes de la statistique linguistique* (Hachette, 1973), and *Principes et méthodes de statistique lexicale* (Hachette, 1977); and Daniel Dugast's *La Statistique lexicale* (Geneva, Slatkine, 1980). I am also aware that Zola himself would have been amused that his work could be subjected to this type of statistical analysis, based on counting words and letters. The critic begins to feel like M. Vabre in *Pot-Bouille*: '"Ces chers enfants!" dit M. Josserand, absorbé, la voix tremblante, à M. Vabre qui, depuis le commencement de la cérémonie, s'occupait à compter les

cierges allumées, se trompant toujours, et reprenant son calcul' (*RM*, III, 148). An average is a method of expressing numerically a central tendency within a corpus. The first type of average which will be examined is the mean, which is arrived at by counting the scores of individuals, adding them cierges allumées, se trompant toujours, et reprenant son calcul' (*RM*, III, 148). An average is a method of expressing numerically a central tendency within a corpus. The first type of average which will be examined is the mean, which is arrived at by counting the scores of individuals, adding them together and then dividing by the number of scores in the sample. This type of average is what is usually symbolised in statistics by $\bar{x}$ or x-bar.

20. For the purpose of this statistical exercise a sentence has been defined as follows: a sequence of words where the initial word has an initial capital letter immediately preceded by a full stop, an exclamation mark, a question mark or three full stops ('les trois points de suspension') and which is terminated by one of those punctuation signs. This is admittedly arbitrary but it is based on objective criteria and since exactly the same ones have been applied to the sentences chosen at random it follows that a comparison between sentence-lengths of the *explicit* and of sentences in the larger corpus is more valid than would otherwise have been the case.

21. The z-score or 'écart réduit' is obtained by dividing the difference between the raw score and the mean by the standard deviation for that population. This allows for meaningful comparison and variance from the mean in different populations having different means and different standard deviations.

22. 'Désirée battit des mains' (*RM*, I, 899).

23. Etienne Brunet, *Le vocabulaire de Zola* (Geneva, Slatkine, 1985), I, 119.

24. *Ibid.*, p. 133.

25. I am grateful to Philip Walker for this insight.

26. Brunet, *op. cit.*, I, 432.

27. J. Dubois, *L'Assommoir: société, discours, idéologie* (Larousse, 1973), pp. 135–40.

28. Armine Mortimer, *La Clôture narrative* (Corti, 1985), p. 15.

29. *Ibid.*, p. 172

30. *Ibid.*, p. 19.

31. *Ibid.*, p. 29.

32. *Ibid.*, p. 21.

33. F. Kermode, *The Sense of an Ending* (New York, Oxford University Press, 1967), p. 29.

34. Frank Kermode, 'Sensing endings', in *Nineteenth Century Fiction*, 33 (1978), 154.

35. L. Kamm, *The Object in Zola's* Rougon-Macquart (Madrid, Turanzas, 1978), p. 73.

10

ZOLA AND THE LIMITS OF CRAFT

Robert Lethbridge

The preceding chapters of this book testify to what Colette Becker calls 'la liberté du constructeur'.[1] To explore Zola's fictional constructions is to be reminded that they are the product not only of a powerful imagination, but also of a properly strategic conception of the forms in which his particular vision can find expression. The preparatory *dossiers* of *Les Rougon-Macquart* give us privileged access to that premeditation. From sketch and outline to quasi-definitive shape, the plans speak of technical invention rigorously subordinate to the imperatives of narrative organization. What remains to be asked is the extent to which this deliberation is not merely transcended by the intuitive and the poetic. For it can also be suggested that Zola's novels themselves question the very efficacy of that craftsmanship, with implications beyond its exclusively literary operations.

L'Assommoir, for example, has rightly been seen as the text in which Zola comes closest to a euphoric staging of the craftsman at work.[2] Goujet is no ordinary blacksmith. The character is obviously inseparable from the modern incarnation of Vulcan (evoked in Philip Walker's conclusion) which occupies so prominent a place in Zola's work as a whole.[3] 'Maître du feu', as David Baguley writes, 'chaste et civilisateur, comme le forgeron antique, il incarne la mesure, l'harmonie, la science';[4] and 'l'art même', he adds, recalling the curious detail of Goujet's collection of 'gravures coloriées' in a room decorated with 'images du haut en bas', extracted from illustrated volumes with the equanimity with which he cuts rivets from metal (*RM*, II, 473-4, 529). From the autobiographical perspective adopted by John Lapp,[5] to the thematic resonance and rhythmical assimilation underlined by Auguste Dezalay,[6] there is widespread critical agreement that the figure of Goujet is implicitly associated with Zola himself. What has gone virtually unnoticed, however, is that, alongside Goujet's characteristically valorized forge, *L'Assommoir* presents us with another which is its inverted correlative. In their own 'atelier' lit up by a 'petite forge', the Lorilleux couple may indeed be engaged in what Naomi Schor terms 'une espèce d'alchimie obscène'.[7] That is not to deny that, with his sister's help, the 'chaîniste' elaborates a structure (the 'colonne') as painstakingly and as methodically as does Goujet with his 'martèlement continu'. In contrast to the latter, the labour results not in a functional shape wrought from impure material, but rather in a refined (if unpolished) abstraction devoid of both purpose and significance. 'Continuellement, mécaniquement', and with technical precision, Lorilleux's gold chain is extended in interminable repetitions, compelling rhymes without reason: 'cela avec une régularité continue, les mailles succédant aux mailles, si vivement que la chaîne s'allongeait peu à peu sous les yeux de Gervaise, *sans* lui permettre de suivre et de bien comprendre' (*RM*, II, 426; my emphasis). At one level this is doubtless yet further evidence of Zola's predilection for antithetical symmetries, an episode to be juxtaposed with Gervaise's admiration for Goujet's productive skills. But we would also do well to bear in mind Alain Pagès's remark (echoing Zola's own; *RM*, V, 1739) that 'le romancier du cycle pense par *enchaînements*', and the far-reaching consequences of his being 'tout entier pris dans cette mécanique'.[8] To do so is to superimpose on the heroic version of craftmanship, projected by Goujet, the possibly ironic mirror held up by the 'chaîniste', in which we can see reflected a more problematic self-representation of the Zola who had planned *La Chaîne des êtres*.

This book has tried to demonstrate the ways in which Zola's 'craft of fiction' manifests itself in an artistic practice consistent with his Goujet-like efforts to master an initially shapeless materiality. Philip Walker lists those 'goals' as 'unity, order, harmony, coherence, clarity, simplicity, solidity',[9] traditional aesthetic values given renewed urgency by the contrary contemporary movement of dissolving definitions. The organizing principles of Zola's creative work can thus be located in cyclical superstructures and microcosmic cycles, topographical categories and taxonomical frames, narrative 'blocs superposés' (*RM*, V, 1743) and the calculated distribution of combinatory effects. In his 'conscious artistry', the writer as craftsman can be metaphorically related to other pragmatic professions; he is, by turn, architect, military strategist, cartographer, *metteur-en-scène* and engineer. And if the last of these seems the most apposite it is because mastery of the world's complexity and apparent confusion presupposes an understanding of its workings. Zola's commentators accordingly have recourse to a language of analysis which mirrors his own, in which literary procedures correspond to those of the mechanical, rather than natural(ist), sciences. The terminology informs, of course, the very heading of Zola's 'Notes générales sur la *marche* de l'œuvre' (*RM*, V, 1742–5; my emphasis), his translation of biological heredity into 'le *mécanisme* de l'organisation'(*RM*, V, 1694), and his ambition to study 'le *mécanisme* intérieur' (*RM*, V, 1737) of a family. It is not surprising, therefore, that several of the essays in this book, in stressing the functional role of character and scene, refer us to Michel Serres's thermodynamic model, in which the entire *Rougon-Macquart* series is cast as a gigantic *machine*, emblematic of the nineteenth century's utilitarian experience and collective imagination.[10] In both literal and figurative terms, Lorilleux's 'mechanical' (artistic) activities have to be situated in this context; as does the Goujet ultimately unable to resist the efficiency of the 'fabrication mécanique' (*RM*, II, 535).

While it may seem purely a convenient verbal association, there are thus other reasons why this last essay should be largely devoted to *La Bête humaine* (1890), in which a machine, precisely, plays so central a part, and in which the 'mécanicien' offers us the most satisfying variant of the novelist as craftsman. The importance of *La Bête humaine*, within the development of Zola's novel-cycle, is undeniable. Not least in its ubiquitous title, it represents the culmination of preoccupations whose origins can be traced as far back as *Thérèse Raquin* over twenty years earlier.[11] For Jean Borie, 'c'est dans ce roman que se fait sentir de la façon la plus nette, la plus obsédante même, un besoin de formulation de ce que nous avons appelé l'anthropologie mythique des *Rougon-Macquart*'.[12] But it is not simply as a thematic *summa* and private catharsis that *La Bête humaine* can be considered as a turning-point in Zola's career. If some readers feel that never again would he write so good a story, it may also be because it is in this novel that he returns, for the last time, to the kind of plot-structure fashioned during his literary apprenticeship, here spun out to the limits of its possibilities. And it provides us with a fitting conclusion to this book, in so far as it brings into focus the vicissitudes of Zola's craftsmanship. For *La Bête humaine* not only displays that technical mastery characteristic of his art; in a sense, it also dramatizes it, foregrounding its self-generating imbrications in such a way that, as for Gervaise mesmerized by the 'chaîniste', elucidation is frustrated and omniscience denied. It is a text in which Zola's 'craft of fiction', taken to its limits, finds itself reflected in (as it were) the fictions of that craft.

Certainly Zola himself has done much to legitimize *La Bête humaine*'s emblematic status, In his preliminary notes for the series, the very phrasing of 'une famille qui s'élance vers les biens prochains, et qui roule détraquée par son élan lui-même' (*RM*, V, 1739) seems to anticipate *La Bête humaine*'s closing pages. And this is by no means the only metaphorical substitution awaiting concretization in its textual scenarios. But nowhere is Zola more explicit, in this respect, than in his thoughts on his future 'roman des chemins de fer': 'Je voudrais que mon œuvre elle-même fût comme le parcours d'un train considérable, partant d'une tête de ligne pour arriver à un débarcadère final, avec des ralentissements et des arrêts à chaque station, c'est-à-dire à chaque chapitre'.[13] Responding to the suggestive potential of such a *mise-en-abyme*, Auguste Dezalay has extended it all the way from the surrogacy of 'le héros de la répétition monté sur le coursier du progrès' to the significance of the 'régulateur' which controls both steam-engine and textual machine, setting them both in motion and yet ultimately unable to bring them to the closure of the 'débarcadère final'.[14]

Further justification for considering Jacques Lantier in this perspective might be found in those elements of his characterization which point to an oblique self-portrait of his creator. Living in the 'quartier des Batignolles', he also has something of Zola's moral rectitude, 'enfermé comme un moine au fond de sa cellule' and 'ne buvant pas, ne courant pas, plaisanté seulement par les camarades noceurs sur son excès de bonne conduite' (p. 1045).[15] Some years before Jean Borie's psychoanalytical focus on the underlying erotic obsessions of *Le Bête humaine*, F.W.J. Hemmings had drawn attention to the discreet way in which it 'transposes the emotional and moral "crisis" through which the author, by his own admission, was passing at the time'.[16] It should also be noted, however, that the former student of the 'école des *Arts* et Métiers' (my emphasis) is endowed with a properly novelistic talent. In imagining Roubaud's murder, 'ce canevas d'un drame qu'il arrangeait' (p. 1235), Jacques thereby appropriates the very inventive directions adopted (if eventually discarded) by Zola himself during the preparation of the novel.

As far as the figurative dimension of the machine is concerned, it could be argued that, in the same way as there are, in effect, two locomotives within La Lison - successively in and beyond its driver's control - so *La Bête humaine* contains two kinds of novel, the one obeying generic rules and the other outside its conventions.[17] And this doubling process is overlaid by the importance given (even in the *dossier*) to two *récits* within the story, firstly in the shape of Séverine's confession to her husband (in the opening chapter), and secondly the one she makes to her lover (in chapter VIII). While the former amounts to a conventional flash-back bringing the reader up to date, Séverine's later story-telling is afforded a significance inadequately explained by the psychological 'besoin de l'aveu' (p. 1194). Rather than being merely the narration of a drama, it can more profitably be considered as a drama of narrative itself.[18]

Critical guides to *La Bête humaine* tendentiously underline the formal coherence of its design. Evidence of authorial control takes as its starting-point the 'fusion si parfaite'[19] of the novel's twin subjects, the 'roman du crime' and the 'roman du rail'. Equally impressive is Zola's integration of action and description (through point-of-view), his correlation of individual moods and spatial determinants, and his synchronization of private destinies and public affairs. To this is added the symmetrical construction of his chapters, alternating narrative rhythms, and the repeated thematic and formulaic patterns responsible for the novel's overall unity. Such an achievement sits uneasily, of course, with Zola's declared ambition to write *La Bête humaine* 'sans art visible'.[20] But it does confirm the extraordinary care with which he planned his novel. And one has only to re-read its introductory chapter, which so brilliantly synthesizes the departure of the train and a complicated plot, to subscribe to the view that *La Bête humaine* is the product of a literary craftsman at the height of this powers. That view, however, may need to be qualified. We should not forget that when the train-compartment in which Grandmorin has been murdered is first inspected (by officials and reader alike), there is 'aucun désordre'; the initial impression is that 'tout semblait en place' (p. 1068). Only subsequently is there a growing awareness of the 'sang nauséabond', the hyperbolic and disproportionate 'mare si profonde, si large' at its centre. Similarly, the apparently ordered world of *La Bête humaine* deserves further investigation. Its 'incoherence', at the level of ideas, has already been the subject of critical reflection, most notably in Roger Ripoll's thesis that the contradictions of Zola's philosophical discourse can only be accommodated in the text's mythical dimensions.[21] It is a different matter altogether to highlight the imperfections of this 'perfect' novel, to underline its disorder, illogicality, implausibility and disintegrative dynamic.

The genesis of *La Bête humaine* is thus also doubly instructive. On the one hand, there is, as Ripoll puts it, a concentrated effort to 'déterminer l'enchaînement d'une intrigue criminelle de façon à disposer de motivations cohérentes et de circonstances vraisemblables'.[22] It remains true that its material realization, in the shape of Zola's work-notes, is deceptive. Indeed, all his preliminary *dossiers* largely disguise a process of composition of a less methodical kind. Its scholarly reconstruction is as positivist an exercise as Zola's own classificatory procedures for the benefit of posterity. Those include numbering and sorting systems, cross-reference and synthesis. It is still possible to glimpse the creative chaos behind the reconstituted chronology which fails to register a more haphazard *va-et-vient*. Even without the 'missing' drafts to which Alain Pagès refers,[23] the various stages of the preparation and the actual writing of *La Bête humaine* suggest a labour which is hardly consistent with the 'plume courante' Zola had intended it to be.[24] In his study of the novel's pre-history, Martin Kanes traces its fractured rhythms, its stops and starts, a four-month gap between November 1888 and February 1889, and changes of pace from regressive procrastination to vertiginous acceleration.[25] Rather than being as effortless as Goujet at his anvil, the construction of *La Bête humaine* may have more in common with Lorilleux's painful toil. Certainly its plot was elaborated with self-absorbed uncertainty. And in spite of countless reminders to himself to organize 'la marche très logique d'un bout à l'autre', Zola leaves much of it vaguely unexplained, right up to definitive plans which are never as definitive as the written page.

Nor does the text itself entirely function within those ordered constraints of rationality and logic encoded in the idealized Goujet. More to the point is that *La Bête humaine* can *only* work thanks to what Michel Serres calls 'le contre-ordre, du côté de la fantaisie, du hasard'.[26] This is not to reproach Zola, as contemporary critics did, for taking the novel into the realms of the literally incredible. Admittedly, it would not be difficult to do so, starting with the statistical improbability of Jacques being the only witness of Grandmorin's murder at the very moment the train emerges form a tunnel somewhere in Normandy, and finishing with the aptly named 'véritable miracle' (p. 1275) which allows the protagonist to crawl away, virtually unscathed, from La Lison's catastrophic accident. Rather than encouraging us to measure *La Bête humaine* against the criteria of the real, such incidents are simply a recognition that the novel *depends* on chance and coincidence, at the expense of its proclaimed 'logique' and internally consistent causality. What is more, such coincidences occur at crucial moments in a narrative which ingeniously synchronizes murderous thoughts and passing trains. Jacques and Séverine spontaneously conceive of eliminating Roubaud. Phasie and her daughter die within hours of each other. Cabuche comes across Séverine's corpse at exactly the same time as her husband. The house at the 'Croix-de-Maufras' takes this process beyond the contingent. For, at this crossing, *all* the novel's characters and plots inter-connect; it is the space of violation, illicit meetings, second honeymoons, murders and suicide; it is here that La Lison comes to rest in the snow; it is inevitable that it is here that it should crash.

This aspect of *La Bête humaine* alerts us to the *cracks* in Zola's fictional system, the underlying logical hiatus only compensated for by such necessary mechanisms. Topographically, as well as thematically, as Michel Serres has shown,[27] the novel exhausts the semantic variables of fissure and gap: tunnels and railway cuttings, viaducts and bridges over the void, the crumbling walls of the house in the 'trou reculé' (p. 1025) of La Croix-de-Maufras, holes in the ground and gashes in the flesh, tearing wounds, breakdowns and faults, interstices and intersections. And all this in a novel informed by the multiple structures of a railway network, with the precision of its technical organization, its rules and regulated timetables designed to ensure uninterrupted operation of linkage and interchange. That these artificial structures fail to do so is itself revealing. For it was Zola, we should remember, who set up the analogy between his work and 'le parcours d'un train'; and it can be argued that his encyclopedic machine comes to a shuddering halt when confronted by the dehumanized materiality which blocks its progress.

Its original 'destination' had surely been to 'tout voir'.[28] In marked contrast, the symptomatic optical experience of La Bête humaine is to peer vainly into the murk of a winter evening and political corruption, or to be blinded by driving snow and hallucinatory impulses. Even the locomotive's 'œil vivant de cyclope' (p. 1173) pierces the darkness only to enlarge it. If trains hurtle past 'dans un tel vertige de vitesse, que l'œil doutait ensuite des images entrevues' (p. 1047), their criss-crossing represents the blurring of boundaries and dizzying admixtures of what Zola calls 'le trouble du moment que je peins' (RM, V, 1739); in other words (also his own), the confusion of 'le mouvement moderne', the 'bousculade' of a generation whose displacement is enacted 'trop vite'. The territorial delineations of the railway-employees' apartments are eroded by another pot-bouille, in the 'débandade des deux mobiliers, mêlés, confondus, dans le transbordement' (p. 1242). Marital structures dissolve too, as does the compartmentalization of a train whose hierarchical distinctions are threatened by the 'bousculade' of 'des voyageurs de deuxième et même de troisième classe' (p. 1073). In the same way, the classificatory systems of scientific observation are ultimately unable to accommodate a reality subject to forces undermining the very processes of differentiation: 'toutes les faces se noyaient, se confondaient, comme semblables' (p. 1032).

Zola's awareness, in La Bête humaine, of this fallacy at the heart of his totalizing project may be gauged by looking at the mode of enquiry exemplified by Denizet, which is, as David Baguley notes[29] ('interestingly'), deconstructed. For if all the novel's characters subscribed to the dictum 'Faut voir clair, pour savoir' (p. 1075), the prime responsibility to provide such elucidation falls on the 'juge d'instruction [qui] vous aidera à voir clair dans tout ça' (p. 1075). To this end, Denizet assembles a 'dossier énorme' (p. 1082) supporting deductive practices which override its inner contradictions. 'Avoir surtout la logique de la déduction', Zola had written in the preliminary notes for the Rougon-Macquart series (RM, V, 1742), and his own dossiers constantly invoke it.[30] Preoccupied by the 'vraisemblable' (p. 1087), and bringing to his scientific methodology 'l'amour de son métier' and 'son amour de la vérité' (p. 1077), Denizet offers the reader perhaps the most ironic of all the self-portraits of the Zola who had declared that 'mes livres seront de simples procès-verbaux' (RM, V, 1744). The various hypotheses developed by the examining magistrate not only duplicate, but are drawn from, those adumbrated to no avail in the speculative plotting of La Bête humaine. His proceeding 'mathématiquement' (p. 1311) directly echoes Zola's 'en déduire mathématiquement tout le volume' (RM, V, 1742), subsequently articulated in the Preface to *La Fortune des Rougon* as 'le fil qui conduit mathématiquement d'un homme à un autre homme' (*RM*, I, 3). What Denizet constructs, with the aid of his 'documents' (p. 1083) and their technical vocabulary, is nothing less than a Naturalist edifice, 'un chef-d'œuvre de fine analyse, disait-on, une reconstitution logique de la vérité, une création véritable' (p. 1307). Creative it is, but the real truth, of course, it is not. That truth he dismisses as a mere 'roman' (p. 1314), making it doubly paradoxical that 'cette création de son intelligence' (p. 1116) should become, in the public domain, 'ce roman atroce qui hantait les imaginations' (p. 1315).

By reversing the conventions of the detective novel (the criminal is identified at the beginning and apprehended at the end only by his own confession), Zola ensures that the reader, far from being inscribed in an investigative progression, is the spectator of its empty patterns. Nor is Denizet's enquiry the only one in *La Bête humaine* viewed with such dramatic irony. Misard, for example, taunted (and then haunted) by his wife's *repeated* 'Cherche! Cherche!' (pp. 1245–6), is engaged in a similarly fruitless search which takes him, significantly, *round* in circles. That his movements, too, should be described as 'mécaniques' (p. 1282) may remind us of the Lorilleux of *L'Assommoir*. In a sense, therefore, the thematically seminal 'on aura beau inventer des mécaniques meilleures' (p. 1032) can refer not simply to the bestial drives which contradict the inventions of perfectibility. Denizet's 'mathematical' accretions are also negated. His equations cannot quantify the reasoning of the irrational. His confidence, however, that 'la vérité elle-même aurait semblé moins vraie, entachée de plus de fantaisie et d'illogisme' (p. 1311) is instructively misplaced. For, as it has been pointed out, these are the fracturing agents of a novel which points to pre-determined craftsmanship as an equally fallible instrument with which to explain the indeterminacy of human experience.

It is not only its characters who are subject to 'une désorganisation progressive' (p. 1160). Zola had always feared 'd'éparpiller l'intérêt, en ayant tant de buts'.[31] But the corresponding dislocations of *La Bête humaine* itself are only partly due to the heterogeneity which invalidates Guy Robert's typology of the Zola novel.[32] An essentially narrative disorganization surfaces after the accident of chapter X. It is after this climactic episode that the earlier precision of timetable references disappears and that coincidence and *ex post facto* justification bring destinies together in melodramatic intersections. Above all, it is here that one is aware of an accelerating 'enchaînement' which is simultaneous with the frenetic 'déchaînement' of unbridled men and machines. Martin Kanes has noted, in Zola's work-notes for *La Bête humaine*, such imaginative elaboration 'almost beyond his own control'.[33] Disarrangement is filtered, of course, through derangement. So that (to borrow Naomi Schor's remarks about *La Conquête de Plassans*) one could say of *La Bête humaine*, too, that 'la mise en scène de la folie *dans* le roman est accompagnée d'une mise en cause de la folie *du* roman'.[34]

There is no need to detail the thematic reflection of a decomposition consistent with earlier examples of indistinction and formlessness. It would embrace 'l'inextricable lacis des rails' (p. 1020), 'la complication des voies' (p. 1132) and the 'inextricable détours' (p. 1144) prefiguring Jacques's aimless physical and mental wanderings in the labyrinthine streets which merely bring him back to his point of departure. *La Bête humaine* undergoes a similar process of complication. F.W.J. Hemmings comments that its 'main theme became overgrown by a tangle of collateral ones'.[35] The text may suggest a more appropriate extended metaphor: 'les trois doubles voies qui sortaient du pont, se ramifiaient, s'écartaient en un éventail dont les branches de métal, multipliées, innombrables, allaient se perdre' (p. 997). For *La Bête humaine*'s 'network' of inter-connected story-lines leads not to the unravelling of a 'dénouement', but to a reworking of narrative threads in superimposed intricacies distinguished by their reduplicative effects. Its eight triangular structures,[36] underpinning a drama with at least twelve plots, take consummate craftsmanship well beyond discursive necessity. It is all the more extraordinary that this structuring principle should then spiral off into yet further repeated patterns of the novel we have already read. The belated amorous intrigues bringing together Henri Dauvergne and Séverine, Jacques and Philomène, and Séverine and Cabuche, inevitably usher in the possibility of infinitely re-transcribed homicidal scenarios: 'un meurtre n'avait pas suffi, [...]. Une autre, et puis une autre, et puis toujours une autre [victime]' (p. 1326). So inordinate a narrative dynamic seems inadequately accounted for by the protagonist's own movement from equilibrium to (psychological) disorder. *La Bête humaine* itself 'goes off the rails'.

In doing so, it is not unlike those other nineteenth-century works in which Nathaniel Wing detects 'the rhetoric of mastery [...] violently displaced by the unfathomable rhetoric of madness'.[37] The former consciously encompasses circle and cycle, as the master-narrative of *Le Docteur Pascal* ('bouclant le boucle') would finally be 'l'anneau du serpent qui se mord la queue' (*RM*, V, 1569). Zola's reflections on his craft lay a similar stress on 'la logique [des] chapitres se succédant, [...] se *mordant* l'un l'autre' (*RM*, V, 1743; my emphasis); and the Preface to *La Fortune des Rougon* boldly announces that the entire novel-series 's'agite dans un cercle fini' (*RM*, I, 4). The closure of *La Bête humaine*, on the other hand, which caused Zola such anguish during its preparation, is not only deferred by its 'open ending'. It is almost denied in the *refrains* which accompany the driverless train's onward charge. Unable to proceed towards a desired revelation, the explanatory project is thereby deprived of its teleological impetus. Instead of the resolution of an enigma, we have its endless re-enactment. In other words, repetition is divested of its relational function of assuring intelligible sequence by recall. Narrative sequentiality, as much as descriptive segmentation, doubles back on itself in anaphoric echoes. The 'parcours' of the novel makes *aller* and *retour* synonymous, so that the *circulating* trains on the Paris line lead to the 'haven' of Le Havre only to return, with an appropriate turn-*around* in *Rou*en (where Denizet's constructions go round in circles too, and where the trial is less a turning-*point* than a new departure). Zola had described *La Bête humaine* as a work with smoothly integrated cogs, 'dont les rouages nombreux mordent profondément les uns dans les autres'.[38] But after a textual journey intended to take this machine 'd'une tête de ligne' to its other end, Pecqueux and Jacques, relinquishing their control, are 'entraînés sous les roues par la réaction de la vitesse', and are found 'sans tête, sans pieds' (p. 1330). There are, in fact, fewer 'arrêts' than 'recommencements', and there is never a 'débarcadère *final*'. Apparent progression reveals itself as narrative digression, propelled not by the 'logic' of causality but by the reiterative incantation of associative resonance. Both text and locomotive are liberated from that logic: 'la machine, libre de toute direction, roulait, roulait toujours [...], comme affolée de plus en plus par le bruit strident de son haleine' (p. 1330).

It is in that 'mad proliferation of textuality'[39] that, as Harry Levin put it some years ago, Zola is 'not the mechanical monster he set out to be in his obiter dicta'.[40] This is now the most familiar of critical positions, whereby the 'liberation' (from Naturalist theory) gives La Bête humaine a poetic unity which transcends logical coherence, not least in the power of its metaphorical disfigurement of the real. Like La Lison's driver, it is a product of 'art(s)' *and* 'métier(s)', and its deforming 'subites pertes d'équilibre' (p. 1043) are themselves responsible for Zola's achievement in conveying (if not explaining) the destabilized experience of his age. That success doubtless has its source less in craftsmanship than in an inspiration the writer habitually rejects, the unscientific Romantic legacy fortuitously confronted in his documentary work-notes for the novel: 'l'âme de la machine est dans les tiroirs. Cela dépend du mystère de la fabrication'.[41]

That is not to say, however, that La Bête humaine reflects the ideal of Goujet as 'un homme magnifique au travail'.[42] His 'science réfléchie' is described as 'le jeu classique, correct, balancé' which has much in common with Denizet's 'enquête judiciaire classiquement menée' (p. 1079). And his creative status may need reassessment in so far as his 'volées régulières' and 'précision rythmée' result in a circular shape, 'polie, nette, sans une bavure, un vrai travail de bijouterie, une rondeur de bille faite au moule', which displays the same structural perfection as Lorilleux's artefact, fundamentally different only in its lack of finish(ing) (in both senses of the word). With his 'bras sculptés qui paraissaient copiés sur ceux d'un géant, dans un musée', Goujet is associated with the anachronistic culture aligned in the Louvre, peopled by 'copistes' and its 'colosses de pierre, les dieux de marbre noir muets dans leur raideur hiératique'. Such statuesque forms are at odds with the modern world of the 'rue *Neuve* de la Goutte d'Or' (my emphasis), so much so that ordered corridors and rectilinear spaces become labyrinthine chambers echoing with the 'vacarme énorme' of the characters' disrespect for institutional rules, social conventions and a mandatory chronologically sanctioned closure. It is Goujet's *rivalry* with the 'unpolished' Bec-Salé which may tell us more about the 'mystère de la fabrication' of La Bête humaine. For this master-craftsman's organically rhythmical control, so often identified with Zola's own, is less impeded (as Dezalay asserts)[43] by Bec-Salé's intoxicated rage, than complemented by it. The latter forges a deformed object, not destined to capture the affection of the sentimental (Gervaise), but nevertheless 'se sentait une sacrée force de machine à vapeur', as, indeed, the pounding wheels of the train in La Bête humaine are equally explicitly likened to 'des volées de marteau sur l'enclume' (p. 1200). To read that Bec-Salé 'sautait du sol comme emporté par son élan' may be an unlikely reminder of Zola's notorious characterization of his art as 'le saut dans les étoiles sur le tremplin de la vérité exacte'. But just as Denizet's enumerated 'preuves classiques' (p. 1115) cannot accommodate gaps in his scored system, so Goujet's aggregated 'musique claire' is a 'menuet ancien' compared to Bec-Salé's dynamically unfinished 'chahut de bastringue'. *La Bête humaine*, conducted with the 'élan' of its 'piano endiablé' (p. 999), introduces a similar discordant note, difficult to reconcile with the orchestration of a classic Naturalist work.

Bec-Salé's salacious mouthings, disrupting the idyllic harmonies of 'la Gueule d'or' (as Goujet is known), are not his only impurity. His blackened teeth and 'sa cotte et son bourgeron sales', as opposed to the 'propreté nue et recueillie' of both the Louvre and Goujet's room and person, are reflected in the material filth which the Lorilleux work with, inhabit and incarnate. To the extent that this is the very modernity of which Zola's novels are made, one might be tempted to see here an ironic response to the charge of 'la littérature putride' of which he was deemed to be so scabrous a practitioner. Certainly *La Bête humaine* was not designed to spare its readers' sensibilities. It was to be 'un drame violent à donner le cauchemar à tout Paris',[44] and its morbid eroticism is taken to lengths almost consciously provocative. Zola described it as a 'monstre'.[45] It is equally 'monstrous' in other ways, both in its generic adulteration and disproportionate effects. For *La Bête humaine* has a brazenness and manic energy which is very different from Goujet's forceful innocence and quietude. As desecrating as the latter's opposition, and informed, at every level, by criminality, deviance and transgression, the novel is energized by its infraction of those Naturalist laws which appropriate Nature into perfect intellectual systems. Its plot depends, as we have seen, on the running-boards which allow displacement between classified compartments, on Roubaud being summoned to Paris for breaking regulations, on the malfunctioning of apparatus and the misunderstanding of personnel. Its integration is a function of accidents which are the obverse of reason. The 'mathematics' of *La Bête humaine* include the statistical illogicality of 'la passion du jeu' (p. 1216) responsible for Roubaud's disintegration, that same 'hasard' which has Flore jump right rather than left, out of the path of the oncoming train. The creative process involved in such imaginings may also have arbitrary, as well as inspirational, origins. For Zola's novel, like its monstrously anthropomorphic locomotive, is a product of another 'jeu' which is the free play of the writer's imagination.

Its 'liberation' from textual taxonomy is perhaps inevitable, given Zola's intention to give *La Bête humaine* 'un côté de mystère, d'au-delà, quelque chose qui ait l'air de sortir de la réalité'.[46] A parenthetical 'force inconnue, à trouver' speaks of a lacuna, both epistemological and inventive, which haunts Zola's project from the beginning. For not the least of the 'bavures' in his own system is the 'mystère' (p. 1072) not only unamenable to the dictates of reality, but also beyond a dictation which would record the all-seeing diagnosis of the 'romancier expérimental'. A number of the many titles Zola considered for *La Bête humaine* may suggest the limits of that enterprise, and are only compatible with the omniscience of the novelist-as-scientist if they anticipate understanding *in the end*: 'En route pour', 'le meurtre incompréhensible', 'sans motif', 'sans cause', 'sans raison', 'ce qu'on ne voit pas', 'd'où vient le crime', 'l'obscure origine'.[47] The last of these tentative inscriptions confirms Peter Brooks's general remarks on the anxiety about origins which characterizes the 'golden age' of nineteenth-century narrative explanations.[48] Rather than overcoming that anxiety, however, *La Bête humaine* encodes it. Roger Ripoll has called the novel 'un roman de l'inconnu'.[49] The thrust of the present essay is that it is, precisely, its '*unfathomable*' rhetoric (to underline Wing's term) which allows us to substitute the 'unknowable' for the merely predicated 'unknown'. Séverine is not the only one for whom writing serves less to elucidate the mystery than to deepen it: 'elle tenait la plume, mais sa main tremblait, sa peur s'augmentait de tout l'inconnu, que creusaient devant elle ces deux simples lignes' (p. 1021).

If there is re-enactment rather than resolution it is because for Zola as much as for Denizet, 'la grande clarté centrale, la cause première, illuminant tout, manquait' (p. 1079). Without that recuperable certainty, *La Bête humaine* spins around the 'grand Pourquoi'[50] at its centre. The indictment of the perpetrator (as well as the originating cause) is itself indicted by 'une *tournure* de plus en plus mystérieuse' (p. 1073; my emphasis). And cognitive frustration engenders compensatory narrative 'enchaînements', as self-sufficient for Jacques as for the examining magistrate:

> Comment? à la suite de quelles circonstances? Poussée par quelle passion ou quel intérêt? Il s'était posé ces questions sans pouvoir clairement les résoudre. Pourtant, *il avait fini par arranger une histoire*: le mari intéressé, violent, ayant hâte d'entrer en possession du legs; peut-être la peur que le testament ne fût changé à leur désavantage; peut-être le calcul d'attacher sa femme à lui, par un lien sanglant. *Et il s'en tenait à cette histoire*, dont les coins obscurs l'attiraient, l'intéressaient, *sans qu'il cherchât à les éclaircir* (p. 1121; my emphasis).

The text is punctuated (literally) by the extraordinary prevalence of interrogatory silences, irrationally filled in the absence of reason: 'Tant de bonnes raisons lui conseillaient le silence! Et les mots étaient inconsciemment sortis de ses lèvres' (p. 1075). So, too, the unanswered questions generate unending stories, as the creation of images resists an encroaching blindness.

This is true of both the experience of its characters and the structures of *La Bête humaine*. While the former look backwards 'pour savoir' (p. 1023), the novel's explanation of irrational human behaviour takes the shape of former episodes repeated. These two levels are brought together in chapter VIII, almost entirely occupied by Séverine's 'long récit',[51] mentioned earlier as primary evidence of the novel's self-reflecting strategies. The chapter has certainly earnt enough critical admiration to repay the amount of work Zola devoted to it.[52] But it should also be seen in the context of Peter Brooks's highlighting of narratives which have 'embedded' within them the principles of their functioning. This episode, which takes place in *bed* and takes story-telling and 'une nuit d'amour' (p. 1190) to consummation in synchronic progression, is surely an exemplary case of his notion of 'narrative desiring'![53] It unfolds in a claustrophobic space characteristic of the novel's topography and, in particular, in the very same room in which *La Bête humaine* opens. The first story there is recalled (p. 1190), retold (p. 1196), and continued (p. 1192) to the familiar accompaniment of the 'branle sourd' of the piano downstairs, so that even the same furnishings 'contaient l'histoire tout haut' (p. 1194). As these are a formless 'débandade' (p. 1193), so the novel's drama of blindness is replayed in the feeble light finally extinguished.

'Quand on se couche, on n'a pas besoin de voir clair' (p. 1190) ironically echoes all its elucidatory quests.

Séverine's story exactly mirrors what we described as the 'two novels' within *La Bête humaine*. On the one hand, it is beautifully crafted: it is introduced in such a way as to provoke the maximum amount of curiosity in the listener (pp. 1194–5); the modulation of tenses (from perfect to past historic) embraces the immediacy of dialogue and *style indirect libre*; recounted action is interspersed with the background movement of passing trains; the telling has pauses (p. 1198) and changes of pace and tone (pp. 1200–1); there is 'la montée ardente de ce long récit' (p. 1204), heightening tension by interruption, up until the point when Séverine 'avait hâte de finir' (p. 1202). With its revelation of motives more complex than had been apparent (p. 1196), it is a narrative such as Zola had hoped *La Bête humaine* might be: 'du récit simplement'.[54] On the other hand, Séverine's too has an inner momentum in the superimposed 'besoin de tout dire à son amant, de se livrer toute' (p. 1192). The long-dormant, but tormenting, 'besoin de l'aveu' (p.1194) brings words to her lips 'malgré elle', and the 'excitation croissante' and 'fièvre heureuse' (p. 1192) are an uncontrollable 'plaisir' (p. 1196). And both her body and her story are inscribed in the repeated 'désir éperdu d'être reprise' (p. 1195). For one effect of her explanation is to make Séverine even less understandable than before, 'maintenant impénétrable, sans fond, de cette profondeur noire dont elle parlait' (p. 1199). Another is that Jacques feels as little 'soulagement' as Roubaud had done on listening to her the first time (p. 1017). He asks for it to be re-told (pp. 1204–5) and then, taking over the role of story-teller in 'une activité cérébrale prodigieuse' (p. 1206), tells it back to himself over and over again, 'vingt fois, trente fois': 'la même hantise recommençait, les mêmes images défilaient, éveillant les mêmes sensations. Et ce qui se déroulait ainsi, *avec une régularité mécanique*' (p. 1206; my emphasis) is, of course, the same story. Because progressive elucidation of the fathomless is always denied, he turns inwards to his own *un*avowable past, generating yet further repetitions of this scenario, imagining the identical murder of Séverine and then various substitutes he follows round the streets, before returning to the significantly named *impasse* Amsterdam where the chapter and the novel had begun.

In the same way, *La Bête humaine* takes us not to an end but to a repeated beginning. It is emblematic, in this sense, of Zola's entire literary project. It was to be, he had admitted to himself, 'quelque chose de pareil à *Thérèse Raquin*'.[55] More important, however, is that each of the *Rougon-Macquart* novels *appears* to extend our knowledge by taking us further along the series. But, up until the composition of *La Bête humaine*, most of them could be considered as simply a re-enactment of the vision of Man articulated in its opening frame. To argue that his novel of 1889 coincides with Zola's recognition of the obstacles in the way of forward-driving ambitions to record 'la vérité humaine' in his textual machine,[56] is to see reflected in its literal and figurative 'impasses' the symbolic Impasse Saint-Mitre of *La Fortune des Rougon*, subtitled, it should be remembered, 'Les Origines'. Denizet's 'vérité', too, is based on an imaginary construct which leads 'logically' to a false conclusion. 'Vision', in *La Bête humaine* is equated with hallucination rather than insight: 'Avait-il bien vu? et il hésitait maintenant, il n'osait plus affirmer la réalité de cette vision, [...]. Ce n'était sans doute qu'une imagination' (p. 1047). If the novel registers a doubt that it may be no more than such 'songeries confuses', it is because it is deprived of that nineteenth-century narrative authority which grounds fiction in fact.[57] The referential illusions of its texture, from contemporary politics and steam-engines to the outbreak of the Franco-Prussion War, may be documented. But *La Bête humaine* relies on an essentially *mythical* scenario as its 'cause première'. In a textual gap which leaves unexplained how Jacques managed to return from his labyrinthine wanderings, geographical and historical co-ordinates are sucked into the 'gouffre noir' of the 'néant, où il n'y avait plus ni temps ni espace, où il gisait inerte, depuis des siècles peut-être' (p. 1212). Such an atemporal fabulation is the prolix master-plot of *La Bête humaine*, played out in 'la première tromperie au fond des cavernes' (p. 1297) and captured in the *verbal* resonance of Zola's *invented* title.[58] Legitimizing the fictions substituted for the unknowable, that universalizing thematic matrix is the only recuperable signal at the heart of the novel's darkness. 'In the beginning' of its fictional world there may be *only* words, the 'sans fond' of its re-presentation. And, in the *aller–retour* of its textual proliferation, the explanation of true origins is not retrospectively illuminated by fictional endings, but endlessly re-inscribed in originating fictions.

The 'parcours' of *La Bête humaine* rewrites a mythical, rather than scientifically verifiable, version of reality; it is thus a perversion of Naturalist discourse as programmatically conceived by Zola himself, 'désobéissant aux signaux' (p. 1162), so that when the train is blocked 'l'ordre naturel était perverti' (p. 1176). Such waywardness restores to the subsequent 'libre de toute direction' its necessary ambiguity. For *La Bête humaine* is less deconstructive than doubting. Its dysfunction posits, but does not go as far as, the verbal delirium which turns Coupeau into a 'machine à vapeur' at the end of *L'Assommoir* (*RM*, II, 791). What needs to be underlined is a doubling process which goes beyond that represented by Goujet and Bec-Salé. For sterile mechanics and creative madness are interchangeable terms when the latter's 'sautant d'un air de singe' is that of Lorilleux's 'vivacité de singe' (*RM*, II, 532, 424), and when Goujet's scientifically regulated rhythms are reflected in Jacques's hallucinatory ones. Séverine's cathartic story-telling and her lover's narrative regeneration, which is also 'affolant' (p. 1206), are as undifferentiable in their embrace (p. 1244) as the 'étreinte' (p. 1330) which binds together the reversible order and disorder of Jacques and Pecqueux. The piano's music is 'endiablé' because it is not so much counterpointed as played by two sets of hands superimposed.

Craftsmanship and its limits are just as closely aligned. Even in describing *La Bête humaine* as the most carefully crafted of his novels, Zola clings to an ideal of 'logic' and integrated imaginative elaboration: 'Je suis très content de la construction du plan, qui est peut-être le plus ouvragé que j'aie fait, je veux dire celui dont les diverses parties se commandent avec le plus de complication et de logique'.[59] This essay has tried to show how such a synthesis breaks down. And, even allowing for 'le mystère de la fabrication', it is not difficult to see why this should have been the case. As Henri Mitterand remarks, *La Bête humaine* is exceptional in placing such a burden on the mechanics of the novel, thus reversing the priority of general idea over plotting.[60] If to do so was incompatible with the Naturalist subordination of *inventio* to mimesis, the self-generating fictions further undermine that theoretical position. Not as much, however, as the enforced chronological and spatial re-arrangement of the *Rougon-Macquart*'s (published) genealogical tree in order to insert a protagonist consistent with those creative (in)directions. Zola's belief in heredity had always been relegated to the internal coherence of this 'tree of Knowledge'. With its vertebral column and branches not unlike the 'embranchements' of *La Bête humaine*'s,[61] here was yet another systematization now (publicly) revealed as arbitrary. The substitution of the newly invented Jacques for Etienne has no consequences for the reader of *La Bête humaine*; but, for its author at least, it is the first, if not the last, of its fictions.

There are numerous other reasons, most of them biographical, why the novel is seen to mark 'a critical turning-point in the *Rougon-Macquart*'.[62] More speculatively, one could suggest that Zola's discovery of photography the year before may have had the effect of 'liberating' him, not just from theory, but also from rigorously mimetic designs appropriated by a less problematical form.[63] We know that his 'après *le Rêve*, faire un roman tout autre, d'abord dans le monde réel'[64] coincides with a belated re-appraisal, by Zola himself, of his artistic procedures. Prompted by critical articulation of the poetic qualities of *Germinal*, it becomes explicit in his 1893 disavowal of 'la rigide méthode du savant'.[65] We should not forget the distance, in terms of Zola's development, between the surrogate artists discernible in Goujet and Jacques Lantier. The former still confidently inhabits a directed structure; Jacques, himself 'libre de toute direction', moves in 'un labyrinthe sans issue, où tournait sa folie' (p. 1042). Authorial doubts may be registered in a sympathy for Séverine: 'elle avait commencé une œuvre interminable [...] qui menaçait de l'occuper sa vie entière' (p. 1136). By the time of *La Bête humaine*, with *Les Rougon-Macquart* coming to a close, Naturalism itself has the institutionalized status of 'l'acte d'accusation classique' (p. 1079).[66] In Denizet's 'certitude' and 'conviction absolue' one can see implicated not only a literary methodology but also that of contemporary scientific discourse confronted by 'l'angoisse du réel' (p. 1108) which is 'l'angoisse de l'inconnu' (p. 1124). *La Bête humaine* destabilizes the perspectives in which acquired certainties are aligned. Its forms are arabesque rather than plotted along the 'fil' of a deterministic 'logic'. And its irruptive force, beyond craftsmanship and convention, is thus properly disruptive. It is to be situated, of course, in a wider crisis of representation, which brings with it the increasing self-consciousness of both its cultural modes and artistic practitioners.[67] Goujet can look outwards while he works; Lorilleux is entirely introspective. In 1889, for reasons both private and public, Zola is uneasily lodged between these two reflections. While it is therefore unsurprising that, as Michel Serres has written, 'au delà des hésitations de Zola, tout un discours contemporain s'éclaire',[68] those uncertainties may well be responsible for a reflection *on* his craft instead of its invisibility within the aesthetics of transparence. *La Bête humaine*, consistent with the dynamic of Zola's circles,[69] *revolves* in the space between fiction and its making.

NOTES

1. See above, p. 64
2. See Sandy Petrey, 'Goujet as God and Worker in *L'Assommoir*', *French Forum*, I (1976), 239–50.
3. See above, p. 41; and Auguste Dezalay, *L'Opéra des* Rougon-Macquart. *Essai de rythmologie romanesque* (Klincksieck, 1983), p. 254.
4. 'Rite et tragédie dans *L'Assommoir*', *Les Cahiers naturalistes*, 52 (1978), 87.
5. *Zola before the* Rougon-Macquart (University of Toronto Press, 1964), pp. 23–7.
6. *Op. cit.*, pp. 254–8.
7. 'Saint-Anne: Capitale du délire', *Les Cahiers naturalistes*, 52 (1978), 108.
8. See above, p. 46
9. See above, p. 28
10. *Feux et signaux de brume: Zola* (Grasset, 1975), pp. 24–7.
11. See F.W.J. Hemmings, *Emile Zola*, 2nd ed. (Oxford University Press, 1966), p. 243.
12. *Zola et les mythes, ou de la nausée au salut* (Seuil, 1971), p. 45.
13. Recorded by Paul Alexis, *Emile Zola. Notes d'un ami* (Charpentier, 1882), p. 125.
14. Dezalay, *op. cit.*, p. 98.
15. Subsequent interpolated page references bearing only a page number are from *RM*, IV (*La Bête humaine*).
16. *Op. cit.*, p. 248.
17. See David Baguley, above, pp. 17–22
18. See Jean Verrier, 'Le Récit réfléchi', *Littérature*, 5 (1972), 58–68.
19. Renée Bonneau, *La Bête humaine* (Hatier, 1986), p. 12; the following general propositions are all patiently substantiated in this 'Profil d'une œuvre'.
20. In the novel's *Ebauche* (*RM*, IV, 1717).
21. *Réalité et mythe chez Zola* (Champion, 1981), pp. 822–41.
22. *Ibid.*, p. 823.
23. See above, p. 47–8.
24. *RM*, IV, 1717.
25. *Zola's La Bête humaine: a study in literary creation* (University of California Press, 1962).
26. *Op. cit.*, p. 79.
27. *Ibid.*, pp. 130–60.
28. See Philip Walker, above, p. 30.
29. See above, p. 21.
30. In that of *Germinal*, for example; see my 'Etienne Lantier "romancier": genèse et mise en abyme', *Les Cahiers naturalistes*, 59 (1985), 49.
31. Work-notes for *La Bête humaine* (*RM*, IV, 1720).
32. Cited by David Baguley; see above, p. 18–19.
33. *Op. cit.*, p. 92.
34. 'Le Délire d'interprétation: naturalisme et paranoïa', in *Le Naturalisme* (UGE, 1978), 237–55 (p. 238).
35. *Op. cit.*, p. 241.
36. Grandmorin–Roubaud–Séverine; Lantier–Roubaud–Séverine; Flore–Jacques–Séverine; Grandmorin–Louisette–Cabuche; Pecqueux–Victoire–Philomène;

Jacques–Philomène–Pecqueux; Jacques–La Lison–Séverine; Jacques–La Lison–Pecqueux.

37. *The Limits of Narrative* (Cambridge University Press, 1986), p. 17.
38. In a letter of 6 June 1889 to J. van Santen Kolff, *Corr.*, VI, 395.
39. Peter Brooks, *Reading for the Plot: design and intention in narrative* (Oxford University Press, 1984), p. 132.
40. *The Gates of Horn: a study of five French realists* (New York, Galaxy Books, 1966), p. 311.
41. B.N., N.a.f., Ms. 10274, fol. 501.
42. All references to the forge episode in *L'Assommoir* are to be found in *RM*, II, 529–34; those to the visit to the Louvre are from pp. 445–8.
43. *Op. cit.*, pp. 256–7.
44. *Ebauche* of the novel (*RM*, IV, 1717).
45. In an interview with *L'Evénement* on 18 March 1889 (cited by Kanes, *op. cit.*, pp. 37–8, n.3).
46. *Ebauche* of the novel (*RM*, IV, 1717).
47. For all 134 of them, see *RM*, IV, 1757–8.
48. *Op. cit.*, pp. xi–xii.
49. *Op. cit.*, p. 805.
50. See *OC*, X, 1185–8, and 1195–9; *Le Roman expérimental* follows Claude Bernard here when Zola writes: 'Il est bien entendu que je parle ici du *comment* des choses, et non du *pourquoi*. Pour un savant expérimentateur, l'idéal qu'il cherche à réduire, l'indéterminé, n'est jamais que dans le *comment*. Il laisse aux philosophes l'autre idéal, celui du *pourquoi*, qu'il désespère de déterminer un jour. Je crois que les romanciers expérimentateurs doivent également ne pas se préoccuper de cet inconnu, s'ils ne veulent pas se perdre dans les folies des poètes et des philosophes. C'est déjà une besogne assez large, de chercher à connaître le mécanisme de la nature, sans s'inquiéter pour le moment de l'origine de ce mécanisme' (p. 1195).
51. Zola notes that once she had told it, she could be eliminated (see Kanes, *op. cit.* n.25, p. 78).
52. See, for example, Hemmings's view of 'one of the most haunting scenes he ever composed' (*op, cit.*, p. 243). On its preparation, see Kanes, *op, cit.*, pp. 77–8.
53. Brooks, *op. cit.*, p. 108.
54. *Ebauche* of the novel (*RM*, IV, 1717).
55. *Ebauche* of the novel (*RM*, IV, 1717).
56. See Zola's reflections on the *Rougon-Macquart* series as a whole: 'Si mon roman doit avoit un résultat, il aura celui-ci: dire la *vérité humaine*, démonter notre machine, en montrer les secrets ressorts' (*RM*, V, 1740).
57. See Brooks, *op. cit.*, p. 276. On the 'Integration of Fact and Fiction', see Kanes, *op. cit.*, pp. 69-72.
58. See Claude Duchet, '*La Fille abandonnée* et *La Bête humaine*: éléments de titrologie romanesque', *Littérature*, 12 (1973), 49–73.
59. Letter to van Santen Kolff of 6 June 1889 (see above, n. 38).
60. *RM*, IV, 1719.
61. 'Ce serpent de fer dont la colonne vertébrale est la ligne, les membres, les embranchements avec leurs rameaux nerveux' (Ms. 10274, fol. 360). Hemmings describes the genealogical tree in precisely these terms (*op. cit.*, p. 61). On the belated invention of Jacques, see Kanes, *op. cit.*, p. 30.
62. Kanes, *op. cit.*, p. 1. The significance of such personal disruptions for *La Bête humaine* is dealt with by Hemmings (*op. cit.*, pp. 241–8).
63. See François Emile-Zola, *Zola photographe* (Denoël, 1979).
64. *RM*, IV, 1717. It is in the *dossier* of *Le Rêve* that a synonymity is established

between 'l'inconnu' and 'l'inconnaissable', and where Kanes detects 'one of the rare moments of self-observation found in his manuscripts' (*op. cit.*, p. 16).

65. Cited by Bonneau, *op. cit.*, p. 73.

66. As Jacques Dubois writes, 'les écrits les plus liés au système institutionnel donnent toujours à quelque degré et éventuellement sous une forme métaphorique une représentation d'eux-mêmes, du faire dont il sont issus. Mais, d'un autre point de vue, la manifestation de l'énonciation dans le texte est rupture de la norme [...], et donc opposition à l'institution'. See *L'Institution de la littérature: introduction à une sociologie* (Brussels, Editions Labor, 1978), p. 155.

67. See Michel Raimond, *La Crise du roman: des lendemains du naturalisme aux années vingt* (Corti, 1966).

68. *Op. cit.*, p. 63.

69. See Introduction, above, p. 10.

POSTSCRIPT

Terry Keefe

It is not necessary to be a specialist to confirm the point made in the Introduction that all the contributors to this book address themselves to the question of how Zola's fictional constructions are made. Moroever, there is a certain continuity in this respect through from James, to Lubbock, to Forster, to the 1963 and 1988 conferences, in spite of considerable differences in critics' precise preoccupations, let alone striking changes in terminology and basic assumptions. Yet few readers will be inclined to doubt the notion of *progress* in literary criticism: each chapter of the volume makes a substantive advance in our understanding of the 'craft of fiction' in Zola's case.

One point that is likely to occur to readers, however, is how much remains to be done before that understanding can be said to be wholly coherent, or can begin to lay any claims whatever to completeness. To take just one obvious kind of deficiency, it cannot escape notice that, although there are references in these pages to Zola's very earliest novels (especially *Thérèse Raquin*), and although there is some discussion of *Les Trois Villes* and *Les Quatre Evangiles*, very little analysis of his craft in these works is attempted. Recognition of the quality of the achievement in *Les Rougon-Macquart* and the sheer scale of that fictional enterprise are, of course, more than enough to account for and justify this emphasis. Nevertheless, in so far as it is typical of the current state of Zola studies in general, this does draw attention to certain aspects of the study of the author's craft in the past and to possible avenues for further investigation.

The debt that Zola scholars owe to John Hemmings - in whose honour the 1988 conference was held and this volume was compiled - is, of course, partly measurable by the number of references to his work made by contributors. But even without examining the detailed aspects of his personal influence, one can see beneath each of the chapters in this book the critical bed-rock laid by John Hemmings and others of his generation. More or less exclusive concentration on *Les Rougon-Macquart*, or, in any given piece of writing, on one of its particular volumes, is consistent with professional self-respect among critics only to the extent, broadly speaking, that others have previously examined Zola's life and work more generally. Not only is a scholar always building upon information gathered by earlier scholars: he or she is necessarily working in relation to - though not, of course, necessarily *within* - critical parameters established by them. It is the penetrating and subtle literary judgements, as well as the extensive and rigorous historical research of John Hemmings and his contemporaries that have made selection possible, have made it possible to see what questions can most appropriately be asked about the craft of Zola's fiction.

That literary value-judgements are always involved is one point that special focus on *Les Rougon-Macquart*, as well as other features of this book, should cause us to meditate upon. David Baguley's opening chapter dwells upon the difficulty of defining the 'novel', and even perhaps in some cases (though not Zola's) of *identifying* which writings are novels. But if this is one preliminary fact that has to be faced before we examine the craft of an author's fiction, another is that we primarily mean his or her 'good' fiction. One can approach this point from a more useful angle by noting that within Lubbock's central concern with how novels are made, two different sorts of question are interwoven: 'By what processes of composition do novels come into being?', and 'What elements characterizable as "craft" are discernible in the final product?' That these *are*, theoretically, quite separate questions in any individual case is clear from the fact that we do not need to know the author, much less his or her method of composition, in order to be able to talk about the craft of a given novel. Prior literary judgements are at play in the asking of *both* types of question, none the less, since 'craft' is a value-laden term. That is, we are preoccupied, by and large, with the craft of 'good' novels, and interest ourselves, for the most part, in the method of composition of authors who have written (at least some) 'good' novels. One interesting question that this volume leaves wide open, therefore, is whether further investigation in connection with Zola's early novels, as well as *Les Trois Villes* and *Les Quatre Evangiles* will eventually come to cast further light on how the volumes of *Les Rougon-Macquart* were made and are made.

In the meantime, the chapters of this book have valuable and diverse things to say about the craft of Zola's fiction in relation to both process and product, both craft*ing* and craft*ed*. Because of its very nature, the book does not tackle in order, or in calculated proportions, the different aspects and stages of Zola's craft that are touched upon. But the framework or the ground-plan for a systematic study is clearly discernible here, encompassing: the author's stated aims or intentions; the 'preparatory mechanisms' of *dossiers*, *plans*, *notes de travail*, *ébauches*, etc; the method(s) of composition in the narrowest sense; and the innumerable different facets of craft that can be 'read off' the completed novels. (Is it too simple to think of *all* craftsmanship as involving, in principle: some kind of blueprint, raw materials, specific techniques and a finished product?) Some contributors tackle Zola's craft from one end of this continuum, others from the other; virtually all take account, to some degree, of more than one of the different aspects or phases.

By virtue of the very variety of approaches, moreover, certain points or preoccupations recurring in a number of chapters take on special significance. And of these, the *programmatic* nature of Zola's undertaking in *Les Rougon-Macquart* deserves particular mention. Every one of the critical enquiries initiated here illustrates, in its own way, that any single question asked about Zola's craft, even the most specific of questions about a given novel, has ramifications that immediately extend into the series, or at least one of its cycles, as a whole - if not directly and analytically, then by an insistent pressure of analogy and contrast. In the only chapter to bear the title of a particular volume of *Les Rougon-Macquart*, Jean-Pierre Leduc-Adine concentrates more than most on one novel, but still sets his detailed analysis firmly within the context of a theory concerning the relation between text and pictorial representation in Zola's fiction as a whole. To this extent, his task differs only in its range of references from that of, for instance, Colette Becker, who sets out to show the influence of melodrama upon Zola's craft.

If one common pattern in these chapters, then, consists in investigating a *general* feature of the author's craft - whether it be his treatment of space (Henri Mitterand), or his handling of a certain system of images (Joy Newton), or his incursions into the baroque (David Baguley) - and illustrating that feature in depth by careful reference to a small number of novels, another pattern involves focusing on aspects of the novel-making process as such that have a significant bearing on the series in its entirety. Philip Walker's sweeping account of the conflicting forces at work in the construction of *Les Rougon-Macquart* can be bracketed with the final three chapters of the book, in which Geoff Woollen concentrates on Zola's summaries of individual novels and of the series; Colin Boswell examines characteristics of the endings of *all* of the novels; and Robert Lethbridge argues that the 'self-reflecting strategies' of *La Bête humaine* have implications for the craft of the whole of *Les Rougon-Macquart*.

The content of these concluding chapters in particular confirms that the need for commentators to take account of Zola's use of cycles and series is more than a formality. The fact strongly brought out by the book is that virtually all of the questions to be asked about his craft *have* to be asked at a number of different levels. Not only is there an obvious similarity (as well as strong built-in contrasts) between the matters of how Zola ends particular novels and how he ends a series (or a cycle); how he summarizes a novel and summarizes a series; how he makes transitions between novels and between series; how a novel is disrupted and a series is disrupted - not only this, but each of the 'phases' of an examination of his craft outlined above generates a multi-layered enquiry. Just as his declared intentions for any particular volume are embedded within his intentions for a series (even, perhaps, a series of series), so the question of the relationship between his work-notes or plans and the finished product ('Intention et réalisation dans les *Rougon-Macquart*' ...) must be raised at the level of the volume *and* the series. Again, 'method of composition' is a concept that can be applied broadly as well as narrowly, and, as Alain Pagès shows, the feedback mechanism of reception by readers can operate on the composition of a particular novel (or even before!), as well as in the middle of a series. Finally, formal properties and other elements of 'craft' are discernible in a series as much as in an individual, completed work of fiction: this is one reason why the idea of emblems and *mises en abyme* figures with some prominence in these pages, and possibly the reason for the fascination with the image of the snake biting its own tail.

But in the ways that Zola's fiction turns back on itself, so too, perhaps, does study of the craft of that fiction in this volume. The craft*ed*, in the critical as in the creative process, comes to govern the craft*ing*. That is, the elements of craft discovered in the final product - whether they be features describable in terms of musical harmony, architecture, art, photography, or theatre - come to be recognized as guiding principles in Zola's method of composition; as organizing principles in his *dossiers*; and even as central aspects of his aims. The dialectical movement whereby this, in turn, sends us back to the finished novels themselves is not in itself unusual in criticism, but it does take on quite special significance in any study of Zola's craft, because of the fact - of which we are reminded more than once in this volume - that there is probably more material extant relating to Zola's preparation for writing than in the case of any other major novelist.

This fact throws into great relief any 'mystery' that remains attached to the actual passage from Zola's copious notes and plans to a completed novel, or the completed series ('le *saut* de l'écriture', a 'dynamic beyond the scope of genetic reconstruction', etc) - 'mystery', it might be added, greatly accentuated by the suggestion that writing, for Zola, was 'une abominable torture', and by his efforts to hide his need to amend and re-write. This, furthermore, raises the question of the relationship between such mystery and those features of the novels that need to be described by some term deliberately *contrasted* with 'craft'. Since there obviously is craft in Zola's novels, what *else* is there? (Candidates presented in this volume include 'imagination', 'poetry', 'myth', 'ornamentation' and so on.) And whatever the something else is, does it pass into the novels in the same way as (and at the same time as) the craft, or by some other, more obscure procedure, like 'inspiration'?

In one form or another, these questions will continue to be asked as long as the topic of Zola's craft of fiction itself is one of interest, and there was never any likelihood of full answers to them in this volume. Nonetheless, the book has a prominent part to play in the continuing process whereby the terms in which these and other issues about Zola's craft are constantly refined and the boundaries surrounding its 'mystery' constantly pushed back. Each reader will have his or her own view on the desirability, and even the very possibility, of envisaging a definitive resolution of such questions. In any case, for the foreseeable future some degree of sheer wonderment in the face of Zola's own achievement will continue to be appropriate, as will the measure of excitement expressed by Mallarmé, in a letter to Zola dated 18 March 1876 (cited in *RM*, II, 1507–8), about the latter's contribution to the novel form: 'Quelle acquisition subite et inattendue pour la littérature que les Anglais appellent la *fiction*.'

Index of Names

*n–indicates an endnote number

Subject Index

* n–indicates an endnote number

Apprenticeship,
  and fictional shapes, 8
  and plot-scructures, 135
  and the art of synopsis, 99-100
  stress on Manet's, 3
Architecture, 153
  architectural similes, 5
  as model, 9, 28-9
  contemporary as emblematic, 9
  materials of contemporary, 91
  of modern Paris, 9
  Zola as classical architect, 80
Art, 39
  and critical reception, 5
  distinction between craft and, 1, 44-5
  negation of novelist's, 4
  preoccupation with artistic transposition,
    3
  'vérité vraie' not the domain of, 4

Baroque, 27 n41, 27 n43, 27 n44, 80, 152
  Nana as baroque novel, 24-5
Beginnings,
  and endings of narrative, 113
  exposition, 3
  first pages of *L'Œuvre*, 81
  opening of *La Bête humaine*, 136
  structural modulation of, 6 simplicity of,
    6
  the *incipit*, 112

Cartography, 84-5, 134
  See also Topography
Centrifugal
  Zola's centrifugal artistic aims, 29-33, 34,
    38, 39-41
  See also Generic Models
Centripetal
  centripetal plot of *Nana*, 24
  Zola's centripetal artistic aims, 28-9, 34-5,
    38-9, 42 n1
  See also Solidity; Harmony; Symmetry
Chance, and accidents, 137

  and coincidence, 139
  at the expense of causality, 137
Chapters,
  and numbers, 80-1
  and the 'dénouement., 6
  economy of, 6
  length of, 6
  logic of sequence of, 7
  rounding-off, 7
  organization of, 96 n3
Characterization, 29, 34, 36, 39
  and autobiography, 32, 33-4
  character destiny and spatial organization,
    80-4
  characters borrowed from melodrama, 55,
    56, 60, 62-3.
  functional role of character, 8, 13 n73, 134
  in the *Ébauches*, xii
  lack of psychological complexity, 5
  Paris as character, 94-5
  'personnages lisibles', 49, 51 n17
Colour,
  and panoptic, 5
  function of in description, 95-6
  organization of colour-values,3
  See also Painting
Combinatory effects, 8, 135
  'combinatoire romanesque', 6
  expansive accumulation, 6
  process of accumulation and
    multiplication, 5
  See also Numbers; Symmetry
Composition,
  by 'tableaux', 58-9
  Daudet's, 3
  habits and account of, 6, 47-8, 50
  importance of, 3
  See also Work-notes
Copy,
  copyists in the Louvre, 141
  exactitude of, 2
  vulgar transcription of life, 2
  See also Realism

NOTES ON CONTRIBUTORS

David Baguley is Professor of French at the University of Western Ontario. He is the author of a book on *Fécondité* (1973), the monumental *Bibliographie de la critique sur Emile Zola* (1976; and supplement, 1982), and has edited *Critical Essays on Emile Zola* (1986). His study of Naturalist fiction will be published as *The Entropic Vision* by Cambridge University Press in 1990.

Colette Becker has recently been appointed Professor of French at the University of Amiens. She is co-editor of Zola's *Correspondance*. Her publications include *La Fabrique de* Germinal (1986) and a large number of articles devoted to Zola's early years and literary apprenticeship.

Colin Boswell was formerly Lecturer in French at Goldsmith's College, in the University of London. The author of *The French Language: its history and structure* (1988), he is primarily a linguist and lexicologist.

Terry Keefe was a colleague of John Hemmings for some twenty years at the University of Leicester before his appointment to the Chair of French at the University of Lancaster. He is a twentieth-century specialist, and his publications include *Simone de Beauvoir* (1983) and *French Existentialist Fiction* (1986).

Jean-Pierre Leduc-Adine teaches at the Université de Paris-Sorbonne Nouvelle. He recently co-authored a book on *La Curée* (1987). Most of his publications have been devoted to late nineteenth-century art criticism, and the relationship between Zola's aesthetic and the visual arts.

Robert Lethbridge is a Fellow and Senior Tutor of Fitzwilliam College, Cambridge, and a Lecturer in the University's Department of French. His publications include *Maupassant:* Pierre et Jean (1984) and numerous essays on Zola.

Henri Mitterand is recognized as the leading Zola scholar of this generation. He is Professor of French at the Université de Paris-Sorbonne Nouvelle. As well as having edited the Pléiade *Rougon-Macquart* and Zola's *Œuvres complètes*, he has made available a substantial part of the novelist's work-notes in *Emile Zola: carnets d'enquêtes* (1987). Other recent publications include *Le Discours du roman* (1980), *Le Naturalisme* (1986) and *Le Regard et le signe: poétique du roman réaliste et naturaliste* (1987).

Joy Newton is Senior Lecturer in French at the University of Glasgow. Her major areas of publication and research are concerned with Zola and the artists of his time, a field she was one of the first to open up and in which she has become the leading specialist.

Alain Pagès teaches at the University of Rheims. He has contributed a considerable part of the scholarly documentation for Zola's *Correspondance*, and has recently succeeded Henri Mitterand as the Director of the specialist Zola journal, *Les Cahiers naturalistes*.

Philip Walker is Professor of French at the University of California at Santa Barbara. A career devoted to Zola has recently culminated in Germinal *and Zola's Philosophical and Religious Thought* (1984) and a new biography, *Zola* (1985).

Geoff Woollen is Senior Lecturer in French at the University of Glasgow. He has published a large number of articles on Zola, notably on *Germinal* and *L'Assommoir*